Applied Shakespeare

"I was excited to find this valuable contribution, demonstrating the transformative power of Applied Shakespeare."

—Tom Magill, *Artistic Director ESC Film*

"Adelle Hulsmeier's energetic account of how Shakespeare's plays are applied to educational, community and therapeutic contexts is inspiring. Meticulously researched and accessibly written, this book demonstrates why and how Shakespeare's plays can engage people living in complex environments in ways that are socially equitable and emotionally powerful. *Applied Shakespeare: A Transformative Encounter?* asks important questions about how Shakespeare's plays can create worlds that shape and change lives today."

—Professor Helen Nicholson, *Professor of Theatre and Performance at Royal Holloway University*

Adelle Hulsmeier

Applied Shakespeare

A Transformative Encounter?

Adelle Hulsmeier
University of Sunderland
Sunderland, UK

ISBN 978-3-031-45413-4   ISBN 978-3-031-45414-1   (eBook)
https://doi.org/10.1007/978-3-031-45414-1

© The Editor(s) (if applicable) and The Author(s), under exclusive licence to Springer Nature Switzerland AG 2024
This work is subject to copyright. All rights are solely and exclusively licensed by the Publisher, whether the whole or part of the material is concerned, specifically the rights of translation, reprinting, reuse of illustrations, recitation, broadcasting, reproduction on microfilms or in any other physical way, and transmission or information storage and retrieval, electronic adaptation, computer software, or by similar or dissimilar methodology now known or hereafter developed.
The use of general descriptive names, registered names, trademarks, service marks, etc. in this publication does not imply, even in the absence of a specific statement, that such names are exempt from the relevant protective laws and regulations and therefore free for general use.
The publisher, the authors, and the editors are safe to assume that the advice and information in this book are believed to be true and accurate at the date of publication. Neither the publisher nor the authors or the editors give a warranty, expressed or implied, with respect to the material contained herein or for any errors or omissions that may have been made. The publisher remains neutral with regard to jurisdictional claims in published maps and institutional affiliations.

Cover illustration: Maram_shutterstock.com

This Palgrave Macmillan imprint is published by the registered company Springer Nature Switzerland AG.
The registered company address is: Gewerbestrasse 11, 6330 Cham, Switzerland

Paper in this product is recyclable.

ACKNOWLEDGEMENTS

I would like to thank Dr. John Kefala-Kerr, who was a key advisor throughout my research journey, for his advice, encouragement, and support.

Dr. Fritz Wefelmeyer for his endless positivity, encouragement, and motivating emails.

Tom Magill and Professor Helen Nicholson for their encouragement, support, and very kind words.

Poppy Joe for initiating my love affair with the works of Shakespeare.

Finally, I would like to acknowledge with gratitude, the support and love of my family—my parents Elaine and Peter, my brother Callum, and my partner Karl.

CONTENTS

1   Introduction: The Praxis and Scope of Applied
Shakespeare   1

Part I   The Challenges of Applied Shakespeare as a
Transformative Encounter   9

2   Shakespeare as the Ultimate Form of Cultural Success,
Individual Healing, and Personal Development   11

3   Shakespeare and Cultural Exclusion   17

4   Shakespeare and Universalisation   25

5   Subverting a Universally and Culturally Biased
Shakespeare   35

Part II   Prison Shakespeare   45

6   The History of Prison Theatre   47

7   The History of Shakespeare in Prison   51

viii CONTENTS

8 Shakespeare's Prison, Prison Shakespeare: A Renaissance
Reading of Shakespeare's Prisons in *Measure for Measure*   61

9 Shakespeare's Criminals, Criminal Shakespeare: A
Renaissance Reading of Shakespeare and the Criminal
Mind in *Macbeth*   73

10 ESC: A Case Study   81

Part III   Disabled Shakespeare   103

11 The History of Disability Theatre   105

12 The History of Shakespeare and Disability Theatre   109

13 Shakespeare's Disabled, Disabled Shakespeare: A
Renaissance Reading of Shakespeare and Disability in
Henry VI Part Two and *Three* and *Richard III*   113

14 Blue Apple Theatre Company: A Case Study   131

Part IV   Therapeutic Shakespeare   141

15 The History of Theatre and Therapy   143

16 The History of Shakespeare and Therapy   151

17 Shakespeare's Therapy, Therapeutic Shakespeare: A
Renaissance Reading of Shakespeare and Therapy in
Hamlet   157

18 The Combat Veteran Players: A Case Study   171

CONTENTS   ix

Part V Conclusion		187
19 Suggestions for Further Research		197
20 Concluding Statement		201
Bibliography		203
Index		217

ABOUT THE AUTHOR

Adelle Hulsmeier Phd, MA, PGCE/PCET, BA (Hons) SFHEA, NTF, CATE, is a senior lecturer and programme leader at The University of Sunderland. She has managed the Faculty of Arts and Creative Industries' (FACI) collaborative relationship with Northumbria Police, a successful collaborative project that runs annually and as an embedded element within performance programmes. She also strategically leads an academic partnership with Live Theatre, Newcastle *(Live)*, which affords students to experience teaching and learning in an operational and professional theatre venue, extending the reach of HE beyond the parameters of a classroom environment. Her publications include *The Arden Research Handbook of Shakespeare and Social Justice ed. David Ruiter (2021)* London: Bloomsbury Press.

CHAPTER 1

Introduction: The Praxis and Scope of Applied Shakespeare

This chapter introduces the reader to the praxis and scope of Applied Theatre as a performance practice. It draws upon theories and purposes relative to Applied Theatre. It introduces the concept of marginalised communities and diverse participants often connected to applied practice. Finally, it introduces the ways in which Shakespeare's works are regarded as a beneficial tool, when used alongside the practice of Applied Theatre, to achieve transformative encounters for a range of diverse participants and communities.

I begin this book with the assumption that readers will be aware of the established history of presenting Shakespeare's work in a range of Applied Theatre settings, and with knowledge of practitioners and companies who have explored his plays in diverse environments that move from the domestic space to amateur dramatic productions, from prisons of war to mental hospitals, school programmes to village workshops, from prisons, old people's homes, schools, heritage sites, and to different countries and for different cultures and communities.

Shakespeare's subtle exploration of moral issues, analysis of human and social problems, and his attempt to grapple with 'timeless' and 'universal' themes have, for many years, made his plays appear an ideal vehicle for Applied Theatre artists concerned with raising public and political consciousness and promoting social and individual transformation amongst marginalised communities. Over four hundred years after his death, Shakespeare's works are still being performed and adapted, and the

© The Author(s), under exclusive license to Springer Nature Switzerland AG 2024
A. Hulsmeier, *Applied Shakespeare*,
https://doi.org/10.1007/978-3-031-45414-1_1

1

cultural impact of his work can be found in the range of theatrical disciplines and the scope of geographical spaces to which his work appears to reach and interact. Through various levels of active participation Applied Shakespeare projects use different drama-focused tools to bring diverse groups of people together to explore the possibilities for change, and the results are suggested to be transformative for those involved.

Applied Theatre can be understood as a practice that attempts to promote the alternative method of drama and theatre to engage socially excluded people, on particular issues for the progressive intention of 'change'. 'Marginalised' is the common and relevant term practitioners of this field use in relation to the communities with which they work, relating to individuals and communities who find themselves in social situations that may prevent their voice from being heard.[1]

The transformative intention(s) of Applied Theatre is celebrated as an important vehicle to break down the increasing exclusion of marginalised groups through various levels of active participation. This can arrive in many forms, via many focuses and through a wide range of formats, from workshops through to conversations with members of the public. It is work that requires ongoing consent and negotiation between artist and participant.

The word 'marginalised' is not intended as derogatory or offensive but rather a term used to recognise participants who find themselves in excluded situations and/or may experience multiple deprivations such as poverty, exclusion, and/or lack of social support. Their future trajectories may be associated with negative outcomes such as reoffending, underachievement, substance misuse, and mental health problems. Applied theatre is predominantly concerned with work that attempts to be pro-social, and therefore its use of the term 'marginalised' is indicative of the way in which the applied discourse has positioned its participants in a variety of roles that look at the participant as being 'at risk', from recidivists to victims, patients to clients.

Applied Theatre, when discussed throughout this book, is informed by the works of J.L. Moreno (1889–1974, Psychodrama), Bertolt Brecht (1898–1956, Lehrstruke and Epic Theatre in the early twentieth century), Paulo Freire (1921–1997, Pedagogy of the Oppressed, 1970), and Augusto Boal (1931–2009, Theatre of the Oppressed, 1979), who are regarded as the forerunners of Applied Theatre practice and have all inspired Applied Theatre practitioners due to their collective notion that pedagogy could address issues of social and political concern.[2] They

1 INTRODUCTION: THE PRAXIS AND SCOPE OF APPLIED SHAKESPEARE

recognised the shift in an aesthetic understanding of theatre, its placement outside conventional theatre venues, the dividing line between traditional and new theatre, and the ability theatre has to promote change.

In general terms previous investigation surrounding the use of Shakespeare's work in Applied Theatre settings can be regarded as more peripheral to the field, mostly encompassing justifications, and articulating the benefits of presenting Shakespeare's work within a range of marginalised environments. These arguments move between general, anecdotal, and descriptive reflections, to relevant and progressive accounts of Shakespeare's use(s) and the subsequent challenges of using Shakespeare's plays amongst the marginalised, informed by critical, historical, and political discourse relevant to this practice.[3]

This book builds upon explorations of *where* and *why* Shakespeare's work is used in Applied Theatre settings, by seeking to highlight some of the challenges often inherent in combining Shakespeare's work with Applied Theatre practice for the purposes of a transformative outcome.

Despite widespread and positive claims regarding the healing and transformative nature of Shakespeare's work, I acknowledge from the offset that when the continuous and often compulsory use of Shakespeare's work takes place problems can arise meaning that Shakespeare's works are often negotiated via his 'virtual cultural presence'. Issues may include but are certainly not limited to the use of a universalising discourse, elitism, changes in social, political, cultural and/or historical contexts, and cultural biases.

Many may question whether Shakespeare's work when used alongside an applied format can really foment transformation. Many may also question whether the use of Shakespeare's work can ever extricate itself from the complex universalising discourses and cultural biases to which it is so often and readily attached, so that opportunities to identify transformation can be achieved.

The research responds with the following considerations/provocations/suggestions: (1) That transformation is a shared principle that guides and motivates a range of practitioners who fervently believe in this practice and therefore should remain a central component when considering this practice. (2) Through historicisation[4] and new historicism,[5] as a literary framework, alongside Brecht's verfremdungseffekt[6] as a theatrical framework, universalising discourses and cultural biases may be subverted, helping to move away from being 'comfortable' with the suggestion that we can identify with a culture that existed 400 years ago, and instead seek opportunities to be distanced from the work to identify the differences and not similarities found within the plays, for the purpose of transformation.

Part I explores the challenges associated with using Shakespeare's work as a tool to aid Applied Theatre practice. This section not only recognises the challenges of a format of theatre that attempts to combine disparate areas of practice to achieve transformative outcomes but aims to highlight the political and social agendas bound to the use of Shakespeare's work more specifically.

In this book I present an exploration of a field still very much in creation and development. Whilst Applied Shakespeare as an umbrella term may be seen by many as too inclusive, as fields like prison Shakespeare or Shakespeare and Therapy represent separate areas of practice, they are brought together in this book by the collective intention of Applied Theatre to promote and achieve transformation. I take the stance that the different forms explored throughout Parts II, III, and IV (collectively) have their own histories and epistemologies but connect through the joint intentions of Applied Theatre's focus on transformation and change. As such the book is presented under the umbrella term Applied Shakespeare, whilst recognising the more specific terms Prison Shakespeare, Shakespeare and Disability and Shakespeare and Therapy.

There will be a consistent exploration of the relationship between Applied Theatre discourse and a particular context (e.g., Prison Theatre, Disability Theatre, and Theatre Therapy), Chaps. 6, 11, and 15 seek to establish connections between value and ideology and how these are spoken about in reference to the projects specifically. These fields are in themselves recognised by specific terminologies, theories and practice and I attempt to clarify each field in turn.

Chapters 7, 12, and 16 will look at three main areas where Shakespeare's work has been applied: prison, disability, and therapy. These chapters explore the history of each community's interaction with theatre (Prison and Shakespeare, Disability and Shakespeare, Therapy and Shakespeare). My exploration is of a discipline that holds together forms of theatre which use Shakespeare's work to facilitate change, and with transformation as a shared purpose and guiding principle that motivates so many of Applied Shakespeare's practitioners and participants.

Chapters 8, 9, 13, and 17 offer an historical/Renaissance reading of *Measure for Measure*, *Macbeth*, *Henry VI Part Two* and *Three*, *Richard III*, and *Hamlet* for the culture informing the work to be understood and the lessons of the plays (influenced by their own context and time) to be explored. The readings highlight the importance of the text's historical context in suggesting ways in which Shakespeare's plays are not universal and are often a clear reflection of the time in which they were created, however still offer the participant opportunities to consider change.

These sections aim to match the applied community with specific Shakespearean plays to present a deeper sense of Shakespeare's understanding of these areas of community at the time in which he was writing. It is important to acknowledge that, although a logical combination between Shakespeare's work and the different communities being explored are made, this does not necessarily mean that these texts are used by Applied Theatre practitioners within each specific community. For demonstrative purposes the chapters attempt to logically pair different plays with each applied environment. The penal environment is explored in relation to *Measure for Measure,* crime, and criminals in relation to *Macbeth,* Disability as presented in *Henry VI part one* and *two* and *Richard III,* and mental health in relation to *Hamlet.*

The case studies explored throughout Chaps. 10, 14, and 18 allow for a detailed analysis of Shakespeare's use in specific Applied Theatre settings. They present a range of companies currently working in the UK and abroad who have used Shakespeare's work to engage different marginalised communities. The companies referenced ask their participants to perform or study Shakespeare's work practically, theatrically, and as active participants. They present clear examples of the different environments and communities where Shakespeare's work is 'put to use'. The projects were selected because they represent Shakespeare's use amidst different areas of marginalisation.

ESC Film, although filmic and not theatre-based, remains a relevant example of how Shakespeare's work is used as a tool to achieve transformation.

The case studies selected offer adaptations of Shakespeare's works where the work retains the original structure and much of the language of Shakespeare, but often edits out material and truncates the text with a view to making the language and characters more understandable and/or accessible to the participants and subsequent audiences engaging with the work.

These sections aim to explore who the companies are, why they perceive Shakespeare's work to be beneficial, how they use Shakespeare's work, and interrogate any challenges they face in doing so.

The diverse nature of the selected companies affords an opportunity to consider analytical comparisons of how Shakespeare's work is used within different marginalised communities. The analysis represents projects that celebrate the successes of Shakespeare's use, but also offer important articulations regarding the challenges of the work. All companies represent projects that ask for high levels of active participation, use Shakespeare's work as the focus of the project, work with marginalised communities of people, and explore possibilities for transformation and change. Collectively the companies highlight how Shakespeare's work is used in multifarious environments and diverse communities.

The case studies intend to provide an examination of the companies' own understanding of their work and the role of Shakespeare's plays within it. These sections explore the mission statements, aims, processes, and outcomes of a range of Applied Theatre companies that use Shakespeare's plays as a tool to achieve transformation. The section reflects on the strategies employed to realise various projects that participate with Shakespeare's plays to understand how these companies theorise their own work by examining the company's own understanding of their work and the role of Shakespeare's work within it.

These sections are predominantly concerned with how participants and practitioners are placing and articulating the value of their projects. Therefore, I draw upon artist's written claims and other documentation of practice. This affords greater consideration of the uses of Shakespeare's work and deeper interrogation of the participant's reflections surrounding their engagement with the practice, rather than a presentation of outside theories dictated by the researcher. The benefits of this are founded in the opportunities to reflect upon honest and immediate reactions to the work from the viewpoint of the participants and practitioners engaged with the work and operating within the field. It also allows for a complimentary research position in line with the aims of an Applied Theatre format, which asks for a voice to be given to the participant engaging with the work. This is predominantly concerned with looking at the purpose of social action through the practice of Applied Theatre and how the practitioners and participants of a range of Applied Theatre projects, delivered in marginalised communities, talk about their work. This 'critical lens' helps to identify the nuances of using Shakespeare's work in Applied Theatre settings, and for transformative purposes.

This work is not intended as a criticism to the use of Shakespeare's plays within community and non-traditional settings, but rather an exploration into the existence of Shakespeare in applied environments and potential challenges that surround this field of practice. The work does not aim to make accurate predictions about the uses of the plays, and because of the nature of the work and its subjectivity from the perspective of practitioner and participant, the work does not determine the success of, cause and/or effect. It would also be unrealistic to expect the work to represent the entirety of this discipline; hence, the work draws primarily on a selection of different communities that use Shakespeare's plays within their work.

The conclusion in Part V presents the main provocations of practice. It draws together findings from the readings of Shakespeare's plays and the explorations of the different theatre companies explored throughout the main body of material. The focus of the conclusion is on bringing together the different examples, intentions, and purposes of Applied Shakespeare and to revisit the overarching purpose to explore the challenges that may ensue when using Shakespeare's plays in Applied Theatre settings, ultimately questioning whether Applied Shakespeare can be a transformative encounter.

NOTES

1. See Freebody, K., Balfour, M., Anderson, M. & Finnernan, M. (2018) *Applied Theatre: Understanding Change.* Switzerland: Springer.

   Thompson, J. (2012) *Applied Theatre: Bewilderment and Beyond.* New York: Peter Lang Publishing Incorporated.

   Prentki, T. & Preston, S. (2009) *The Applied Theatre Reader.* London: Routledge.

2. J. L. Moreno: American psychiatrist, psychosociologist, and educator, founded Psychodrama; a form of therapy dramatising conflict.

   Bertolt Brecht: German practitioner, founded Lehrstucke, an experimental form of theatre which helps participants learn about an issue or event. He also founded Epic Theatre, political theatre that addresses contemporary issues.

   Paulo Freire: Brazilian educator and philosopher, advocate of critical pedagogy which explores the possibilities of people becoming active agents in their own education. He is most known for Pedagogy of the Oppressed and critical consciousness.

   Augusto Boal; Brazilian theatre practitioner, drama theorist, and political activist; developed the Theatre of the Oppressed to bring to light exploitation and oppression with common situations.

8 A. HULSMEIER

3. See Dobson, M. (2011) *Shakespeare and the amateur performance: A Cultural History*. Cambridge: Cambridge University Press.

See Pensalfini, R. (2016) *Prison Shakespeare: For These Deep Shames and Great Indignities*. London: Palgrave Macmillan.

Herold, N. (2014) *Prison Shakespeare and the Purpose of Performance: Repentance Rituals and the early modern*. London: Palgrave Macmillan.

Herold, N. & Wallace, M. (2011) 'Time Served in Prison Shakespeare,' Selected Papers of the Ohio Valley Shakespeare Conference, 2 (4): http://ideaexchange.uakron.edu/spovsc/vol4/iss2011/2 (Accessed: 18/07/18).

4. Historicisation: meaning to interpret something as a product of historical development.

5. New Historicism: a form of literary theory which aims to understand history through its cultural context.

6. Verfremdungseffekt: a technique used to alienate/distance an audience to become critical about the issues being explored.

PART I

The Challenges of Applied Shakespeare as a Transformative Encounter

Part I considers the challenge(s) of combining Shakespeare's work with the practice of Applied Theatre for the purposes of a transformative outcome. It is placed to precede the exploration of a selection of Applied Theatre companies who use Shakespeare's work for the purposes of transformation, to highlight the encompassing challenges practitioners and companies may face when embarking on an Applied Shakespeare project.

Academics are divided when it comes to supporting claims for the transformative power of the arts. Although there are a vast range of benefits associated with the form of Applied Shakespeare, any form of Applied Shakespeare that has the intention of providing and producing social transformation needs to remain aware that aesthetic, political, and ethical discourse continually interacts with the practice and may change the way the intentions and outcomes of the work are viewed/received. [1] Although it may be impossible to avoid these implications, there is a need to always be conscious of them.

Whilst this is a book that explores the scope of Shakespeare's use(s) in Applied Theatre settings, it begins with a mixed level of interest in, and reservation towards, the combination of Shakespeare's work with Applied Theatre for the purpose of transformation. Trepidation is born from promoting the notion that Shakespeare's plays are often said to 'transcend' through time because of a 'universalising force' that enables a participant access to cultural excellence.

This chapter also suggests potential solutions for subverting a universally and culturally biased version of Shakespeare's work by proposing the use of new historicism, historicisation and Brecht's verfremdungseffekt, as tools to distance from the text and engage with the differences and not similarities of Shakespeare's work for the purposes of learning, change, and transformation.

NOTE

1. See Prendergast, M. & Saxton, J. (2009) *The Applied Theatre Reader.* London: Routledge.

    Thompson, J. (2006) *Applied Theatre: Bewilderment and Beyond.* New York: Peter Lang Publishing Incorporated.

    Nicholson, H. (2005) *Applied Drama: The gift of theatre.* Basingstoke: Palgrave Macmillan.

    Ackroyd, J. (2001) 'Applied Theatre: Problems and Possibilities', *Applied Theatre Researcher,* 1 (1), pp. 1–12: www.griffith.edu.ac/centre/cpci/atr/journal/article1_number1.htm (Accessed: 05/12/15).

CHAPTER 2

Shakespeare as the Ultimate Form of Cultural Success, Individual Healing, and Personal Development

This chapter considers to what extent Shakespeare has become the embodiment of literary tradition and a sign of the 'ultimate form of literary achievement'. It considers how Shakespeare's works are often negotiated via his 'virtual cultural presence'. Through widespread notoriety Shakespeare's work is attributed to have an 'idiomatic sense of cultural success and widespread notoriety.[1] This is connected to how the value of Shakespeare's work has been sustained and transmitted over time. Shakespeare is believed to be assigned with 'conventional value' and is deemed as 'essential to the progress of this civilisation'. Therefore, the chapter explores how Shakespeare's work is helpful in promoting values of an idealised civilisation, which can perpetuate the 'snobbery that to be clever or important or accepted you have to know some Shakespeare'.[2]

Often people 'are conditioned to accept that such brushes with greatness, like some potent but ill tasting medicine, are good for them'.[3] This is a concept that appears to have endured since the Victorian Era. Then the belief was that Shakespeare represented high culture and excellence, and that simply through accessing Shakespeare's work you could become a better person. Governmental papers have also followed this narrative and often regard 'Shakespeare as our greatest English writer'—the tone of a range of papers appears to promote the notion that exposure to 'good literature' makes for a 'good citizen'.[4] This offers a direct assertion that to study, watch, or participate with Shakespeare's work provides an engagement with elite and high art which equates to being a better and more

© The Author(s), under exclusive license to Springer Nature
Switzerland AG 2024
A. Hulsmeier, *Applied Shakespeare*,
https://doi.org/10.1007/978-3-031-45414-1_2

11

acclimatised individual. This is a slavish subjugation that allows Shakespeare's work to take on a status that pervades the value of the work itself. It also implies that assumptive uses of Shakespeare's work are relevant amongst a range of practices and environments because the work itself equates to an unquestioned excellence.

As an example, in practice, and based upon her time spent watching prison yard rehearsals and performances, interviewing inmates, programme directors and wardens at the Luther Luckett Correctional Complex in Kentucky, Scott-Douglass reflects that Shakespeare is seen to promote the power for an individual to grow by raising 'individual horizons and improving participants' sense of self-esteem'.[5] Shakespeare is in a related fashion held to be transformative because he opens the mind of the individual, captures the imagination of the imprisoned, and provides the tools to become a better, well-adjusted individual. Shakespeare is thus constructed as a 'creative, social, and spiritual life force, a vital and necessary reminder that, no matter what, we are all human beings'.[6] Scott-Douglass argues that the combination of Shakespeare and prison is appealing because Shakespeare's work holds the key to help understand the prisoner's crimes explaining:

> Shakespeare approaches philosophical issues about how we live and order society, what a healthy relationship is, what boundaries we should mountain. These are issues that the [prisoners] didn't reflect on before they committed their crimes.[7]

Although taking care to acknowledge that 'Shakespeare is not a cure-for-all', Scott-Douglass often counters that engaging collaboratively with Shakespeare's work 'can help you remember that you're a person', reminding us that many regard Shakespeare's currency as being able to help individuals and groups engage with opportunities for self-identification and personal development.[8]

Often the articulated benefits of Shakespeare's use in these environments are limited to passionate accounts as to why someone may hold Shakespeare's works so dear, expounding the issues of 'taken-for-granted' beliefs often in operation when exploring Shakespeare's plays in these settings. The critical stance here is one founded in 'feelings and honesty' rather than engagement with criticism and theory.[9] There are often many assertions about Shakespeare's significance and the idiosyncratic perspectives that can inform these kinds of projects are often evident.

As an example, Weinberg and Rowe's text *WILL POWER! Using Shakespeare's Insights to Transform Your Life* promises to offer their readers 'a compassionate revealing book, that lets Shakespeare help you with your job, your friends, and your personal and romantic life' through Shakespeare's 'humanistic, everyday psychology'.[10] Shakespeare assumes the role of 'therapist and guide; teaching you to understand yourself and other people better [...] discovering a lifestyle called Will Power'.[11] The London Business Forum's Inspirational Leadership workshops claim to offer 'timeless lessons' for leaders from Shakespeare's *Henry V*, a fictional figure existing over four hundred years ago. Participants need 'no prior knowledge of the play or author, the characters and their situations will take us on a journey that is self-explanatory'.[12]

The putative healing nature of Shakespeare's work is also widely articulated. Although Shakespeare is peripherally mentioned in relation to psychotherapy and healing in many studies, it is Cox who offers an account of a mission to use Shakespeare's plays 'to restore and rehabilitate those with broken minds'.[13] In relation to his work at Broadmoor, Cox professes that 'the opportunity of experiencing great drama in the heart of the hospital was an almost miraculous possibility for all those present' and 'the performances were thus "therapeutic" in the widest possible sense'.[14, 15] According to Cox, after an encounter with Shakespeare, participants are likely to experience the surroundings charged with meaning and even to 'see the world in a new way'.[16] It is argued that because of 'Shakespeare's profound grasp of the human predicament and unequalled capacity to express what needs to be said', he has an astonishing capacity to facilitate the therapeutic process and augment 'conventional clinical observation and discernment'.[17] Shakespeare is presented as a considerable advantage to forensic psychotherapy's endeavour 'to facilitate the process through which unconscious material enters consciousness and is subsequently integrated and accepted by the patient'.[18]

Cox explains that 'Shakespeare is an incomparable inspiration in therapeutic work, by reason of his deep knowledge of the mind, his poetic language ... and his oscillation between concrete and abstract statements'.[19] Thus, Shakespeare's subject matter is held to be a means of identification and self-development, providing opportunity to facilitate 'the confrontation with self'.[20]

Cox and Theilgaard progress the analogy of Shakespeare's value in relation to therapy. They argue, on the one hand, 'Shakespeare can prompt therapeutic engagement with 'inaccessible' patients who might otherwise be out of therapeutic reach', and, on the other, he 'can enlarge the therapist's options when formulating interpretations' because his image-laden and metaphorical language can be used to 'reach the deepest levels of experience'.[21] According to Cox and Theilgaard, there is a technical element to this: 'the imaginative precision of Shakespeare's poetry is such that it has the capacity to prompt clinical precision' and stimulates 'the necessary collision with self'.[22] Cox and Theilgaard explain that Shakespeare's language is key to developing views of human nature and describe how:

> Our approach is [...] concerned with drawing out the latent energy in the particular stratum where Shakespearean language touches the language "of all sorts and conditions of men" –irrespective of education, social class, political affiliation, ethnic group or religious persuasion – when confronted by the universal depths of experience. By this we mean life in limited situations such as facing the stark choices between hating and loving, killing and being killed, causing loss or experiencing losses.[23]

Furthermore, according to Cox and Theilgaard, Shakespeare not only speaks directly to repressed areas of experience, 'he enables us to discern and tolerate what integration demands of us'.[24] Thus, Shakespeare is constructed as having a considerable contribution to make to the general aim of psychotherapy, facilitating 'a process in which the patient is enabled to do for himself what he cannot do on his own'.[25]

The combined debates say something significant about Shakespeare's influence upon individuals and communities. From academic interrogation to psychoanalytical exploration, Shakespeare's work is clearly an area of interest for drama practitioners, therapists, medical practitioners, and academics, and current debate depicts a range of benefits when combining applied theatre with Shakespeare's work.

Notes

1. Bristol, M. (1996) *Big time Shakespeare*. London: Routledge, p. 0.
2. Irish, T. (2008) *Teaching Shakespeare: A History of the Teaching of Shakespeare in England RSC*: https://cdn2.rsc.org.uk/sitefinity/education-pdfs/articles-and-reports/rsc-education-history-of-teaching-shakespeare.pdf?sfvrsn=2 (Accessed: 04/04/18), p. 10.
3. Adams, R. (ed.) (1985) *Teaching Shakespeare: Essays on approaches to Shakespeare in school and college*. London: Robert Royce. P. 2

2 SHAKESPEARE AS THE ULTIMATE FORM OF CULTURAL SUCCESS... 15

4. See The Newbolt Report (1921) *The Teaching of English in England London*. London: HM Stationery Office: http://www.educationengland.org.uk/documents/newbolt/newbolt1921.html(Accessed: 04/04/18).
   The Newsom Report (1963) *Half Our Future A report of the Central Advisory*. Council for Education (England) London: Her Majesty's Stationery Office 1963: http://www.educationengland.org.uk/documents/newsom/newsom1963.html (Accessed: 04/04/18).
5. Scott-Douglass, A. (2007) *Shakespeare inside: The Bard behind bars*. London: Continuum books, p. 97.
6. Ibid., p. 129.
7. Ibid., p. 21.
8. Ibid., p. 129.
9. Cox, M. (ed.) (1992) *Shakespeare comes to Broadmoor: The performance of tragedy in a secure psychiatric hospital*. London: Jessica Kingsley Publishers. P. viii.
10. Weinberg, G. & Rowe, D. (1996) *Will Power! Using Shakespeare's Insights to Transform Your Life*. New York: St Martin's Press. p. 1.
11. Ibid, pp. 1–5.
12. Olivier, R. (2013) *Inspirational leadership: timeless lessons for leaders from Shakespeare's Henry V*. London: Nicholas Brealey Publishing. p. 8.
13. Cox, M. (ed.) (1992) *Shakespeare comes to Broadmoor: The performance of tragedy in a secure psychiatric hospital*. London: Jessica Kingsley Publishers. p. 19.
14. Ibid., p. 9.
15. Ibid., p. 4.
16. Ibid., p. 168.
17. Ibid., p. 163, 133.
18. Ibid, p. 255.
19. Ibid, p. 172.
20. Ibid, p. 133.
21. Cox, M. & Thielgaard, A. (1994) *Shakespeare as prompter: the amending imagination and the therapeutic process*. London: Jessica Kingsley Publishers. p. 3.
22. Ibid, p. 3, 13.
23. Ibid, p. 14.
24. Ibid, p. 6.
25. Ibid, p. 30.

CHAPTER 3

Shakespeare and Cultural Exclusion

This chapter acknowledges that whilst Shakespeare's cultural influence is undeniable, there remain limitations to his work's cultural influence. The idea that Shakespeare is the ultimate form of cultural success remains a contentious one. It is rooted in Western-centric biases and when Shakespeare's plays are viewed as the pinnacle of Western literary achievement it ignores the rich literary traditions of other cultures around the world. The chapter suggests that Shakespeare's works are products of their time, written in a specific historical and cultural context, and some aspects of his work may be outdated or problematic by contemporary standards. The chapter argues that the canonisation of Shakespeare may limit diverse artistic expression and the cultural dominance of Shakespeare's works may lead to a narrow view of what constitutes great literature, potentially stifling the development of new and diverse artistic voices and preventing transformative opportunities from being identified and achieved.

Shakespeare is a term that has 'multiple and ambiguous valences, especially in its vernacular usage, where it may also signify privilege, exclusion, and cultural pretension'.[1] Suppliers of this version of 'Shakespeare' often represents the elite and powerful. They exercise their persuasions over a minority who are delivering, presenting, and exploring Shakespeare. Accusations of elitism are relevant and Irish argues that the issue is twofold when explaining that:

© The Author(s), under exclusive license to Springer Nature Switzerland AG 2024
A. Hulsmeier, *Applied Shakespeare*,
https://doi.org/10.1007/978-3-031-45414-1_3

17

some feel it is wrong to impose the writings of a white male, whose plays promote questionable values about class and women. Others counter that to deny [people] access to a man generally regarded as the world's greatest playwright was simply reverse snobbery.[2]

Elitism manifests itself in many forms. It is identified in a society who forces forward worth and value in the form of 'exclusive culture'. The links to power and privilege often mean those outside of this culture are told of the opportunities in accessing the values and authority found inside Shakespeare's works. It is also a society motivated by profit-making which governs Shakespeare's work as a cultural good or service for monetary gain. 'Shakespeare' as a profitable brand can often become attached to agenda-based incentives. These are predominantly financial and result in the un-relentless promotion of his works as valuable to serve a range of ulterior purposes, suggesting that 'Shakespeare's strength as a brand has not faltered. In fact, it's ubiquitous'.[3]

Shakespeare's work is a 'cultural good' and 'through hype, aggressive commercial promotion, and even relentless encouragement from parents, successive generations promote value in Shakespeare, however problematically'.[4] This can reinforce a sense of cultural hierarchy, where certain forms of art and literature are seen as inherently superior to others. This can lead to a devaluing of other cultural forms that do not conform to this narrow standard of excellence. The association of Shakespeare with elitism can be exclusionary, in that it can make his works less accessible to certain groups of people. For example, students from marginalised communities may feel alienated or disengaged from Shakespeare's plays due to their perceived cultural distance or exclusivity. The association of Shakespeare with elitism can obscure the diverse range of interpretations of participants from a variety of backgrounds, meaning that Shakespeare's work is imposed on, rather than a representation of the community the applied theatre project is intending to help.

Whether for purposes of elitism or financial gain there remains the need to be aware of the politics that Shakespeare's works can be bound to, ultimately questioning whether 'such artefacts [can] actually widen and enhance democratic participation in our public culture, or just reinforce acrimonious social division?'[5]

This area of critique bridges the gap between applied theatre's intentions for using Shakespeare's work for transformative purposes versus where complex cultural values may take precedence in practice generally.

This is connected to the implications bound to commissioning Applied Shakespeare, which is traditionally by governmental organisations, charitable trusts, arts councils, varying funding organisations and agencies, NGOs/NPOs, businesses, sponsorships, patrons (to name a few) and all become stakeholders of the work. Tofteland references hierarchy and structural boundaries, rules and regulations, the mission of an overseeing department, and the scope of the stakeholder's power.[6] Pensalfini references agendas and the need to satisfy the 'keeper of the keys'.[7]

Prentki and Preston warn of governmental agendas that may make stipulations as to the content and context of the applied theatre project. They state that:

> it is commonplace in the UK today for applied theatre projects to be undertaken directly or indirectly at the behest of the Government's social inclusion policies but a critique of those policies or an examination of the deeper causes of exclusion typically fall outside the scope of these projects.[8]

Governmental use of Shakespeare's works can provide a way of promoting a sense of national identity and cultural heritage. Shakespeare's work can be seen as embodying 'Englishness' and can be used to promote the country's cultural heritage. These factors can be influenced by political considerations such as funding priorities or political affiliations, and often Shakespeare's work remains the chosen body of literature to interrogate due to a preoccupation with Cultural Excellence. Shakespeare's work is thus at risk of becoming political propaganda; adapted and used to support political agendas. For example, politicians may quote or reference Shakespeare's works in speeches or use them to support a particular political ideology.

Money is not always given to the 'oppressed' who want to find a voice through the process of theatre but rather funding is closely tied to a range of instrumentalist outcomes such as from reducing crime or cutting the number of teenage pregnancies. But is often given to those who 'tick the boxes' that fulfil the funder's criteria. Projects are squeezed to fit the funding criteria (possibly at the expense of the community), and the starting point of a project becomes the funding and not necessarily the idea or desired outcome. The danger of being co-opted by funding agencies is a challenge for a range of applied theatre projects. It can create divisive funding politics across projects, between practitioners and participants, and across various social communities and geographical locations.

Often funding is readily available to support the use of Shakespeare's plays because they are widely considered to be some of the greatest works of literature in the English language. They have been performed and adapted countless times and have a proven track record of commercial success. This can make it easier to secure funding for a Shakespeare project, as investors and producers may be more willing to invest in a project with a built-in audience. The plays being in the public domain also means they can be freely adapted and used without the need for licensing or royalties, significantly reducing the costs associated with producing an Applied Shakespeare project. As a 'cultural icon' and a 'cornerstone of Western culture', investing in work that uses Shakespeare's plays can also be a way of supporting and promoting cultural heritage and educational enrichment, attractive to government or philanthropic investors. These considerations are particularly interesting when considering how the UK government have included Shakespeare as the only compulsory playwright on the English curriculum and have done so since the 1990s.

Therefore, Shakespeare's works are often a significant influencing factor in the commissioning process because of their cultural significance, universal themes, and potential for widespread notoriety. In this way agendas can be at odds with the direct needs of the community. The use of Shakespeare's plays can be tokenistic if they are included simply to fulfil a diversity or cultural quota, rather than as an integral part of the artistic or social mission of the project. This can result in a superficial engagement with the issues at hand and can undermine the potential impact of the work and disconnect between the goals of the production and the needs and desires of the community.

Commissioning then is a complicated endeavour that can often present diverging interests, intrapersonal conflicts, power positions, and various values which attach themselves to the projects and present political challenges in achieving applied theatre's overarching purposes. The process of commissioning Shakespeare's work is also incredibly political, and it can involve navigating complex political landscapes including securing funding, negotiating intellectual property rights, and balancing artistic vision with commercial viability. But not one of these reasons appears to align to the consideration of what might benefit the community or participant, or indeed whether Shakespeare's work as the main source material is the most relevant, appropriate, helpful, or transformative. The commissioning of Shakespeare's plays can therefore be in danger of adhering to a top-down approach to undertaking the work.

3 SHAKESPEARE AND CULTURAL EXCLUSION   21

The top-down approach can be curriculum-centred, outcome-driven, and funder-controlled, and can cause challenges to the intentions of achieving transformation. Although the aim of applied work may be to 'progress' or 'transform' the participant, there is a simultaneous risk that under a top-down approach applied theatre's transformation is *on* rather than *for* the participants and can instead prove bad, dangerous, damaging, oppressive, poison, disappointing, and propaganda.[9]

This top-down perspective suggests that applied theatre can unknowingly support institutes of power and exacerbate existing problems. Often practitioners believe they can make a change to the participants and their subsequent struggles. However, this world of change is created from their own heads, rarely informed by the community's experience of the strife they want to make a difference to. Ultimately top-down messages are at risk of promoting results that participants find difficult to relate to themselves, 'in this top-down manner the theatre becomes didactic, where messages are put across to audiences, often by practitioners who are not from the community, with no discussion, debate or community participation'.[10]

There is a risk of manipulation and coercion for work that is delivered by someone not necessarily part of the community, who could be potentially promoting change, with little validation from the community in relation to its use or relevance. Furthermore, the area of change may have been decided because the person in power has a motive ulterior to the community's needs and consequently the position of the practitioner becomes synonymous with power, authority, and control. Participation is therefore a powerful tool for change and simultaneously capable of being used to reiterate the power of an existing authority enforced to control groups of citizens. This demonstrates how applied theatre can be used to curtail freedom, progression, and transformation as much as facilitate it.

Kershaw's Welfare State version of King Lear in Barrow presents challenges in relation to funding the project, and the complex agendas connected to community theatre. *The Tragedy of King Real* (commissioned by Adrian Mitchell and inspired by Shakespeare's King Lear) took place in the 1980s and culminated in a 'community film'. The work was captured over a seven-year period from 1983 to 1990, on location in Barrow in a desolate warehouse. About 50, mostly unemployed locals were involved in its production. The project's aim was to 'develop a concept of vernacular art whereby we respond continually to local demand, producing plays, bands, dances, songs [...] generating a social poetry of a high order within a very specific community context'.[11] What the work ultimately

22   A. HULSMEIER

demonstrates is 'a fundamentally *participatory* tradition, in which the community had control', demonstrating the Welfare State's ability to use Shakespeare's plays in applied theatre settings by addressing the relationship between performance text and socio-political context.[12] Kershaw documents the adaptation of Shakespeare's work but warns of the challenges of producing work in which a diverse and specialised community is involved in its consideration. He touches upon the 'naivety' of reconstituting King Lear, 'where the storyline simplifies frequent power struggles into crude black-and-white issues'.[13] There are also complications between the two traditions, the community's and Shakespeare's and Kershaw argues that *King Lear* only makes sense to the audience because of its intertextuality and contextuality, and the variable positions that the audiences may have in relation to the text. He highlights major complications with the form and the challenges of an agenda-driven, funding-based incentive and explains that his project was:

> obliged to generate more product rather than process and work to rapid (and to an extent commercial) deadlines in strange lands [...] we could not respond to or follow up the longer term needs of the community, because essentially we were not part of any community'.[14]

Kershaw also explains how there were issues behind a company entering a community different to their own. Barrow represented a community known for its shipyards, submarines, and manufacturing of artillery weapons. *Real Lear* focussed on a Shakespeare for the nuclear age where the outbreak of peace was considered bad news. The welfare state was concerned with dramatising the dynamics of the local community, at a micro-political engagement. It played into some of the youth's fears of the closure of the shipyards and tangibly worked to include the community (e.g., a submarine was constructed by young apprentices and featured as a central aesthetic focus throughout the film). However, all of this was captured with no pre-existing congruence between participants and practitioners, therefore the Welfare State were met with 'the Barrovian cold shoulder'.[15]

This example draws attention to how this work is limited by context (education, health education, prison, etc.), content (issues that are wide ranging but may include crime, teenage pregnancy, unemployment), and the people who are deciding on what exactly these aspects should be (e.g., the government, funders, stakeholders, gate-keepers). What this establishes is that, in a cultural climate where much public funding prioritises certain criteria, outcomes and values, applied theatre needs to question whether engagement reflects a genuine commitment to providing change.

The view of transformation and its realisation amongst communities need to be carefully considered, as many people have multiple affiliations, needs, and values; and one method or model applied by the practitioner may not engage *all* participants at *all* times or may not be transformative to *all* participants involved in the project.[16] While the use of Shakespeare's plays in applied theatre can be a powerful tool for promoting social change and critical engagement, it is important to be mindful of the potential negative consequences of being bound to a particular agenda or political intention. It is crucial to balance the artistic and literary quality of the play with the social or political goals of the production, and to engage meaningfully with the community for which the project is aimed. It is up to educators and policymakers to consider these arguments and make informed decisions about the inclusion of Shakespeare's work in a range of endeavours.

NOTES

1. Bristol, M. (1996) *Big time Shakespeare*. London: Routledge. p. ix.
2. Irish, T. (2008) *Teaching Shakespeare: A History of the Teaching of Shakespeare in England RSC*: https://cdn2.rsc.org.uk/sitefinity/education-pdfs/articles-and-reports/rsc-education-history-of-teaching-shakespeare.pdf?sfvrsn=2 (Accessed: 04/04/18). p. 10.
3. Boston, M. (2016) *Six reasons Shakespeare remains relevant 400 years after his death*: https://news.usc.edu/91717/six-reasons-shakespeare-remains-relevant-400-years-after-his-death/ (Accessed: 18/07/18).
4. Bristol, M. (1996) *Big time Shakespeare*. London: Routledge. p. ix.
5. Ibid, p .xii.
6. See Tofteland, C. (2011) 'The Keeper of the Keys' in Shailor, J. (ed.) *Performing New Lives: Prison Theatre*. London: Jessica Kingsley, pp. 231–246.
7. See Pensalfini, R. (2016) *Prison Shakespeare: For These Deep Shames and Great Indignities*. London: Palgrave Macmillan.
8. Prentki, T. & Preston, S. (2009) *The Applied Theatre Reader*. London: Routledge. p.14.
9. See Jackson, A. (2007) *Theatre, Education and the Making of Meanings*. Manchester: Manchester University Press.

Thompson, J. (2006) *Applied Theatre: Bewilderment and Beyond.* New York: Peter Lang Publishing Incorporated.

Nicholson, H. (2005) *Applied Drama: The gift of theatre.* Basingstoke: Palgrave Macmillan.

Ackroyd, J. (2001) 'Applied Theatre: Problems and Possibilities', *Applied Theatre Researcher,* 1 (1), pp. 1–12: www.griffith.edu.ac/centre/cpci/atr/journal/article1_number1.htm (Accessed: 05/12/15).

10. White, G. (2013) *Audience Participation in Theatre: Aesthetics of the Invitation.* New York: Palgrave Macmillan. p.302.
11. Kershaw, B. (1991). 'King Real's King Lear: radical Shakespeare for the nuclear age', *Critical Survey,* 3(3), pp. 249–259: http://www.jstor.org/stable/41556515 (Accessed: 14/12/17). p. 8.
12. Ibid, p. 257.
13. Ibid, p. 250.
14. Ibid, p. 250.
15. Ibid, p. 250.
16. See Nicholson, H. (2005) *Applied Drama: The gift of theatre.* Basingstoke: Palgrave Macmillan.

CHAPTER 4

Shakespeare and Universalisation

This chapter argues how for centuries Shakespeare's works have been an important source of inspiration for academics and practitioners alike, and many artists are motivated to 'borrow' from the bard. His canonical texts appear to inspire and impact those who interact with his plays. His works are also transformed to diverse geographical spaces, alternative cultural environments, and delivered via a range of different theatrical forms. The chapter considers how the longevity of Shakespeare's work and the lesson to be found therein, appear to connect ideas of relatability and timelessness which is promoted as a reason for his work's continued use. Shakespeare's work is justified as being able to 'transcend' through time because of its 'universalising force', promoting the notion that Shakespeare's plays deal with 'eternal' struggles that can be used to teach an audience lessons about humanity 400 years after they were created.

This version of Shakespeare ignores any external influences upon Shakespeare's work and stands against the idea that Shakespeare may have borrowed from other sources himself. This places Shakespeare as the ultimate sign of literary greatness, providing him with the national identity of essential 'Englishness'. This begs the question, is Shakespeare universal, or do we need him to be?

In the application of universality there becomes a 'glossing over' of cultural difference, contextual influences, and human diversity to suggest that Shakespeare holds 'universal powers' that speak to 'all people, all communities, all cultures'.[1] Through a universalising discourse, we are

© The Author(s), under exclusive license to Springer Nature Switzerland AG 2024

A. Hulsmeier, *Applied Shakespeare*,

https://doi.org/10.1007/978-3-031-45414-1_4

told to engage with Shakespeare's work for what it may help an individual achieve (e.g., psychological healing, business leadership strategies), and are afforded an 'unreflective affirmation' of a range of ideals found in the play's universalising powers. As Bristol argues, 'we may say that neither Shakespeare himself nor his contemporaries knew the 'great Shakespeare' that we know today' and our current versions and understandings of Shakespeare's work can be fraught with assumptive and taken-for-granted beliefs.[2]

The justification behind universalising Shakespeare's work appears to be founded in the notion presented by English-speaking cultural authorities as 'good for you', and despite all scholarly activity to contest the cultural and ideological biases that made Shakespeare 'top-poet', many continue to be comfortable with the promotion of Shakespeare's universal relevance.

For example, Scott-Douglass works from a critical perspective that is deeply committed to the idea of Shakespeare's timelessness and the possibility of using this timelessness as a technique for change. Scott-Douglass explains that through 'focusing on what Shakespeare wrote about 400 years ago and applying this in their lives [...] enables prisoners to learn from their own mistakes'.[3] As such she situates the work as 'encompassing all that life has to offer'.[4] This demonstrates the appeal of reading Shakespeare as an example of a 'moralising force'.[5] Scott-Douglass heralds Shakespeare's work as the tool for change through their ability to touch all with their universal relevance. She claims that the promotion of prison Shakespeare provides a means 'of freedom, social activism and even revolution. Shakespeare provides inmates with opportunities for personal liberation in spite of institutional restrictions'.[6]

Another example can be found in the reflections of the contributor at Broadmoor, actor Sir Mark Rylance, who explains that the appeal of the Shakespeare at Broadmoor project is his sense that in Broadmoor he may find 'brothers of Hamlet', 'people who really have experienced some of the things that we as actors pretend to do in plays'.[7] In this regard, the inmates at Broadmoor promise to be 'authentically' Shakespearean. The concern is that this appears to suggest that Shakespeare's work represents a 'blue-print' for learning about and transforming oneself, simultaneously promoting beliefs about Shakespeare's work that are presumed rather than validated.

This is where the use of Shakespeare's work in an applied environment becomes the most challenging and/or contested. This is because it is often the case that Shakespeare's work is universalised for the sole purpose of exacting change.

The promoted notion that Shakespeare's plays deal with 'eternal' struggles that can be used to teach an audience lessons about humanity four hundred years after they were created is obviously questionable. Whilst the longevity of his work and the lesson to be found therein appear to connect ideas of relatability and timelessness which is promoted as a reason for his work's continued use, the way 'self-discovery' leading to 'transformation' is identified (through the forms and purposes of Applied Theatre projects using Shakespeare's work) is problematic.

In a range of applied theatre projects the way 'self-discovery' leading to 'transformation' is achieved is by being able to identify with, and explore parallels to, the characters in Shakespeare's plays. There are a wide range of academics and practitioners who believe in the positive (and often therapeutic) power of interacting with Shakespeare's characters to achieve individual transformation.[8] These transformative intentions promote two major complications to practice. Firstly, it brings attention to the ethical difficulties often found in work that aims to transform an individual, potentially causing risk to the participant.

For an applied theatre project, the promotion of character identification can often combine the use of a universalising discourse with the promotion of value found in Shakespeare's works to achieve transformation. It may ask for vulnerable individuals to identify with complex characters and situations, which may result in individuals being too closely connected to the issue, making it difficult to extricate themselves from it emotionally, therefore complicating their ability to identify opportunities for change. This immediately draws attention to how transformative intentions are fraught with ethical difficulties.

Ko grapples with how universalising Shakespeare's work can bring about moral and ethical dilemmas. He argues that we run the risk of embedding tensions between straight moral instruction and sympathy for evil.

The importance here lies in questioning whether Shakespeare's complex characters are helpful in promoting transformation amongst communities exploring his play texts, or whether in fact further damage can ensue. The inferences here are not only specific to the historical implications of the play text, but also hold significance within the often therapeutic intentions of applied theatre projects. Ko states:

28 A. HULSMEIER

> This difficulty gets ratcheted up in unpredictable ways when actual inmates who are in prison for violent crimes, including murder, perform the play in prison […] From a different angle, one might argue that it aestheticizes or takes pleasure in the representational fidelity of violence and victimhood.[9]

Ko discusses the dangers for the participant when 'fostering sympathy for characters who are very deeply compromised morally'.[10] He explains how participants may be at risk of 'identifying with a hallucinating murderer given to fits of nihilistic fury and apocalyptic monomania'.[11] He also questions the validity of 'defining Shakespeare's greatness by means of a moral vocabulary'.[12] This alignment is linked to the 'corollary of Shakespeare's universality' suggesting that this 'moral vocabulary' is compromised because Shakespeare often seemed to write without any moral purpose.[13] Ko is very direct, but relevant, in addressing the *challenges* of using Shakespeare's texts for transformative purposes.

As an example, inserted here to demonstrate Ko's point more firmly is a profound case study presented in Scott-Douglass' *Shakespeare Inside: The Bard Behind Bars* project. The example documents how a practitioner might ask a participant to 'relate the universal themes of Shakespeare to the lives of other human beings and to society at-large', through the moral purpose of the action and the feelings cultivated by the play the project aimed to use *Othello* to illuminate the complex processes behind criminal activity and the example suggests 'how it can be the moments of the text when Shakespeare's 'purposiveness without [moral] purpose seems most visible' that the prisoners are asked to explore.[14]

In 1999 Sammie Bryon was asked to play the role of *Othello*. He reflects that 'the death scene… was similar to the crime I committed'.[15] His best friend states that 'the play mirrors his crime to the point where it was just, like, identical, and I get goose bumps right now just talking about it.'[16] Sammie was incarcerated in 1983 for raping and strangling his mistress to death. He was sentenced to 25 years in prison. Then, 15 years later, he theatrically recreates an eerily similar scene when suffocating a fellow inmate playing the role of Desdemona. The project asks Sammie to 'face his monster' and discusses the 'cathartic experience' the project affords when asking Sammie (as Othello) to suffocate Desdemona to death. They explain how they are not worried about Sammie: 'yes he had committed a crime of passion. Yes, he has been given a life sentence. But since then he had served 20 years. More importantly, he truly changed'.[17]

The example of Sammie is complex. It adheres to the assumptive suggestions of Shakespeare's benefits to the incarcerated particularly in reference to how Shakespeare's combination with therapy can induce levels of healing. It seems to take no responsibility for the participant interacting with the work and instead the project appears to place Shakespeare in the role of a psychotherapist. It also assumes that because the prisoners have committed crimes they will automatically identify with Shakespeare's fictitious criminals, which might be simultaneously untrue and/or dangerous. Any level of identification with complex characters is compromising. Companies using Shakespeare's characters for moral instruction therefore need to be careful as to how interactions with the work might unfold.

The universalising discourse means that our culture makes certain assumptions about Shakespeare's work and the perspective from which Shakespeare operates, how we assume he intended his works to be understood, and/or how we believe his works should be used. This suggests that the universalising discourse often employed when using Shakespeare's texts offers an implied validity in the use of his plays. Furthermore, Shakespeare's works can be used to promote a romanticised view of the past, where the play's historical context is idealised or romanticised. Productions that present a sanitised or idealised view of the past can promote a cultural bias that reinforces a particular view of history, rather than engaging critically with it.

That Shakespeare's work is to be taken at 'face-value', and because his plays deal with supposed versions of humanity that will 'always remain relevant'; the universalising discourse implies that his works should never be questioned or interrogated but delivered to a range of communities as a 'blue-print' for learning about and transforming oneself. When bringing Shakespeare's work in line with applied theatre, projects which embed universalisation for the purposes of transformation may not offer the most beneficial or useful lessons for its participants, as applied theatre's aims and intentions are predominantly concerned with promoting diversity and offering the marginalised a voice, which a universalising discourse potentially counteracts.

The idea of universalising Shakespeare's work is not only unimaginative but can be potentially dangerous when used within applied theatre practice. This is because the universal discourse is socially engineered and universalises experience. It does not acknowledge that Shakespeare has a different purpose at different times, and instead, as the Newsom Report explicitly states:

> All [participants], including those of very limited attainments, need the *civilizing experience* of contact with great literature, and can respond to its *universality*.[18]

To use the term 'for all time' can be regarded as absurd and simply plays into the hands of those stakeholders who want Shakespeare to be culture-reinforcing and morally uplifting.

Ultimately, work that intends to transform an individual can simultaneously be at risk of achieving the opposite, and this is because Applied theatre, as a form intending to be mutually progressive, inclusive, diverse, and transformative is at risk of being sacrificed to promote universal ideology which may not be compatible with the people it needs to help. In this way Shakespeare's plays can be used as a means of supporting, rather than resisting the establishment that promotes his work as valuable, which is in juxtaposition to applied theatre's purposes, values, and ambitions.

Shakespeare's universality promotes cultural plurality asking cultures to not get in the way of political progress and/or economic change by sharing a set of universal values and responding uniformly to change. This is tied up with community sacrifice, and Conquergood's idea of 'the enthusiast's infatuation' which looks at the idea of sacrifices which trivialise the community by asking, 'aren't all people really just alike?'[19] This favours a glaze of generalities and the identification with the community here is superficial and surface. This may attend *only* to similarities, therefore being in danger of becoming a vehicle for exploitation and community sacrifice. Projects become unconcerned with specific cultures, and instead aim towards a sacrifice for 'the universal'. This is a process of appropriating, decontextualising, representing, and sacrificing cultures through its direct connection to the political process. Projects that only address the similarities of the community universalise all participants and present them as one and the same and can be seen as a programme of activity that does little more than confirm the social order. This is an example of intersectionality in which the oppression and discrimination becomes the result of an individual's social identity. Therefore, instead of emancipating 'marginalised' communities from their oppression, they are intersectionalised and disadvantaged by race, class, gender identity, sexual orientation, religion, and/or other identity markers. Grady argues that it is often an application that oppresses those:

who are not European, white, male, middle-class, Christian, able-bodied, thin, and heterosexual. The ideal in much of the literature in critical pedagogy is encouragement to speak with "authentic voices" [...] However, White women. Women of colour. Men of colour. White men against masculine culture. Fat people. Gay men and lesbians. People with Disabilities and Jews do not speak of the oppressive formations that condition their lives in the spirit of "sharing"".[20]

Transformation then is often in danger of being used and presented as a vehicle to undermine collaborative reflection by situating human experience as an individualistic transaction, rather than a communal negotiation. This links the work to neoliberalism, shifting from the community and social to the individual and personal.

It is important to recognise the tension of entering a community and promoting your own values and ideals at odds with what the community needs and/or would benefit from assuming that the starting point of the project is representative of an outsider going into a community, rather than specific groups working in partnership to help define the practice. The sacrifices made for transformation can often be at the behest of a community.

To avoid any element of sacrifice is difficult, but there must be an attempt to try and promote an open dialogue with those involved in the work to share political values and an ethics of practice that is not based on pre-established methods and models of change. It is important to recognise that applied Shakespeare, whilst intending to achieve inclusion, progression, and transformation, may simultaneously, and perhaps unknowingly, achieve its antithesis.

Universalising Shakespeare or attempting to apply his works in a way that disregards their original context and meaning, is problematic. As his plays are deeply rooted in the historical, cultural, and social context in which they were created, by losing the context of the plays, Shakespeare's works can become distorted. When Shakespeare's works are universalised, they are often interpreted in a way that reflects the values and beliefs of the person or group doing the interpretation. This can result in a misinterpretation of the work and can lead to a distortion of its original meaning, which may be appropriated by those who seek to use the work for their own (potentially biased and agenda bound) purposes. This can result in the exploitation of Shakespeare's work for political or ideological purposes, which can undermine the integrity and value of the work.

32   A. HULSMEIER

Relative to Applied Theatre practice, when Shakespeare's works are universalised for a marginalised community, it can result in a disregard for the unique perspectives and experiences of that community. This can result in a failure to recognise and address the specific issues and challenges faced by that community, which can further marginalise and exclude them. Shakespeare's works are not universally applicable, as they are rooted in a specific time and place and reflect the perspectives and experiences of a particular group of people. Universalising his works can result in the erasure of diversity and the promotion of a narrow and homogeneous view of the world; this can reinforce existing power structures and perpetuate the marginalisation of that community. This can further entrench the social and cultural barriers that prevent applied practice from achieving full inclusion and equality and suggesting that while Shakespeare's works can be valuable for applied practice, universalising them as the sole basis for such practices are at risk of preventing full participant/community engagement and opportunities for transformation and change.

NOTES

1. Irish, T. (2008) *Teaching Shakespeare: A History of the Teaching of Shakespeare in England RSC*: https://cdn2.rsc.org.uk/sitefinity/education-pdfs/articles-and-reports/rsc-education-history-of-teaching-shakespeare.pdf?sfvrsn=2 (Accessed: 04/04/18). p. 8.
2. Bristol, M. (1996) *Big time Shakespeare*. London: Routledge. p.11.
3. Scott- Douglass, A. (2007) *Shakespeare inside: The Bard behind bars*. London: Continuum books. pp. 24–25.
4. Ibid, p. 28.
5. Ibid, p. 23.
6. Ibid, p. 97
7. Cox, M. (ed.) (1992) *Shakespeare comes to Broadmoor: The performance of tragedy in a secure psychiatric hospital.* London: Jessica Kingsley Publishers. p. 29, 27.
8. See Walsh, F. (2012) *Theatre and Therapy*. London: Palgrave Macmillan.
   Cox, M. & Thielgaard, A. (1994) *Shakespeare as prompter: the amending imagination and the therapeutic process.* London: Jessica Kingsley Publishers.
   Cox, M. (ed.) (1992) *Shakespeare comes to Broadmoor: The performance of tragedy in a secure psychiatric hospital.* London: Jessica Kingsley Publishers.
9. Ibid.

10. Ibid.
11. Ibid.
12. Ibid.
13. Ibid.
14. Ibid.
15. Herold, N. (2014) *Prison Shakespeare and the Purpose of Performance: Repentance Rituals and the early modern.* London: Palgrave Macmillan. p. 89.
16. Scott- Douglass, A. (2007) *Shakespeare inside: The Bard behind bars.* London: Continuum books. p. 35.
17. Ibid, p. 35, 38.
18. The Newsom Report (1963) *Half Our Future A report of the Central Advisory.* Council for Education (England) London: Her Majesty's Stationery Office 1963: http://www.educationengland.org.uk/documents/newsom/newsom1963.html (Accessed: 04/04/18). p. 155.
19. Read more on Conquergood, D. (1985) *Performing as a Moral Act: Ethical Dimensions of the Ethnography of Performance*: http://www.csun.edu/~vcspc00g/301/perfasmoralact.pdf (Accessed: 05/12/15).
20. Grady. S. (2003) 'Accidental Marxists? The Challenge of Critical and Feminist Pedagogies for the Practice of Applied Drama'. *Youth Theatre Journal,* 17 (1), pp. 65–81, DOI: 10.1080/08929092.2003.10012553: http://www.tandfonline.com/doi/pdf/10.1080/08929092.2003.10012553 (Accessed: 07/12/17). p. 75.

CHAPTER 5

Subverting a Universally and Culturally Biased Shakespeare

This chapter suggests that while Shakespeare's cultural significance, educational value, and national heritage make a strong case for his inclusion in a range of applied theatre projects, there remain criticisms relative to his relevance, accessibility, universality, and cultural bias. The chapter suggests combining historicisation and new historicism, as a literary framework, alongside Brecht's verfremdungseffekt as a theatrical framework as a method of subverting the universalisation of Shakespeare's plays and overcoming some of the culturally biased challenges found in combining Shakespeare's work with applied theatre formats.

This proposition informs Chaps. 8, 9, 13, and 17 which are concerned with exploring lessons that may be found within (a selection of) Shakespeare's plays. The method demonstrates how participants are afforded an opportunity to grapple with unresolved questions and concentrate the mind to find relevant and appropriate opportunities to create change and transformation.

A critical and historical reading of Shakespeare's plays remains important to applied theatre practice and identifies three main provocations of practice to (1) offer the participants a safe distance when exploring opportunities for transformation, (2) subvert the universalising discourse to avoid assumptive and taken-for-granted beliefs about Shakespeare's work, (3) challenge the concept of universal truth, demonstrating that if the mind is concentrated on the past and can recognise the differences and *not*

© The Author(s), under exclusive license to Springer Nature
Switzerland AG 2024
A. Hulsmeier, *Applied Shakespeare*,
https://doi.org/10.1007/978-3-031-45414-1_5

similarities between then and now; opportunities for change and transformation can be more appropriately identified and achieved.

The suggestion here is to move away from being 'comfortable' with the suggestion that we can identify with a culture that existed 400 years ago, and instead seek opportunities to be distanced from the work to identify the differences and not similarities found within the plays. To do this it is suggested that an historical/Renaissance reading of Shakespeare's plays would be helpful so that the culture informing the work can be understood and the lessons of the plays (influenced by their own context and time) can be explored. This considers the opportunities for participant's minds to be more concentrated upon the opportunities for change and transformation through viewing the plays as a product of the past at a safe distance from the issues of the present.

Overcoming the challenging cultural influence of Shakespeare requires a multifaceted approach that involves re-evaluating our understanding of Shakespeare's works. Engaging with Shakespeare's work within the applied environment needs to be culturally sensitive and inclusive, and it should be remembered that Shakespeare may not be the best resource to capture these ambitions. Moving beyond accepting Shakespeare as the ultimate form of cultural brilliance is important generally in promoting works from diverse cultures and perspectives, and for an applied theatre practitioner specifically it means that the correct resource is chosen for the culture and perspective being explored, rather than from an overwhelming need to adhere to outdated Western literary traditions.

Mindfulness towards the cultural and historical context of Shakespeare's works, while also acknowledging the diversity of experiences and perspectives, is paramount. Encouraging critical engagement with Shakespeare's works to foster a more critical understanding of cultural success is also important.

By adopting a more diverse and inclusive approach to cultural achievement, we can overcome Shakespeare as a cultural bias and create open dialogue relevant to the community engaging with the practice. This can promote cultural exchange and understanding, which is much more clearly aligned to the ambitions of applied practice.

It is important to approach Shakespeare's plays with a critical eye and to be mindful of the potential negative consequences of selectively interpreting or essentialising the characters and themes in his works.

To overcome the association of Shakespeare with elitism, it is important to approach his works with an open mind and to explore their cultural and historical significance critically. Overcoming the elitism attached to the use of Shakespeare involves challenging the assumption that Shakespeare's plays are only for the cultural and intellectual elite. This can be achieved by actively seeking out new audiences and creating opportunities for people from diverse backgrounds and communities to engage with the plays, potentially focusing on the differences and not similarities between the plays and their own cultures, to more closely identify where change and transformation can be achieved.

There is often a tendency to 'deflect attention from and displace the potentially more relevant social history that underlies the play's original discursive field, for a modern day reading or identification of the work [via a] timeless universality'.[1] Therefore, another way to overcome cultural bias is to provide historical and cultural context for Shakespeare's plays. This involves acknowledging the biases and assumptions of the time in which the plays were written and exploring how these biases may have influenced the content of the plays, offering a subversion of the universal.

What is not being suggested here is that the historical reading can provide something like a guaranteed meaning but rather promotes an avoidance of personal interpretation and criticism. Therefore, the value of historical scholarship in the study of literature is founded on accepting that different meanings for different generations do exist. That generally audiences have different histories and various baggage that may affect their reading(s) of a play. Plurality is important in highlighting the plethora of interpretations that may be found in reading and studying Shakespeare's plays and characters. The insinuation towards multiple meanings is clearly positioned in direct opposition to a universal discourse. All audience members do not respond the same way to a piece of theatre, and this is recognised and acknowledged within the application of an historical reading of Shakespeare's work. The application of an historical reading to the play is justified. Firstly, it keeps the participants at a safe distance from the issue being addressed, looking at history to help focus and concentrate their minds on the opportunity for change and transformation. Secondly, it helps to subvert the assumptive considerations encapsulated in the idea that there exist 'universal powers' within his plays. This is a recommendation that may allow practitioners to be more aware of the challenges involved in not acknowledging that character motives, themes, and beliefs pervasive during the Renaissance period may be very different to those held and understood today and therefore important in helping to identify opportunities for transformation and change.

38   A. HULSMEIER

Undertaking an historical reading of the work offers a method in which the works of Shakespeare and their uses within applied theatre react against the cultural systems that surround his encouraged (and often compulsory) use.

Bertolt Brecht (1898–1956) is an important figure in understanding why one would benefit from reading Shakespeare's works historically. His links to applied theatre are also acknowledged. Brecht recommends the technique of historicisation which is a device used to interpret the play as a product of historical development. It acknowledges that different points in history produce different values, behaviours, and opinions. Brecht argues that because present day differs (often substantially) from earlier periods there is a necessity to recognise the work in its original context.

It is in relation to Brecht's concept of verfremdungseffekt that the historical reading of Shakespeare's work becomes coherent. The distancing effect attempts to create a cognitive change where the granted is no longer taken-for-granted. By distancing oneself from the issues of today and reading them through the lessons of yesterday the mind is concentrated on opportunities for change. According to Brecht, '[a] representation that [estranges] is one which allows us to recognize its subject, but at the same time makes it seem unfamiliar'.[2] For Brecht, verfremdungseffekt used alongside historicisation 'keeps impermanence always before our eyes, so that our own period can be seen to be impermanent too'.[3] By stressing the impermanence of social conditions, Brecht explains that change can happen whilst simultaneously discrediting the idea of universalisation. Brecht explains that conditions are created by man and that they can be changed by man, through learning and changing things based on looking back to similar things that have happened in history. Once conditions are no longer seen as universal or permanent, but as changeable, the audiences will say (in Brecht's words), '[t]his person's suffering shocks me, because there might be a way out for him' so that the issue can be considered in relation to change.[4]

Heinemann writes that through Brecht's proposition to 'expose the historical bases of Shakespeare's constructions can the authority of those constructions be subverted'.[5] The justification for referencing Brecht is appropriate in finding a technique that can help to subvert the assumptive appropriations of Shakespeare's plays and concentrate the participant's mind upon the values that can be uncovered when considering Shakespeare's plays as a product of his time, rather than something that can be universally applied. The combination of Brecht's historicisation and verfremdungseffekt with Shakespeare's plays thus appears complimentary of the purposes of reading the texts with historical implications in mind.

Complimentary of Brecht's theatrical vision for Shakespeare's work is the literary work of new historicists who are similarly concerned with a reading of Shakespeare's work as a product of history. New historicists aim to understand Shakespeare's work through the context of its own time, comparing this to how the plays have been used in English culture since the seventeenth century. Greenblatt, who co-founded new historicism, offers a method of understanding literature by examining elements in history that may have been previously ignored.[6] In order to reinterpret Shakespeare's plays by 'constructing closer relationships between play text and history, and exploring topical concerns when current cultural politics are projected onto the past', new historicists are concerned with exploring opportunities to subvert and contain current understanding of early modern texts when universalisation takes place.[7]

New historicism is aligned to considerations that explicitly explore and challenge the concept of universal truth and rationality. Thinkers that hold the notion that Shakespeare's work offers an engagement with universal themes, ideas, and concepts overlook opportunities for interpretation as the universal is offered as an unchanging truth. The new historicists reject the universalising discourse and emphasise that literary texts are influenced by biographical, social, and historical contexts. They suggest that literary texts should be rarely explored in isolation to their historical contexts. They argue that 'history matters and reinforce a shared desire to resist 'presentism".[8] New historicists do not favour history over modernity, but rather seek an:

> approach to the past which asks present-minded questions but refuses present-minded answers; which concerns itself with the traditions but allows for their continual reinterpretation; and which notes the importance of unintended consequences in the history of historical writing as well as the history of political events.[9]

New historicism offers a literary method that affords:

1. An historical discourse from which to analyse Shakespeare's plays to subvert the universalising discourse often used when applying Shakespeare's work in a range of contexts.

40   A. HULSMEIER

2. Acknowledgement of any important political and cultural values important at the time in which the plays were created that are different to the values that operate today.
3. An opportunity to distance the participants from the issue addressed in the work to identify opportunities for transformation more safely.

The importance of this method is founded in how it situates the literary text in the political situation of its own day.[10] It is interested in the historical situation of Shakespeare's time. The methodology follows the logic that literature and history occupy the same area and should be given a similar weighting when analysing, evaluating, and interpreting a play text within the context of the history of the author. The method subverts the assumption 'that texts had some universal significance and essential ahistorical truth to impart, [and] reads literary texts as material products of specific historical conditions'.[11]

The intention here is not to suggest that because a text is influenced by a particular time-period, it is therefore of no use to a modern audience. Contrarily, it is suggested that lessons of the past may be of importance to the participant, particularly in an applied theatre setting, where the participant can be safely distanced from the implications of the issue whilst simultaneously offering opportunities to explore transformation and change. The discourse is important as 'new historicism insistently raises the question of whether dominant forces in culture are essentially producing their own versions of 'the real''.[12] New historicism therefore acknowledges and embraces the ideas that, as times change, so will our understanding of great literature, making universality redundant.

It is important to establish that what is not being suggested is that Brecht's recommendation of historicisation and verfremdungseffekt should be captured in its holistic entirety, that the theories of new historicists are the only ones through which to interpret Shakespeare's plays, that modernisations of the work are not relevant, or that those using Shakespeare's works need to present an historically dogmatic version of the plays; but rather that an historical *understanding* of Shakespeare's plays is important (especially in applied formats) to explore more thoroughly the transformative opportunities afforded by the work and to subvert the use of a universalising discourse. The recommendation is ultimately concerned with the idea that theatre should allow the audience to view the events critically, not merely accept them, which is also a complimentary recommendation in line with applied theatre.

This book maintains a reservation towards a universalisation of Shakespeare's works for the purpose of transformation and therefore undertakes an historical reading of a range of Shakespeare's plays to gain an understanding of the political, cultural, and historical contexts influencing Shakespeare's plays. An exploration of *Measure for Measure, Macbeth, Henry VI Part 1 & 2, Richard III,* and *Hamlet* is present in subsequent sections to demonstrate the application of a Renaissance reading and offer provocations to Applied Shakespeare practice.

Summary

From academic interrogation to psychoanalytical exploration, Shakespeare is clearly an area of interest for drama practitioners, therapists, medical practitioners, and academics, and there are a range of reasons to combine applied practice with Shakespeare's plays.

Shakespeare's placement and use in applied environments is a well-documented area of study. It is far-reaching and presents an area that has a good amount of research dedicated to its practice. Although the reiteration of anecdotal, 'taken-for-granted', and assumptive beliefs regarding Shakespeare's uses appears consistently present in a range of reflections from practitioners articulating the benefits of using Shakespeare within their work, articulations also demonstrate the popularity and purposes of Applied Shakespeare. Their work goes far to reference the impacts upon a range of participants involved and affected by the work and Applied Shakespeare is regarded as an important endeavour to develop and nurture.[13]

The discourse surrounding transformative principles remains a contested area of investigation and the journey towards, or the achievement of transformation will never be an easy one. This investigation demonstrates the constraints and tensions between a form that hopes to be transformative, and a form that is heavily reliant upon accessing complex cultures, implementing agenda-driven incentives, exploring diverse contexts, and making sacrifices to achieve transformation. When Applied Shakespeare is to be used for transformative purposes it is important to recognise that the form will automatically embody a particularly acute version of these tensions as transformation is part of a complex political web of funding, agenda, governmental initiatives, cultural biases, and universalising discourses which pose an imposition on communities of people.

These complications need to be acknowledged but do not completely detract from the successes of work that helps marginalised communities engage with Shakespeare's plays. There is evidence that the use of Shakespeare's work in the arena of applied theatre can be positive and widespread, and the following sections aim to explore a range of applied theatre communities who experience a mixture of both challenge and reward when applying Shakespeare's work for the purposes of achieving transformation.

NOTES

1. Ko, Y. J. (2014) *Macbeth Behind Bars* in Jensen, M. P. *What Service is here?* Borrower and Lenders article: http://www.borrowers.uga.edu/ (Accessed: 04/04/18).
2. Brecht, B. & Willett, J. (1992) *Brecht on theatre: The development of an aesthetic.* New York: Hill and Wang. p. 190.
3. Ibid. p. 190.
4. Martin, C., & Bial, H. (2000) *Brecht Sourcebook.* Worlds of Performance. London: Routledge. p. 26.
5. Heinemann, M. (1985) 'How Brecht read Shakespeare', in Dollimore, J. & Sinfield, A (ed.) *Political Shakespeare: New Essays in Cultural Imperialism,* Manchester: Manchester University Press, pp. 226–251. p. 132.
6. Read *Greenblatt, S. (2000) Practicing New Historicism.* Chicago & London: University of Chicago Press.
7. Smith, C. (2000) 'Healthy Prisons': A Contradiction in Terms? *The Howard Journal,* 4 (39), pp.339–553: https://onlinelibrary.wiley.com/doi/abs/10.1111/1468-2311.00174 (Accessed 26/02/19). p.57.
8. Cochrane, C. (2015) *Theatre history and historiography: Ethics, Evidence and Truth.* London: Palgrave Macmillan. p. 5.
9. Bratton, J. (2003) *New Readings in theatre history.* Cambridge: Cambridge University Press. p. 14.
10. See Barry, P. (2017) *Beginning Theory: An Introduction to Literary and Cultural Theory.* Oxford: Oxford University Press.
11. Brannigan, J. (1996) *New Historicism and Cultural Materialism: A Reader.* Hampshire: Macmillan International. p. 3.

12. Harpham, G, G. (1991) Foucault and the New Historicism. *American Literary History*, Volume 3, Issue 2, 1 July 1991, Pages 360–375: https://doi.org/10.1093/alh/3.2.360 (Accessed 20/03/19). p. 360.
13. See Bates, L. (2015) *Can Shakespeare help prisoners reform?*: https://www.britishcouncil.org/voices-magazine/can-shakespeare-help-reform-prisoners (Accessed: 07/12/17).

    Scott-Douglass, A. (2007) *Shakespeare inside: The Bard behind bars.* London: Continuum books.

    Trounstine, J. (2007) *Shakespeare behind bars: One Teacher's story of the power of drama in a women's prison.* USA: The University of Michigan Press.

PART II

Prison Shakespeare

Angelo: ... I do not deny,
The jury, passing on the prisoner's life.
May in the sworn twelve have a thief or two
Guiltier than him they try; ... What know the laws,
That thieves do pass on thieves?[1]

Part II addresses how and where Shakespeare's work is used within penal environments. The chapter begins with an exploration of the history of prison theatre generally, before addressing the use of Shakespeare's work in penal environments specifically, where it currently exists and the articulated benefits of combining the two areas of practice. *Measure for Measure* and *Macbeth* are used as demonstrative texts in exploring Shakespeare's presentation of prison and crime within his work via an historical/Renaissance reading of the two plays to demonstrate how New Historicism, Historicisation and Verfremdungseffekt can be used to personally separate the participant from the issues being addressed so that their focus can remain on change. Finally, this chapter concludes with a case study analysis of ESC as an example of a community who uses Shakespeare's work for the purposes of transformation. This chapter will explore how the company articulates the benefits of using Shakespeare's work to transform their participants, and analyses challenges that may ensue in the application of Shakespeare's plays alongside prisoners at Maghaberry maximum-security prison, Ireland.

NOTE

1. Shakespeare, W. in Craig, W.J. (1991) (ed.) *The Complete works of Shakespeare*. Oxford: Oxford University Press. p. 76.

CHAPTER 6

The History of Prison Theatre

This chapter explores the history of theatre in prisons and the scope and expanse of applied work that uses the tools of theatre to engage the incarcerated. Prison theatre represents a variety of arts-based programmes with criminal offenders and 'a repeated theme in the discourse on theatre practice in prisons can be summarised as theatre and drama projects [that] have a positive effect on those incarcerated and may contribute towards rehabilitation'.[1]

Many believe that the incarcerated need opportunities in prison to improve themselves; therefore, prison theatre is regarded as an alternative method of rehabilitation and as an alternative response to crime. Ultimately prison theatre is viewed as:

> impacting recidivism by giving the incarcerated vital life skills, transforming them on a social and personal level and by instilling hope and a feeling of worth with the aim that these individuals leave prison with a new outlook on life, a new motivation, and an assured sense of self.[2]

Generally, prison theatre has been documented as showing how exposure to the arts can benefit its participants, 'it provides a place of sanctuary', 'a crucible for transformation', and an 'effective vehicle for (re) integration into society'.[3] It may help with issues of self-worth, confidence, and empowerment. It can help contribute to the development of an

© The Author(s), under exclusive license to Springer Nature
Switzerland AG 2024
A. Hulsmeier, *Applied Shakespeare*,
https://doi.org/10.1007/978-3-031-45414-1_6

48 A. HULSMEIER

inmate's self-expression and exploration and can play a role in improving their motivation, social and life skill.

Historically, the use of theatre as either recreation or rehabilitation in a prison context dates to be over two centuries old. The Australian convict theatres of the late eighteenth and early nineteenth centuries provide clear and historical evidence of theatre's role in a penal environment. In the twentieth century, the prison's applied theatre movement is argued to have begun in 1957 with Herb Blau's production of *Waiting for Godot* at San Quentin Prison, California. There is also evidence of prison theatre and artwork during the Second World War, or performances in concentration camps, in ghettos, in internment camps, and in the community Gulags.[4]

The oldest prison project still running in the UK is Clean Break Theatre, formed in 1979 by two female prisoners in Askham Grange, UK. The largest prison theatre project in the UK is represented by Geese Theatre Company of which Clark Baim was the founder and first director. To date there are over 30 theatre companies in the UK providing theatre training and productions for inmates including, but not limited to: Synergy Theatre Project, Theatre in Prison and Probation (TIPP), Playing for Time, Kestrel Theatre Company, Escape Artists, Clean Break Theatre Company, and Open Clasp Theatre Company. Although the companies presented here do not necessarily interact with Shakespeare's plays; some have included his plays within their work.[5]

NOTES

1. Keehan, B. (2015) 'Theatre, prison & rehabilitation: new narratives of purpose?' *Research in Drama Education: The Journal of Applied Theatre and Performance*, 3 (20), pp. 391–394: http://www.tandfonline.com/doi/abs/10.1080/13569783.2015.1060118?journalCode=crde20 (Accessed: 7/12/17). p. 391.
2. Donham, M. (2016) *Theatre in Prison: How It Is Making A Difference*: http://digitalcommons.chapman.edu/cgi/viewcontent.cgi?article=1207&context=cusrd_abstracts (Accessed: 7/12/17).
3. Shailor, J. (2011) *Performing New Lives: Prison Theatre*. London: Jessica Kingsley Books.
4. See Balfour, M. (2001) *Theatre and War, 1933–1945: Performance* in Extremis. UK: Beghahn Books.
   Berghaus, G. (ed.) (1996) *Fascism and Theatre*. Oxford & New York: Beghahn Books.

Jelavitch, P. (1993) *Berlin Cabaret*. London: Harvard University Press. Berghaus, G. & Wolff, O. (ed.) (1989) *Theatre and Film in Exile*. Oxford: Berg Books. Solzhenitsyn, A. (1975) *The Gulag Archipelago*. London: Collins & Harvill Press.

5. See Landy, R.J. & Montgomery, D.T. (2012) *Theatre for Change: Education, Social Action, and Therapy*. London: Palgrave Macmillan.

Balfour, M. (ed.) (2004) *Theatre in Prison: Theory and Practice*. UK: 4Edge.

CHAPTER 7

The History of Shakespeare in Prison

This chapter references some of the major applied theatre programmes (predominantly in the UK and the United States), which have shaped the field and developed this area of study. With world conferences, publications, journal articles, and a range of varied projects dedicated to the use of Shakespeare's plays in prisons, Shakespeare has a long and now established role within penal settings.[1]

The specific performances and/or projects that include Shakespeare's work in penal settings are mostly recent with recorded origins in the 1980s. Pensalfini states:

> since the seminal Prison Shakespeare projects in the 1980s and 1990s, the phenomenon has grown to where performances of Shakespeare's plays by prisoners are annual occurrence in many parts of the world [...] however, it was not until 2013 that prison Shakespeare practitioners came together under their own banner, at a two-day conference held at Notre Dame University in Indiana [...] and Prison Shakespeare emerged.[2]

The field is very changeable with new projects beginning and old projects coming to their end. Shakespeare in penal settings has now become so expansive that, as Pensalfini reflects, 'every time I thought I had all of the materials [...] I learned about some new article or review, or a new project would emerge that I had not investigated'.[3]

© The Author(s), under exclusive license to Springer Nature 51
Switzerland AG 2024
A. Hulsmeier, *Applied Shakespeare*,
https://doi.org/10.1007/978-3-031-45414-1_7

52   A. HULSMEIER

In 1984 Cicely Berry, in collaboration with the RSC, was invited to Her Majesty's Prison Dartmoor to make a film with prisoners based on *Julius Caesar*. Pensalfini documents that 'Berry was interested in taking Shakespeare into prisons to see whether prisoner's responses to his heightened language might help them to become more articulate about their own ideas and feelings'.[4] The project involved the prisoners and guards devising a tale about the early life of Caesar; however, 'due to the lack of funding the project was not completed until 2012 when *String Caesar* was filmed in prisons in South Africa, Wales, and Canada'.[5] Although Berry's work did not culminate in a performance by the prisoners, her work represents one of the earliest examples of Shakespeare's use within the penal field with the aim of helping prisoners progress or transform.

The United States were close to follow Berry with their first Shakespeare prison project led by Jean Trounstine. Her projects ran in Framingham (MA) Women's Prison, Massachusetts from 1988 to 1998. This led to her accompanying publication *Shakespeare Behind Bars: One Teacher's Story of the Power of Drama in a Women's Prison*.[6]

Trounstine's book (2007) documents ten years' teaching at Framingham (MA) Women's Prison and predominantly focuses on six inmates who discover, through Shakespeare's work, a way to live with the constraints of incarceration. Her supporting article *Texts as Teachers: Shakespeare Behind Bars and Changing Lives Through Literature* speaks of the capacity inherent in Shakespeare's work to help prisoners believe more deeply in their abilities and help create a community where they value themselves enabling 'offenders to leave prison with more assurance that they will be better citizens'.[7]

Trounstine's regard for Shakespeare's work is that it provides the prisoner:

> The chance to feel heard within the text; it engaged their emotions and allowed the text to resonate with their experiences. But it was Shakespeare's ideas, characters, humour and pathos that had the power to engage. The text was the teacher.[8]

According to Trounstine, 'self-realisation and personal growth is a by-product of engagement with Shakespeare's plays. Shakespeare provides the potential for better experiences that hopefully will be the way to better lives'. She states that Shakespeare can help prisoners believe more deeply in their abilities and help create a community where they value themselves.[9]

Trounstine offers a complex account of Shakespeare's place in prisons. Her reflections consider her own initial ignorance concerning the 'world of women behind bars' and discuss the difficulty of pre-conceived notions that prisoners 'deserved to be punished'.[10] She explains, 'I discovered that learning often becomes collaborative because both student and teacher are creating in an environment that does not want creativity'.[11]

Trounstine documents her journey from naiveté to raised awareness of what can be accomplished and facilitated in the prison setting when explaining that:

> from the beginning, I did not believe education behind bars was to reform the women-that is, to enlighten them about what society says is the 'best' way to be, to teach socially accepted behaviour as an antidote to crime. I saw crime as politically driven and often as action without conscience.[12]

Trounstine's acute knowledge of the contradiction between setting and endeavour is an ever-present consideration throughout her work. Trounstine explains that 'Theatre is transformative because it opens the mind. When minds open behind bars, you are working against the nature of prison: confinement of mind as well as confinement of body'.[13] This allows her to write about the difficulty of Shakespeare's use as a tool for change in a penal environment and she states that 'I saw the potential of Shakespeare to affect the internal life, but I also saw that Shakespeare could be enormously political'.[14] Trounstine in this respect highlights the difficulty of separating the roots of what it means to be incarcerated from the impact of Shakespeare upon women within a penal setting. She is very realistic in documenting the impact of recidivism upon the prisoners and discusses the inherent complications of the environment itself when stating that:

> by now I knew that many had returned to prison, in part because people getting out often are without jobs and unsettled relationships, questionable housing, and minimal support from the community... though I saw change, I also saw the limitations of the gruelling day-to-day of incarceration.[15]

54 A. HULSMEIER

Trounstine's work represents an important example of Shakespeare's use within a penal environment and, when referring to her accompanying text, promotes an awareness of the politics to which this work is bound.

The Shakespeare Behind Bars programme (SBB) (formerly known as Books Behind Bars) began as a prison programme in Kentucky in 1991 by Dr. Curtis Bergstrand.[16] It now represents one of the longest running, most established, and developed Shakespeare in prison programmes throughout the world.[17] In 1993 Curt Tofteland (then the Producing Artistic Director of the Kentucky Shakespeare Festival) was invited to introduce Shakespeare's plays to the programme. The programme began as a small project, never intending to be shared with a public audience, but became an independent programme in 1995, with the company meeting nine months of the year to work on material. From 2003 to 2008 the company toured to other prisons and performances are still being created today. Many have written about the company. Scott-Douglass focuses most of her publication *Shakespeare Inside: The Bard Behind Bars* on the SBB programme at the Luther Luckett Correctional complex. Throughout the publication a lot of emphasis is placed upon the redemptive power of Shakespeare. Scott-Douglass discusses the ways in which SBB use Shakespeare's works to provide 'one of the most positive impacts on recidivism', his plays providing 'more than a welcome distraction from the tedium, deprivation and dangers of prison life'.[18]

The 2000–2002 prison project led in collaboration between Agnes Wilcox and the Women's Eastern Reception, Diagnostic and Correctional Centre (WERDCC) in Vandalia, Missouri, is largely Charlebois and Dufresne.[19] The project witnesses Wilcox's use of *Hamlet* with female prisoners showcasing how through the play the prisoners 'experienced their own metamorphoses while studying the play'.[20] Charlebois draws attention to how incentive can play a role in the inmate's desire to participate in the project when stating that 'the prisoners have the potential to earn college credits at Fontboone University, which heightens their appreciation for the class as a bona fide experience in higher education'.[21] Charlebois importantly includes participant Virginia's reaction that Shakespeare wasn't the right choice for prison. She states that Shakespeare is 'typically claimed by an elite group of individuals who by virtue over class or education have had access to his play in the 'normal' course of their lives'.[22] The statement alone is incredibly important in highlighting that prisoner's themselves are aware of the complex political web in which Shakespeare is weaved. Dufresne also a volunteer in WERDCC for over several years, offers a discussion regarding Shakespeare's benefits when suggesting that 'the youth enjoy being exposed to new forms of entertainment' and 'when we finally understood *Hamlet*, we saw how it applied to our lives'.[23] Although Dufresne states that she saw behaviour change, she adds, 'there is no way I can pinpoint the why of the change'.[24]

Both authors briefly indicate the challenges that were faced, particularly in reference to assessing the impact of the value of Shakespeare's work, and the difficulty found in trying to convince everyone involved in the project that it was a worthy endeavour. However, both authors overall appear to write with the intention that the praise should be for the creator of the programme, rather than a concern with the assessment of the programme itself, its participants, or Shakespeare's role within the project. Although there are interspersions of helpful reflections, Dufresne's conclusion highlights most profoundly the work's preoccupation when she states:

> although minimal research exists to show whether or not programs like Prison Performing Arts work, talking with some of the participants is convincing evidence that their lives were changed thanks to Agnes and her dedication and belief in them.[25]

The Shakespeare in Shackles programme, ran by Dr. Laura Bates for ten years from 2003, is a unique programme that focuses on prisoners in Solitary Confinement in the Pendleton Correctional Facility at Indiana Federal Prison, a Level 4 maximum-security prison. Bates, an English professor at Indiana State University, expanded her programme into other prisons in the state and across the United States. She continues to teach Shakespeare's 'criminal tragedies' to the prisoners to help with skills such as communication, comprehension, analysis, critical thinking, and looking at issues and characters from multiple perspectives. Bates believes in the redemptive powers of studying Shakespeare and her work provides an example of maximum-security prisoners, and life-serving offenders who interact with Shakespeare's work. Although Bates' work does not necessarily have an impact on prisoner's reintegration back into society (as they are serving a life sentence), she believes that it has an impact on their approach to their time in confinement.

Her accompanying book *Shakespeare Saved My Life: Ten Years in Solitary with the Bard* is a diary-like, anecdotal publication that documents the relationship between prisoner Larry Newton and Dr. Laura Bates

56 A. HULSMEIER

throughout their time together on the Shakespeare in Shackles programme. The book unfolds over the ten years Bates worked with prisoners in solitary confinement at Indiana's Correctional Facility in Wabash Valley and links to Bates' Shakespeare in Shackles programme.

In her accompanying article for the British Council: *Can Shakespeare Help Prisoner's Reform,* Bates' standpoint on Shakespeare in prisons is clear when she explains 'how the world's most famous playwright can help bring about prisoner reform', stating:

> Shakespeare can help modify prisoners' behaviour in a way that counselling cannot. Counsellors typically begin with the premise: 'you are "broken"; I know how to "fix" you'. Naturally, this kind of approach meets with resistance. Inviting a prisoner to read Shakespeare begins with the opposite premise: 'I believe you are capable of reading the most challenging of literature. Flattered, and often surprised by such an invitation, many prisoners relish, and rise to, the challenge'.[26]

The majority of Bates' 2013 book reflects amazement at the prisoner's levels of perception and interpretation of Shakespeare's work, when she explains that 'I never heard such an enthusiastic Shakespearean discussion in any college or course I'd taken or taught'.[27] She also responds to critics who suggest that the prisoners are only interested in 'time off' their sentence when explaining that:

> I have two responses to that, one: why is a prisoner's motivation to earn a degree so that he can return to his family sooner viewed more negatively than a campus student's motivation to earn a degree so he can make more money? And, two: what about the motivation of a prisoner like Larry Newton, who is serving a sentence of life with no possibility of parole?[28]

The format of the work is presented as a workbook with lessons and prisoner responses. These sections of work discuss the readings of a range of play texts, mainly *Macbeth* and *Richard III,* and appear as part of a guided discussion. A lot of the pages are given over to Newton, and his deep realisations about his crimes. His personal reflections include insights into how:

> Shakespeare offered me the opportunity to develop new ways of thinking through these plays. I was trying to figure out what motivated Macbeth, why his wife was able to make him do a deed that he said he didn't want to

do just by attacking his ego. I had to ask myself what was motivating me in my deeds, and I came face to face with the realisation that I was fake, that I was motivated by this need to impress those around me, that none of my choices were truly my own. And as bad as that sounds, it was the most liberating thing I'd ever experienced, because it meant that I had control of my life. I could be anybody I wanted to be.[29]

The project foregrounds the benefits of the work and continues to believe in the transformative opportunities an encounter with Shakespeare's work may incite.

Shakespeare's placement and use in prisons is a well-documented area of study. It is far-reaching and presents an area that has a good amount of research dedicated to its practice. The work goes far to reference the impacts upon a range of participants involved and affected by the work.

These examples foreground some of the leading projects within this practice, and from the examples presented, the scope and expanse of the work is evident. Shakespeare's work has been used across a wide range of penal settings and with a diverse range of prisoners, from those serving short sentences to those incarcerated for life. What all projects appear to have in common is a desire for the work to promote transformation amongst its participants through the exploration of Shakespeare's plays. These opportunities continue to appeal to applied theatre practitioners and highlight Shakespeare's continued use within projects of this nature.

Notes

1. See Pensalfini, R. (2016) *Prison Shakespeare: For These Deep Shames and Great Indignities*. London: Palgrave Macmillan.
   Shailor, J. (2011) *Performing New Lives: Prison Theatre*. London: Jessica Kingsley Books.
   McAvinchey, C. (2011) *Theatre and Prison*. London: Palgrave Macmillan.
   Balfour, M. (ed.) (2004) *Theatre in Prison: Theory and Practice*. UK: 4Edge.
2. Pensalfini, R. (2016) *Prison Shakespeare: For These Deep Shames and Great Indignities*. London: Palgrave Macmillan. p. 85.
3. Ibid, p. 14.
4. Ibid, p. 25.
5. Ibid, p. 27.

6. Trounstine, J. (2007) *Shakespeare behind bars: One Teacher's story of the power of drama in a women's prison.* USA: The University of Michigan Press.
7. Trounstine, J. (2004) '*Texts as Teachers: Shakespeare behind bars and changing lives through literature*', Arts and Societal Learning: New directions for adult and continuing education, 116, (Winter) pp. 65–77: https://onlinelibrary.wiley.com/doi/pdf/10.1002/ace.277 (Accessed 26/02/19). p. 241.
8. Trounstine, J. (2007) *Shakespeare behind bars: One Teacher's story of the power of drama in a women's prison.* USA: The University of Michigan Press. p. 247.
9. Trounstine, J. (2004) '*Texts as Teachers: Shakespeare behind bars and changing lives through literature*', Arts and Societal Learning: New directions for adult and continuing education, 116, (Winter) pp. 65–77: https://onlinelibrary.wiley.com/doi/pdf/10.1002/ace.277 (Accessed 26/02/19). p.72.
10. Trounstine, J. (2007) *Shakespeare behind bars: One Teacher's story of the power of drama in a women's prison.* USA: The University of Michigan Press. p. 56.
11. Trounstine, J. (2004) '*Texts as Teachers: Shakespeare behind bars and changing lives through literature*', Arts and Societal Learning: New directions for adult and continuing education, 116, (Winter) pp. 65–77: https://onlinelibrary.wiley.com/doi/pdf/10.1002/ace.277 (Accessed 26/02/19). p. 247.
12. Trounstine, J. (2007) *Shakespeare behind bars: One Teacher's story of the power of drama in a women's prison.* USA: The University of Michigan Press. p. 67.
13. Trounstine, J. (2004) '*Texts as Teachers: Shakespeare behind bars and changing lives through literature*', Arts and Societal Learning: New directions for adult and continuing education, 116, (Winter) pp. 65–77: https://onlinelibrary.wiley.com/doi/pdf/10.1002/ace.277 (Accessed 26/02/19). p. 73.
14. Trounstine, J. (2007) *Shakespeare behind bars: One Teacher's story of the power of drama in a women's prison.* USA: The University of Michigan Press. p. 116.
15. Trounstine, J. (2004) '*Texts as Teachers: Shakespeare behind bars and changing lives through literature*', Arts and Societal Learning: New directions for adult and continuing education, 116, (Winter) pp. 65–77: https://onlinelibrary.wiley.com/doi/pdf/10.1002/ace.277 (Accessed 26/02/19). p. 73.
16. For SBB see also, Tofteland's chapter in Shailor's (2010) *Performing New Lives: Prison Theatre*

Herold, N. (2011) *Time Served in Prison Shakespeare*, focuses on the 2010 Shakespeare Behind Bars production of *The Winter's Tale*.

17. See Scott- Douglass, A. (2007) *Shakespeare inside: The Bard behind bars*. London: Continuum books. Thompson, J. (1998) *Prison Theatre: Practices and Perspectives*. London: Jessica Kingsley Publishing.
18. See, Scott- Douglass, A. (2007) *Shakespeare inside: The Bard behind bars*. London: Continuum books.
19. See Charlebois, E. (2010) Their minds transfigured so together imaginative transformation and transcendence in *Midsummer Night's* in Shailor, J. (ed.) *Performing New Lives: Prison Theatre*. London: Jessica Kingsley Books, pp. 256–269.

    Dufresne, J. (2006) 'Crime is Easy, Shakespeare is Hard', *Reclaiming children and youth* 14 (4), pp. 245–248.
20. Charlebois, E. (2010) Their minds transfigured so together imaginative transformation and transcendence in *Midsummer Night's* in Shailor, J. (ed.) *Performing New Lives: Prison Theatre*. London: Jessica Kingsley Books, pp. 256–269. p. 256
21. Ibid, p. 253
22. Charlebois, E. (2010) Their minds transfigured so together imaginative transformation and transcendence in *Midsummer Night's* in Shailor, J. (ed.) *Performing New Lives: Prison Theatre*. London: Jessica Kingsley Books, pp. 256–269.p. 260.
23. Dufresne, J. (2006) 'Crime is Easy, Shakespeare is Hard', *Reclaiming children and youth* 14 (4), pp. 245–248. p. 246.
24. Ibid, p. 247.
25. Dufresne, J. (2006) 'Crime is Easy, Shakespeare is Hard', *Reclaiming children and youth* 14 (4), pp. 245–248. p. 248.
26. Bates, L. (2015) *Can Shakespeare help prisoners reform?*: https://www.britishcouncil.org/voices-magazine/can-shakespeare-help-reform-prisoners (Accessed: 07/12/17).
27. Bates, L. (2013) *Shakespeare Saved my Life: Ten years in solitary with the Bard*. Naperville, Illinois: Sourcebooks. p. 28.
28. Ibid, p.11.
29. Ibid, p. 46.

CHAPTER 8

Shakespeare's Prison, Prison Shakespeare: A Renaissance Reading of Shakespeare's Prisons in *Measure for Measure*

The chapter that follows will examine Shakespeare's presentation of prison and punishment throughout the play *Measure for Measure*. It will explore Shakespeare's presentation of justice and its uncertainties, alongside changing law and law enforcement in reference to the penal system of the seventeenth century to which Shakespeare may have been reacting.

Generally, Shakespeare was writing plays that depict prison and law enforcement as a reflection of the penal system in operation during the seventeenth century. Imprisonment was not a punishment; it was a waiting room or holding area whilst prisoners were brought to trial, the punishment was decided, or they were released. Time served in prison had no set limit and people in this space often died of starvation or the cold, or from poor exercise or sanitation. Sentences and punishments, when they were finally decided were various, but often brutal.

The audiences who originally watched Shakespeare's plays were used to seeing punishments inflicted on perpetrators. Punishment from arrest, imprisonment, and to penalty was very much at the heart of Renaissance life with flogging, branding, stoning, mutilation, and whipping being common and public. This is seen throughout a range of Shakespeare's plays:

> *Macbeth* is accused of treason and sentenced to death without trial. Lady Macduff affirms that traitors "must be hanged". In *The Winter's Tale* and *The Twelfth Night*, the characters mention the practice of boiling a convict in oil or lead. Drowning is mentioned in *The Tempest*, and hanging appears

© The Author(s), under exclusive license to Springer Nature Switzerland AG 2024
A. Hulsmeier, *Applied Shakespeare*,
https://doi.org/10.1007/978-3-031-45414-1_8

in *All's Well that Ends Well, Henry IV*, and *The Merry Wives of Windsor*. Restrain and humiliation is mentioned in *The Taming of the Shrew, Measure for Measure,* and *The Two Gentlemen of Verona,* and other types of punishment documented in Shakespeare's work include the wheel, stocks, the press, whipping, branding, the wisp, and defacement.[1]

Specifically, Shakespeare was writing his plays around the time when law; its intentions, purposes, and science were being more thoroughly explored, and when 'English society in the 17th century found itself in a phase of transition between two penal systems: the system/age of terror (punishment of the body), and the system/age of confinement (punishment of the soul)'.[2] Werkman explains that:

> The new system made an end to the autonomy of the monarch and started a new method of investigation and judgment; and punishment such as torture disappeared and instead were related to the body in a different manner such as imprisonment, confinement, forced labour, penal servitude, prohibition from entering certain areas, and deportation; the main object of punishment now was no longer the body but the soul of the convict; [...] the aim of the punishment was to correct the wrong inflicted on society, but also to punish just enough to avoid repetition.[3]

The terms of confinement and terror were initially termed by Foucault in his seminal text *Surveiller et Punir: Naissance de la Prison* which is important to acknowledge in line with Foucault's general consideration of the prison and concepts of power.[4] However, it is important to remember that Foucault's analysis is an historical reading depicting certain patterns at a particular time in history (eighteenth century) and Shakespeare's plays are literary texts not completely based on reality and influenced by a different time in history (seventeenth century). Werkman warns that 'this combination can indicate an anachronistic situation in which ideas and perspectives of the 20th century on the 18th century are used to interpret the 17th century'.[5] However the justification behind combining Foucault's terms with a reading of Shakespeare's plays can be found in the argument that, although the major changes to the philosophy and practice of punishment upon criminals happened after Shakespeare wrote his plays, in the eighteenth century, it is important to reference that the desire for change in law and its enforcement in the seventeenth century could very easily have had an influence upon Shakespeare's desire to write plays that address crime, criminality and law enforcement.

Measure for Measure is to be analysed in reference to the historical and cultural events reflected in the seventeenth century and supported by Foucault's understanding of the subsequent changes that were made in the eighteenth century to highlight more specifically the seventeenth century as a time of judicial transition and unrest. By not reading Shakespeare's plays through this historical context, the historical traditions surrounding the time in which the play was originally created, against the changes to the legal system that were subsequently made, may go unnoticed.

The shift during the early 1600s saw an important move away from the power to punish, to a deeper consideration of mercy and justice. The cause of transition and the way Shakespeare's work reflects upon it are an important consideration to make to explore Shakespeare's reactions to the penal system that was in existence at the time in which he was writing his plays.

It is *Measure for Measure*, a play that operates around the uncertainties of justice that perhaps most closely shows us the purpose of prisons during Shakespeare's time. The environment Shakespeare presents 'shows the workings of a prison- the presentation of warrants, the preparations for execution [...] and the prison has sucked in all of the diseases that float in the surrounding cesspool of Vienna'.[6]

Regarded as a problem play generally, the biggest complication surrounds the idea that no one really knows what the best or most just decisions are and therefore the uncertainties of justice and its potential subjectivity and elevation of judgement promote the ambiguities of the legal system through the choices the characters make throughout the play. This is a play of antithesis and the characters themselves become personifications of the problems and questions addressed throughout. The play ultimately attempts to show what an ineffectual justice system can do to the people who live by its rules and demonstrates how people wanted change.

The play predominantly focuses upon the application of sexual law to demonstrate the inefficiencies and confusions relative to justice and its enforcement. The application of the law throughout the play is regulated by the absurd sentencing of Claudio to death for his practice of pre-marital sexual activities. Claudio is deprived of procedural right in relation to his access to a counsel for his defence, or the following of the due process of law. Foucault highlights this as 'an element of the old system, since the changes in the new model saw the influence of advisers in jurisdiction'.[7] It is Angelo's precise enforcement of sexual law, his strict temper, and stricter rule that provoke a confused response from the people of Venice, as highlighted in the exchange between Pompey and Mistress Overdone:

Pompey:	Yonder man is carried to Prison.
Mistress Overdone:	Well! What has he done?
Pompey:	A woman.
Mistress Overdone:	But what's his offence?
Pompey:	Groping for trout in a peculiar river.[8]

The existing complex rule of sexual law asks Angelo to judge Claudio through a specific enforcement of punishment. In Renaissance England, church and state struggled to control sexuality and it is documented that 'the ecclesiastical courts tried so many cases of sexual offences like prostitution and bastardy that they were called the 'bawdy courts'.[9] Constables could bring to court anyone they felt to be a suspect of sexual crime, as Elbow does with Pompey. Those accused of sexual deviance could not escape punishment simply by marrying, and as Angelo does with Claudio, offenders would undergo penance and public humiliation. Although death was not often the final punishment, whipping until blood was drawn would be used.

Claudio's punishment is one of the most complicated issues present throughout the play. Legally he has fornicated outside of wedlock and Juliet carries his bastard child. However, socially, he is betrothed to Juliet, she is his fiancée, and they are promised to each other in marriage. Although Claudio's fate throughout the play may appear to a modern audience as extreme, the ambiguities surrounding marriage at the time in which Shakespeare was writing may in fact play a role in Angelo's exercise of the sexual law. According to Sokol and Sokol:

> The fact that no specific language existed to confirm marriage merely added to the ambiguity. A variety of signs, not all of them even verbal, was accepted as sufficient to indicate the existence of this consenting state. Not surprisingly, there were often difficulties in the interpretation of such signs.[10]

Therefore, the interpretation of whether a marriage exists is rendered from a subjective judgement. Angelo does not follow the 'law precisely; he is instead rendering a subjective judgment on an act that may or may not even constitute a crime'.[11] Marriage is an interesting device to not only make commentary on marriage as an institution dogged with confusion, but a commentary upon law in general and its ambiguities and uncertainties in the consideration of justice. Ingram explains that:

the late sixteenth and early seventeenth centuries—the era in which Shakespeare wrote—constituted "an uneasy transition period" for marriage law: despite widespread acceptance of church marriage and the decline of spousals even as a preliminary to ecclesiastical solemnization, the fact that an informal contract could still create a binding union entailed uncertainty, moral ambiguities and opportunities for deceit and fraud.[12]

Therefore, Shakespeare depicts 'Angelo's understanding and practice of the law to reveal the inconsistency at its core'.[13]

Although marriage or engagement represents the conclusion of the play, its impacts are far from positive, from Isabella's silence in reaction to the Duke's proposal, Angelo's commitment to Mariana, to the reunion and subsequent marriage between Claudio and Juliet, all appear as unstable, confusing, and contradictory conclusions to fix the problems presented throughout the play. Although marriage for Claudio and Juliet had been their desired goal from the start, their marriage now appears unstable in relation to the legal judgements surrounding it and point again to the complicated nature of the law that punishes crime and the corrupt use of power residing in those that judge crime. Shakespeare asks the audience to question whether the law should be incited 'to the letter', or whether it should take account of the special characteristics and extenuating circumstances of each offender. The play in this way can be read as work that questions whether the law could be making better judgements in its consideration of punishment to ameliorate crime.

If Angelo is to be seen as a metaphorical representation of the law in place during Shakespeare's time, then he depicts its corruption and right-wing asceticism. He is a manifestation of the age of terror and bodily punishment and Shakespeare is perhaps suggesting the need for a more considered approach regarding both the crime and the criminal, represented to some degree in Duke Vincentio and his left-wing liberalism. The Duke is therefore a manifestation of the age of confinement and as Werkman summarises:

Angelo clearly represents the old system through his excessive use of power, corruption and distance to his people. The Duke however, represents the new system of surveillance, mercy, and his exercises of power over the lives of his subjects instead of their death.[14]

Claudio is used as an example by Angelo, but his corrupt application of using Claudio to teach Vienna a lesson appears to be more about social control. Boal terms this as 'Cops-in-the-head' which alludes to how power can control the mind and discusses its continued role in transforming an individual. 'Cops-in-the-head', by its very name, suggests that 'the world is filled with instructions that are imprinting authoritarian fantasies', based upon the internalisation of one's oppression.[15] That although an individual may seemingly believe they have freedom, the oppression they were made to feel is so ingrained within their psyche that their oppressions are internalised and able to control the individual subliminally. Even upon release from the confines of prison the cops-in-the-head are still working after the prisoner is physically freed. Claudio's punishment is therefore not about the application of a clear legal process, but rather used to incite fear in the minds of himself and others. Depriving Claudio access to considered punishment results in confusion as punishment should never be used:

> merely as a means to promote some other good for the criminal himself or for civil society, but instead it must in all cases be imposed on him only on the ground that he has committed a crime, for a human being can never be manipulated merely as a means to the purpose of someone else and can never be confused with the objects of the law of things.[16]

However, Angelo's zealous pursuit of the written law means he ignores the imperfect justice in which he attempts to operate and continues to provide a confused and seemingly unfair application of a punishment at odds with the crime.

The complex legal backdrop for *Measure for Measure* is clearly established in the earliest stages of the play, but it is the way the characters interact with the law that highlights most specifically the side of transition to which they fall, the side of terror, or the side of confinement.

Isabella is the first to 'give argument for the more lenient and humanitarian penal system of the 18th century'.[17] Isabella appeals to Angelo to 'condemn the fault and not the actor of it'.[18] She also criticises the punishment Angelo chooses for Claudio when stating, 'who is it that died for this offence? /There's many have committed it'.[19] Isabella highlights a desire to implement a system of confinement and considers the 'self' in punishment and prosecution. Although Isabella herself is not imprisoned or tried for a crime, she consciously decides to punish her soul through her confinement in the nunnery and 'is determined to abjure physical pleasure, public life, and procreation' when at the beginning of the play she asks for 'more restraint'.[20] Throughout the play, however, she is repeatedly removed from her pursuit of salvation and instead required to deal with the business of body, family, and state. Kendall highlights this notion further when stating that:

> Isabella is steadily drawn into the marketplace of the physical, into mentality that thinks more about desire than religion, more about the threat of death than the hope of immortality, more about bodily confinement (a grave) than about spiritual injury (disgrace or damnation) that would be a restraint/ though all the world's vastidity you had.[21]

Although Isabella throughout the play cries out for a new system of confinement in relation to the consideration of the soul in punishment, she exists in Angelo's age of terror and he affirms, 'I talk not of your soul'; instead, Angelo proposes a bodily exchange to save her brother.

Angelo:	Now took your brother's life, or, to redeem him,
	Give up your body to such sweet uncleanliness, as
	She that he hath stain'd?
Isabella:	Sir, believe this,
	I had rather give my body, than my soul
Angelo:	Might there not be a charity in sin
	To save this brother's life?[22]

The Duke as the undercover overseer of Vienna also represents an age of confinement and a move towards a new penal system. Werkman explains how:

> the choice of the Duke very much resembles the surveillance in the panoptical in order to control the people [...] it's the Duke's aim to position the characters in confessional subjection, which he does by repressive tolerance, not oppression.[23]

The panoptical was one of the techniques regarded by Foucault in being able to regulate people via non-violent means. Mason discusses how 'the panopticon offered a powerful and sophisticated internalized coercion, which was achieved through the constant observation of prisoners. Constant observation acted as a control mechanism; a consciousness of constant surveillance internalized'.[24] Power is achieved via the position of observing others, often from a distance, which marks the change in punishment to a disciplinary power where movements are supervised instead of bodies punished. This can be seen when in Act Five the Duke reveals he has been concealed as Friar Lodowick. Angelo states:

Angelo: O my dread lord,
I should be guiltier than my guiltiness,
To think I can be undiscernible,
When I perceive your grace, like power divine,
Hath look'd upon my passes. Then, good prince,
No longer session hold upon my shame,
But let my trial be mine own confession:
Immediate sentence then and sequent death
Is all the grace I beg.[25]

Although the Duke does not explore the possibilities of the prison as a form of correctional punishment, his notion that counselling, therapy, and mitigating and aggravating circumstances should be considered is important and offers an indication of the changes surrounding how punishment is conceived. This links to Foucault's suggestion of penitentiary or correctional behaviour. For example, Pompey is excused of execution, which would be 'needless cruelty'; and is instead required to be separated from bad company and rehabilitated through therapy and 'correction and instruction'.[26] This was recommended to not only help Pompey become a more sociable human 'but also to provide him with job skills so that he might become a more productive member of society'.[27] In this way the Duke is modernity in his consideration of self-repression and through experimenting with abandoning:

> public violence in return for the private discipline of its citizens. Increasingly during that period, the therapeutic idea began to gain ground although its implementation differed from the contemporary therapeutic notions a healthy dose of labour discipline was deemed to be a panacea for criminality.[28]

Despite evidence of progressive thought regarding the penal system through some of Shakespeare's leading characters, 'the age of terror' is still present in the play. The prison remains a place where criminals wait for punishment instead of it being a method of punishment itself. Both the Duke and Angelo demonstrate unyielding power, criticised by Isabella: 'Oh it is excellent/ to have a giant's strength, but it is tyrannous/ to use it like a giant'.[29] They also both decide punishment without consultation; their power is Machiavellian and relates to a sovereign's freedom of action. Through Angelo specifically, Shakespeare depicts the techniques and methods of the old system. Angelo's power is presented as infinite and not restricted, he repents and confesses to show the fault first and the punishment to come next, and he highlights how the body can be punished via penance. Angelo's monologue in Act Two, Scene Four represents an important moment in the play where Angelo is struggling with sexual desire for Isabella. Confessing his sins to God to no avail he 'becomes fixated on a punishment to his physical state and his self-lacerating language in the speech that follows, suggests that Angelo might actually flagellate himself during this speech'.[30]

Angelo: When I would pray and think, I think and pray
          To several subjects. Heaven hath my empty words
          Whilst my intervention, hearing not my tongue,
          Anchors on Isabel; heaven in my mouth,
          As if I did but chew his name,
          And in my heart the strong and swelling evil
          Of my conception.[31]

Angelo is a representation of the old system and not just in his decision to whip as a form of physical punishment, but his aim behind the strict penal system 'is to make an example, prevent others from committing crime and thereby expand his authority, which all fits in the penal system of the Age of Terror'.[32]

The elements of transition that Shakespeare's work depicts highlights the turmoil of the penal system in place at the time *Measure for Measure* was written. Angelo is an example of old law, unyielding and unable to consider the circumstances of the prisoner due to overriding strict law and enforcement. The Duke is the new system of surveillance and mercy, exercising power over his subjects instead of sentencing them to death. The two characters allow Shakespeare to present the transition between the two penal systems. *Measure for Measure* 'is a mirror for magistrates, then, in which Angelo, who begins his rule "hoping [to] find good cause to 'whip them all' discovers that the quality of mercy is such as to subjugate more completely than the axe or leash"".[33] *Measure for Measure* documents changes in a penal system, considers a new notion of mercy, and presents the consequences of an ineffectual justice system. Shakespeare is profoundly concerned with the balance between justice and mercy, and how that can be achieved when the law is applied by a zealot.

Shakespeare was perhaps ahead of his time in his consideration of alternatives to crime and punishment and it was not until the eighteenth century when punishment became focused upon changing the souls of the criminals (as presented by the Duke and Isabella). Although we can never truly say what Shakespeare's intentions were in his depiction of prison within the play *Measure for Measure*, what is evident within the text is a demonstration of a type of justice that needs much greater consideration in relation to the implementation of strategies to achieve discipline.

The play suggests something about the nature of crime, how it is considered, and how it should be punished. Shakespeare's presentation of the difficult nature of a penal system suggests that regardless of the way crime is punished and:

> although we are told of engagement within the space of prison, it is important to remember that no matter how the system is developed, it remains a 'detestable solution' to much broader and complex questions about the nature of crime, the politics of power and the type of society in which we choose to exist and operate.[34]

The play offers clear considerations to the penal environment and questions whether its structures are beneficial for those inside the prison and/or overseeing/managing the environment. In concentrating the mind upon the historical implications of the work the play offers a beneficial opportunity to interrogate the criminal and justice system. *Measure for Measure* provides important questions to law enforcement and punishment. The historical terrain at the time in which the play was written highlights the ambiguities of the legal system in operation during the Renaissance and presents something significant about the transition from the age of terror to the age of confinement. English society in its phase of transition between two penal systems allows Shakespeare to depict and question the legal choices in operation and the demands for a new and more just system of punishment. The historical investigations into the work highlight important questions that are tantamount to the challenges of a penal environment in general terms and offer a clear base from which participants can consider the penal setting through Shakespeare's play.

NOTES

1. ShakespeareMag. (2013) *Crime and Punishment*: http://www.shakespearemag.com/fall98/punished.asp (Accessed: 07/12/17).
2. Werkman, A. (2015) *Shakespeare and Prison: A critical reflection on Richard Wilson's Foucauldian reading of William Shakespeare's Measure for Measure*. Netherlands: Utrecht University. p. 6.
3. Ibid, pp. 7–9.
4. See more here Foucault, M. (1975) *Surveiller et Punir: Naissance de la Prison*. France: Editions Flammarion.
5. Werkman, A. (2015) *Shakespeare and Prison: A critical reflection on Richard Wilson's Foucauldian reading of William Shakespeare's Measure for Measure*. Netherlands: Utrecht University. p. 15.
6. Knowles, R. (2002) *Shakespeare's argument with history*. London & New York: Palgrave Macmillan. p. 64.
7. Foucault, M. (1969) *The Archaeology of Knowledge*. France: Éditions Gallimard. p. 21.
8. Shakespeare, W. in Craig, W.J. (1991) (ed.) *The Complete works of Shakespeare*. Oxford: Oxford University Press. p. 73.
9. Bawdy Courts. (no date) *Policing Sex*: http://hfriedberg.web.wesleyan.edu/engl205/wshakespeare/policingsex.htm(Accessed: 07/12/17).
10. Sokol B.J. & Sokol, M. (2003) *Shakespeare, Law, and Marriage*. Cambridge: Cambridge University Press. p. 14.
11. Funk, J. (2012) *Measuring Legal Fictions: Law and Sovereignty in Measure for Measure*. Clemson University: Tiger Prints. p.17.
12. Ingram, M. (1987) *Church Courts, Sex and Marriage in England (1570–1640)*. New York: Cambridge University Press. p. 133.
13. Sokol B.J. & Sokol, M. (2003) *Shakespeare, Law, and Marriage*. Cambridge: Cambridge University Press. p. 15.
14. Werkman, A. (2015) *Shakespeare and Prison: A critical reflection on Richard Wilson's Foucauldian reading of William Shakespeare's Measure for Measure*. Netherlands: Utrecht University. p. 22.
15. Cohen-Cruz, J. & Schultzman, M (ed.) (2002) *Playing Boal Theatre, Therapy, Activism*. London & New York: Routledge. p. 5. See also Boal, A. & Epstein, S. (1990) 'The cop in the head: three hypotheses' *The Drama Review*. 34 (3), pp. 35–42: http://www.populareducation.co.za/sites/default/files/Boal%20cop%20in%20the%20head.pdf (Accessed: 31/08/18).

72   A. HULSMEIER

16. Kant, I. (1985) *Metaphysical Elements of Justice: Part I of The Metaphysics of Morals, Part 1.* Cambridge: Hackett Publishing Company Inc. p. 21.
17. Werkman, A. (2015) *Shakespeare and Prison: A critical reflection on Richard Wilson's Foucauldian reading of William Shakespeare's Measure for Measure.* Netherlands: Utrecht University. p. 18.
18. Shakespeare, W. in Craig, W.J. (1991) (ed.) *The Complete works of Shakespeare.* Oxford: Oxford University Press. p. 79.
19. Ibid, p. 79.
20. Kendall, G.M. (ed) (1998) *Shakespearean Power and Punishment: A Volume of Essays. Shakespeare Quarterly,* Volume 52, Issue 1, Spring 2001, Pages 159–161, https://doi.org/10/1353/shq.2001.0012. p. 144.
21. Ibid, p. 144.
22. Shakespeare, W. in Craig, W.J. (1991) (ed.) *The Complete works of Shakespeare.* Oxford: Oxford University Press. pp. 81–82.
23. Werkman, A. (2015) *Shakespeare and Prison: A critical reflection on Richard Wilson's Foucauldian reading of William Shakespeare's Measure for Measure.* Netherlands: Utrecht University. p. 17.
24. See, Mason, M.K. (2018) *Foucault and His Panoptican*: http://www.moyak.com/papers/michel-foucault-power.html (Accessed: 08/04/18).
25. Shakespeare, W. in Craig, W.J. (1991) (ed.) *The Complete works of Shakespeare.* Oxford: Oxford University Press. p. 98.
26. Ibid, p. 86.
27. Time, V. M. (1999) *Shakespeare's Criminals, Criminology, Fictions and Drama.* London: Greenwood Press. p. 135.
28. Ibid, p. 22.
29. Shakespeare, W. in Craig, W.J. (1991) (ed.) *The Complete works of Shakespeare.* Oxford: Oxford University Press. p. 80.
30. McCandless, D. (no date) *"I'll Pray to Increase Your Bondage": Power and Punishment in Measure for Measure*: http://college.holycross.edu/projects/isp/measure/essays/bondage.html (Accessed: 30/10/16). p. 10.
31. Shakespeare, W. in Craig, W.J. (1991) (ed.) *The Complete works of Shakespeare.* Oxford: Oxford University Press. p. 81.
32. Werkman, A. (2015) *Shakespeare and Prison: A critical reflection on Richard Wilson's Foucauldian reading of William Shakespeare's Measure for Measure.* Netherlands: Utrecht University. p. 23.
33. Wilson, R. (1993) 'The Quality of Mercy: Discipline and Punishment in Shakespearean Comedy', in Wilson, R. (ed.) *Will Power: Essays on Shakespearean Authority.* Hemel Hempstead: Harvester Wheatsheaf, pp.118–157. p. 127.
34. Foucault, M. (1977) *Power/ Knowledge: Selected interviews and other writings 1972–1977.* Hemel Hempstead: Harvester Wheatsheaf. p. 215.

CHAPTER 9

Shakespeare's Criminals, Criminal Shakespeare: A Renaissance Reading of Shakespeare and the Criminal Mind in *Macbeth*

This chapter analyses what lessons Shakespeare's depiction of the criminal mind may be able to provide to participants of applied theatre projects who are accessing criminal characters to achieve transformation. The play *Macbeth* with specific focus on the character Lady Macbeth will remain the focus of this chapter's attention underpinned by an interrogation of the Elizabethan and Jacobean environments that influenced Shakespeare's presentation of crime and the criminal mind.

Many ascertain that prisons across the globe are filled with people who think like the criminals found in Shakespeare, and there are many who believe Shakespeare's canon largely addresses crime and its accountability. If this is true, then a reading of Shakespeare's presentation of the criminal mind is important in understanding how and, to a lesser extent, why (as there is often no one reason why people commit crime) criminals in Shakespeare's plays violate human rights.

The reader is presented with a number of crimes and criminals that are continuously part of the tragic structure of Shakespeare's plays. Obvious criminal behaviour can be seen throughout his canon of work. Thieves, rogues, and vagabonds are found in *Timon of Athens*. Forgery, embezzlement, and false pretence can be found in *Richard III*, and adultery is found in *Cymbeline* and *The Winter's Tale*.[1] It would be beyond the remit of this work to consider all the criminals found in Shakespeare's work

© The Author(s), under exclusive license to Springer Nature Switzerland AG 2024
A. Hulsmeier, *Applied Shakespeare*,
https://doi.org/10.1007/978-3-031-45414-1_9

73

74   A. HULSMEIER

however it is acknowledged that of the more serious crimes, Goll selects six criminal types from Shakespeare's plays: the political criminal (Brutus and Cassius), man of ambition (Macbeth), woman criminal (Lady Macbeth—does not commit crime for her own benefit but to elevate her husband to power), born criminal (Richard III), criminal of pure malice (Iago).[2]

Criminals therefore exist in a range of social, religious, governmental, business, military, and familial settings and a range of Shakespearean criminals are seen to plan and commit crime for a range of reasons—always criminal in nature—but linked to ideas of political power and/or rivalry, war, revenge, murder, ambition, and betrayal.

Although Lady Macbeth does not physically commit a crime and is regarded as an 'accessory before and after the act', her explicit articulation of criminal behaviour and intent are some of the most intense and detailed of any of the criminal characters within Shakespeare's canon.[3] Her thoughts and interactions regarding criminal behaviour are referenced throughout her monologues and soliloquies and appear to point to a very specific crime that can only be fully understood in relation to its historical placement and significance. This is the crime of patrilineal castration and its links to maternal agency, patrilineal identity, and infanticide which are consumed in Lady Macbeth and presented throughout her soliloquies. Lady Macbeth's interactions with these crimes help to present an explicit interaction with issues that are firmly embedded within Renaissance history.

Lady Macbeth's character throughout the play is attached to chaos, both political and social, but she does not attempt to seize masculine power; instead, she follows the female construct that means she does not lift a dagger but is able to consider criminal behaviour in explicit detail. At a time in history where patrilineal order was to be rigorously maintained, and masculine anxiety regarding the power of the female in relation to maternal authority existed, the character of Lady Macbeth speaks clearly to her Renaissance audience regarding their cultural fears. Chamberlain states that 'although many academics have read Lady Macbeth's invocations relating to maternity and motherhood as a desire to seize masculine power; her power is in fact conditioned on maternity, an ambiguous, conflicted status in early modern England' and 'perhaps no other Shakespearean character better represents the threat of maternal agency than she does'. [4]

In Act One, Scene Five upon receiving Macbeth's letters before his return from war, Lady Macbeth is so encouraged by the letter's contents that she summons spirits:

9 SHAKESPEARE'S CRIMINALS, CRIMINAL SHAKESPEARE: A RENAISSANCE...

> That tend on mortal thoughts, unsex me here,
> And fill me from the crown to the toe top-full
> Of direst cruelty. Make thick my blood.
> Stop up the access and passage to remorse,
> That no compunctious visitings of nature
> Shake my fell purpose, nor keep peace between
> The effect and it! Come to my woman's breasts,
> And take my milk for gall, you murd'ring ministers,
> Wherever in your sightless substances
> You wait on nature's mischief.[5]

In very quick succession throughout the speech Lady Macbeth subverts the early modern period's expectation of motherhood. Within this speech alone she asks for her milk to be 'turned to gall', 'to be 'unsexed', and for her body to be filled 'from the crown to the toe top-full of direst cruelty'.[6] Two significant things are referenced within her speech. Firstly, Shakespeare mentions breastfeeding, which was regarded by the early modern period as a fundamental and biological trait of woman, and then Lady Macbeth turns it into something evil. Secondly, Lady Macbeth asks to be unsexed so that her body is unable to reproduce, again a subversion of female expectation but simultaneously a suggestion that would put a stop to Macbeth's lineage. Garber explains that 'heirs are important to political as well as social outcomes is too apparent throughout this play [...] the play is as urgently concerned with dynasty, offspring, and succession as any in Shakespeare'.[7] Shakespeare therefore plays on the cultural fears of his audience that are different to those held today.

Lady Macbeth's second speech goes even further in referencing her criminal thoughts. She states:

> I have given suck, and know
> How tender 'tis to love the babe that milks me.
> I would, while it was smiling in my face,
> have plucked my nipple from his boneless gums
> and dashed the brains out, had I so sworn as you
> have done to this.[8]

Although this is a speech predominantly interpreted as a method to persuade her husband to murder King Duncan, the references in her speech to motherhood and infanticide cannot be underestimated or ignored. They again link to specifically placed cultural fears and Sokol and Sokol explain that historically:

> no other early modern crime better exemplifies cultural fears about maternal agency than infanticide, a crime against both person and lineage. Treated as a sin in medieval England, one punishable through ecclesiastical penance, infanticide, by the early modern period, had been deemed a criminal offence, one punishable by hanging.[9]

Lady Macbeth is seen in the image of a lactating mother who goes on to brutally kill her baby. This use of juxtaposition is important in showing the:

> loving image of nurturing mother [...] which immediately gives way to one of absolute horror, as a demonic mother butchers her yet-smiling infant [...] that this savagery surfaces at a moment of greatest intimacy between mother and child only adds to its incomprehensible brutality.[10]

It matters little whether Lady Macbeth ever nursed children, it is more prevalent that 'Lady Macbeth uses and appeals to the maternal [by] calling up the chilling image of infanticide'.[11] This may be referencing the cases of infanticide that led to the 1624 Infanticide Act which made it a criminal offense to secretly bury or conceal the death of their [lewd women's] children.[12] Between 1558 and 1688 there were 230 recorded cases of infanticide.[13] The play *Macbeth* was written in 1606 by which point the rate of infanticide was 3 per 100,000.[14] What is interesting about this figure is that 'the passage of the 1624 statute that targeted infanticide represents unusually severe punishment, and the exceptionally high execution rate for convicted infanticides that punctuated the seventeenth century' appears at odds with the low number of crimes being committed. This is significant as it highlights not necessarily how common infanticide was as a criminal act, but rather how significant the fear of the population was in attempting to control maternal agency, whilst simultaneously fearing it.[15]

Maternal agency is explored throughout the speech and suggests that Shakespeare is attempting to 'reveal much [...] about the early modern anxiety surrounding mother's roles in the perpetuation of patrilineage'.[16] Botelho suggests that 'murder and the forgetting of maternal duty serve as a way for any women to resist or subvert subordination or confinement'.[17] Her empowerment is instead based on the dependent:

loving relationship with the one she will shortly slaughter: a lamb sacrifice. That a mother could lovingly nurture her infant one moment and spill his brains the next underscores the uncertainties: if not the danger of unchecked maternal agency.[18]

Other literature of the period is not the only source demonstrating the subject of power through mothering; historical sources also depict 'the fear of, fascination with, and hostility toward maternal power in early modern England'.[19] One aspect of this power links to the assurances of matrilineal identity, of which the father lacks similar assurances. The most important aspect of this power, however, is the ability for a woman to undermine and/or control the patrilineal process. Chamberlain states:

> the infanticidal mothers represented in the assize records are all Lady Macbeths, who would lightly dash out the brains of the babes entrusted to their care [...] In doing so, these accounts communicate existing early modern anxieties about the inherent dangers of maternal agency both to helpless children as well as to the patrilineal system dependent upon women for its perpetuation.[20]

Therefore, Lady Macbeth 'embodies both her society's expectations and its anxieties about motherhood by showing motherhood to be at once empowering and destructive'.[21] Shakespeare therefore uses Lady Macbeth's speech to evoke fear in the audience which is relative to early modern England's desire to protect patrilineal rights. Ultimately by dashing the babe's brains, 'Lady Macbeth is happy to kill Macbeth's progeny to secure his succession; but in killing the progeny she must likewise destroy his patrilineage, rendering his short-lived reign a baron one'.[22]

The role of Lady Macbeth as evil is clear, but the clarity is only absolute when it is regarded in the historical vernacular in which the play was created. As Adelman observes, 'the play becomes [...] a representation of primitive fears about male identity and autonomy itself, about those looming female presences who threaten to control one's mind, to constitute one's very self, even at a distance'.[23] By using infanticide, Shakespeare highlights how Lady Macbeth may be able to 'undermine patrilineal outcomes'. Therefore, although Lady Macbeth never wields the dagger, it is her infanticidal fantasy that culminates in Macbeth brooding upon the disappearance of his name. Chamberlain forces forward the point that:

It is this loss of name, of a protected patrilineal identity that proves so destructive to this man who would be the father of kings. For what Lady Macbeth's frightening maternal agency renders is not a coveted line, but rather a barren reign, one which quickly disintegrates when confronted by legitimate political authority.[24]

Lady Macbeth's crimes are not watertight, although appearing indifferent to her insinuations of infanticide:

> what she fails to notice is what will become of her husband given the failure to produce a living heir [...] at no point does she express a concern for Macbeth's extinguished patrilineage [...] and merely cautions 'what's done is done'.[25]

It is this indifference, bred from the negative impact maternal agency provided early modern England, that aroused cultural fears regarding the patrilineal process and thus made Lady Macbeth potentially one of the most feared criminals in Renaissance England.

Taking into consideration the ideas of maternal agency, patrilineal identity and lineage, and infanticide, the extent of Lady Macbeth's crimes can be understood. A historical reading of the work is needed when exploring this character's thoughts on crime, as the true extent of her evil is only comprehended when an understanding of cultural fears and traditions are explored. This may be the case for a range of characters accessed as part of applied theatre. Therefore, one must use the lessons of this play cautiously and tread carefully when suggesting that Shakespeare's plays can provide transformative encounters when engaging with the lessons of the work, as such lessons are complex and can remain tied to beliefs pervasive during the Renaissance, which are different to our own.

NOTES

1. Although they are false charges, the charge of infidelity takes a leading part in Shakespearean plays because of the force it carried during his time.
2. , J. A. (1938) *'Criminal types in Shakespeare', Journal of Criminal Law and Justice*. 5 (29), pp. 1–24: https://scholarlycommons.law.northwestern.edu/cgi/viewcontent.cgi?article=2829&context=jclc (Accessed: 27/09/18). p. 492.

3. See Orten, J.D. (2003) *'That perilous stuff": Crime in Shakespeare's Tragedies*. https://brage.bibsys.no/xmlui/bitstream/handle/11250/147500/Orten.pdf?sequence=1 (Accessed: 18/07/18).
4. Chamberlain, S. (2005) 'Fantasizing Infanticide: Lady Macbeth and the Murdering Mother in Early Modern England'. *College Literature*, 32 (3), pp. 72–91: https://www.wssd.org/cms/lib02/PA01001072/Centricity/Domain/202/Fantacizing%20Infanticide%20Lady%20Mac%20Article.pdf (Accessed 26/02/19). p. 79.
5. Shakespeare, W. in Craig, W.J. (1991) (ed.) *The Complete works of Shakespeare*. Oxford: Oxford University Press. p. 849–850.
6. Ibid, 849–850.
7. Garber, M. (1997) *Coming of Age in Shakespeare*. New York: Routledge. p. 154.
8. Shakespeare, W. in Craig, W.J. (1991) (ed.) *The Complete works of Shakespeare*. Oxford: Oxford University Press. p. 851.
9. Sokol B.J. & Sokol, M. (2003) *Shakespeare, Law, and Marriage*. Cambridge: Cambridge University Press. p. 233.
10. Chamberlain, S. (2005) 'Fantasizing Infanticide: Lady Macbeth and the Murdering Mother in Early Modern England'. *College Literature*, 32 (3), pp. 72–91: https://www.wssd.org/cms/lib02/PA01001072/Centricity/Domain/202/Fantacizing%20Infanticide%20Lady%20Mac%20Article.pdf (Accessed 26/02/19). p. 82.
11. Ibid, p. 81.
12. Fletcher, A. (1995) *Gender, Sex, and Subordination in England? 1500–1800*. New Haven: Yale University Press. p. 277.
13. See Spence, L. (2010) *Women who murder in early modern England, 1558–1700*: https://warwick.ac.uk/fac/arts/history/ecc/emforum/projects/disstheses/dissertations/spence-laura.pdf (Accessed: 08/04/18).
14. See, Sokol B.J. & Sokol, M. (2003) *Shakespeare, Law, and Marriage*. Cambridge: Cambridge University Press.
15. Copeland, S. C. S. (2008) *Constructions of Infanticide in Early Modern England: Female Deviance Demographic Crisis*: https://etd.ohiolink.edu/rws_etd/document/get/osu1222046761/inline accessed (Accessed: 04/08/17). p. 16.
16. Ibid, p. 16.
17. Botelho, K. (2008) 'Maternal Memory and Murder in Seventeenth Century England', *Studies in English Literature 1500–1900*. 48 (1), p.114 https://www.academia.edu/3645009/Maternal_Memory_and_Murder_in_Early-Seventeenth-Century_England._SEL_Studies_in_English_Literature_48_1_Winter_2008_111-130 (Accessed 26/02/19). p. 114.

80   A. HULSMEIER

18. Chamberlain, S. (2005) 'Fantasizing Infanticide: Lady Macbeth and the Murdering Mother in Early Modern England'. *College Literature*, 32 (3), pp. 72–91: https://www.wssd.org/cms/lib02/PA01001072/Centricity/Domain/202/Fantacizing%20Infanticide%20Lady%20Mac%20Article.pdf (Accessed 26/02/19). p. 82.
19. Dolan, F. (1994) *Dangerous Familiars: Representations of Domestic Crime in England, 1550–1700*. Cornwall: Cornwall University Press. p. 283.
20. Chamberlain, S. (2005) 'Fantasizing Infanticide: Lady Macbeth and the Murdering Mother in Early Modern England'. *College Literature*, 32 (3), pp. 72–91: https://www.wssd.org/cms/lib02/PA01001072/Centricity/Domain/202/Fantacizing%20Infanticide%20Lady%20Mac%20Article.pdf (Accessed 26/02/19). p. 77.
21. Staub, S. (2000) 'Early Modern Medea: Representations of Child Murder in the Street Literature of Seventeenth Century England', in Miller, N.J & Yavneh, N. (ed.) *Maternal Measures: Figuring Caregiving in the Early Modern Period*. Aldershot: Ashgate, pp. 333–347. p. 345.
22. Chamberlain, S. (2005) 'Fantasizing Infanticide: Lady Macbeth and the Murdering Mother in Early Modern England'. *College Literature*, 32 (3), pp. 72–91: https://www.wssd.org/cms/lib02/PA01001072/Centricity/Domain/202/Fantacizing%20Infanticide%20Lady%20Mac%20Article.pdf (Accessed 26/02/19). p. 82.
23. Adelman, J. (1987) "Born of Woman': Fantasies of Maternal Power in Macbeth!' in Garber, M. (ed.) *Cannibals, Witches, and Divorce: Estranging the Renaissance: Selected Papers from the English Institute*. Baltimore: John Hopkins University Press, pp. 72–91: https://ssologin.exeter.ac.uk/dist-auth/UI/Login?realm=%2Fpeople&goto=https%3A%2F%2Felibrary.exeter.ac.uk%3A443%2Fidp%2FAuthn%2FRemoteUser%3Fconversation%3De2s1 (Accessed 26/02/19). p. 105.
24. Chamberlain, S. (2005) 'Fantasizing Infanticide: Lady Macbeth and the Murdering Mother in Early Modern England'. *College Literature*, 32 (3), pp. 72–91: https://www.wssd.org/cms/lib02/PA01001072/Centricity/Domain/202/Fantacizing%20Infanticide%20Lady%20Mac%20Article.pdf (Accessed 26/02/19). p. 83.
25. Ibid, p. 84.

CHAPTER 10

ESC: A Case Study

This chapter aims to look specifically at ESC Film's use of Shakespeare's work within their own penal programme and how this programme captures some of the methodologies, impacts, and challenges tied to applied theatre's intentions for achieving transformation.

ESC is an arts education charity and their core work focuses on involving marginalised people in the arts, empowering them 'to find their voice and tell stories through film'.[1] ESC, originally the Educational Shakespeare Company, started by 'working with people experiencing extreme marginalisation within society'[2] and is now an established company with a very developed filmography. In every ESC project, the focus is on the 'creative process and on creating a high-quality end-product, while emphasizing the therapeutic and rehabilitative effects of the work that they do'.[3]

ESC specialises 'in mental health and criminal justice, and work with community and forensic mental health patients, youth at risk, and people who have suffered trauma, amongst many others. They use drama and film to challenge perceptions, tackle social exclusion and change lives'.[4] They have also worked with 'prison officers' widows, medically retired prison officers, young homeless people and young people suffering from cancer'.[5] Given the purpose and nature of this chapter, their work with prisoners will remain the focus throughout.

ESC was founded in 1999 (under the original title of the Education Shakespeare Company) by Tom Magill and Andrew Stocker. Michael Bogdanov (director of the English Shakespeare Company) invited his

© The Author(s), under exclusive license to Springer Nature   81
Switzerland AG 2024
A. Hulsmeier, *Applied Shakespeare*,
https://doi.org/10.1007/978-3-031-45414-1_10

82   A. HULSMEIER

assistant director, Tom Magill, to set up a branch of the company in Belfast to deliver Shakespeare workshops to schools. In 2003 the company moved into filmmaking. This was supported by Peace II funding.[6] In 2007 ESC produced the award-winning film *Mickey B*, a modern adaptation of Shakespeare's *Macbeth* with prisoners from Maghaberry maximum-security prison, Belfast. By 2008, producer Jennifer Marquis-Muradaz founded ESC's first international branch ESC US in Naples, Florida, and in 2014 the company spearheaded Northern Ireland's first mental health arts and film festival.

ESC is concerned with making filmic and not theatre-based adaptations of Shakespeare's plays, which emerged from drama workshops with the prisoners. Following the intentions of applied theatre, captured predominantly by the influences of the work of Boal, the films are a purposefully selected medium by ESC. Firstly, film is relevant to the participant; and secondly, film offers an opportunity to capture important educational skills and developments for the participant. For Magill and Marquis-Muradaz the justification for using film is clear:

> Whilst prisoners generally know little about theatre and Shakespeare, they can and do spend up to twenty-three hours inside a cell with television. So they know a lot about films [...] Making a film which involved several short bursts of work over several days and included long breaks [...] helped to balance out the prisoner's less-developed concentration and listening skills, as well as memorisation/literacy problems [...] Filming allowed us to accommodate unavoidable interruptions and delays (legal and family visits, court dates, alarms, prison jobs, other classes, etc.) and provided important opportunities for those who did not want to appear on screen [...] we have also learnt that film is an extraordinary self-evaluation tool. People will watch their onscreen behaviour [...] and learn from this 'objective' third party vantage point in a way that cannot be replicated in any other medium.[7]

The benefits of the medium are therefore far-reaching as an immediate tool to experience, capture, and then assess change. For Magill, film enables people to be present in their absence. A particularly useful tool, when working in volatile changing circumstances, where access to prisoners is controlled by the whim of the system.

The aims and intentions of ESC go a long way in highlighting their desire for social change. The company are clear about their links to applied theatre. Their manifesto on how to capture change documents their work as being influenced by the purposes of applied theatre and they equate their work to the aims of Boalian praxis and healing. Magill explains that the work undertakes a process of discovery and follows the method of 'teaching by asking instead of telling'.[8] Magill further explains that this method is:

> 'More effective with prisoners especially those labelled high risk and those that have an attitude problem with authority. We encourage prisoners to become independent and to choose their own level of responsibility through the role they play in the film'.[9]

Magill served time in prison where he experienced a profound change leading to a career as an applied theatre artist devoted to serving others in similar circumstances. He was also a student of Boal and became a representative of his techniques and methods in Northern Ireland. This is testimony to the influence of applied theatre upon ESC. They encourage storytelling which 'creates solidarity and support'.[10] They aim to 'create a safe space where people feel free to take risks; the key to empowerment and emancipation' they further 'believe people have the solutions to their own problems and often use Forum Theatre to help them find them'.[11] ESC aims to create work that helps to 'integrate people back into society more easily [...] and use Tom Magill's experiences to help further develop methods of rehabilitating the marginalised through the arts'.[12]

The company also fits the desire to be participatory as the prisoners are actively involved with the filmic productions and prisoners are asked to engage with projects in the role of performance and/or production. The films are shot in prison workshops, firstly to avoid disruptions of the everyday workings of the environment, but an added benefit to this is the opportunity for prisoners to learn a trade, skills like Braille, painting, woodwork, and bricklaying. It provides prisoners with an opportunity to develop multimedia skills acquired in the filmmaking trade, and develop literacy problems with accredited qualifications, such as Active Citizen Awards. Twenty of the prisoners achieved an Educational Certificate, an Active Citizenship Award (ASDAN) for taking part in the film project. Overall, ESC desires to 'use drama and film to challenge perceptions, change lives, tackle social exclusion and encourage civic engagement in order to radically transform people'.[13]

The overarching aims of the company and justification for the work's existence are that the:

ESC wants to enable people to understand and transform their lives, using drama and film to explore and record their stories. Through a core set of values of respect, trust, choice, responsibility, courage, understanding, non-judgementalism and inclusivity, the organisation uses the medium of film and practice of filmmaking to help groups and individuals to understand the potential and power of film for documenting life stories, the practical and technical side of filmmaking, and their own potential for change and personal growth.[14]

Since the film projects began in 2003, ESC has developed a vast filmography. Their prison work includes documentaries such as *Two Sides of the Coin* (2004/5 with The Prison Service Trust, which filmed the stories of medically retired prison officers and widows serving during the Troubles), *The Big Question* (2005/6 made by Magill and Simon Wood in association with Prison Arts Foundation), and *Seen but Not Heard* (2008 with Queen's University Social Work Department and the criminal justice system). Short films include *Inside Job* (2003/4 in association with Prison Arts Foundation), *Extern: The First Course* (207 with Extern AXIS and ex-prisoners and people on probation. This project was funded by Peace II from Proteus in partnership with Prison Arts Foundation), and *Extern: The Second Course* (2008 with a group of volunteer ex-prisoners and people on probation). Of all the work produced by ESC, their feature films are the most important to this research as they use Shakespeare's plays as the main stimulus. These projects include ESC's award-winning *Mickey B* (2007 with HMP Maghaberry, an adaptation of Shakespeare's *Macbeth*) and currently awaiting release is *Prospero's Prison*, a modern adaptation of Shakespeare's *The Tempest* set in a Belfast Prison.

Prospero's Prison will see 'Prospero, a successful criminal set up, framed, and imprisoned by his scheming ambitious brother Antonio and his crew. The Island becomes a prison in post-conflict Northern Ireland'.[15] The company plans to use a cross-community group of ex-prisoners as cast and locate the film in Belfast Prison (Crumlin Road Gaol). Magill states:

> *Prospero's Prison* is timely in the context of Northern Ireland's peace process. For so long in the history of Northern Ireland, revenge has been the reply to violence, perpetuating the cycle of destruction. For this reason, The Tempest is a story worth re-telling for the lessons it can teach us about the wisdom of experience leading to forgiveness and reconciliation.[16]

The vision for *Prospero's Prison* is not just another trouble-related film, but a contribution towards peace building in Northern Ireland, raising forgiveness as the most powerful answer to our histories.[17]

ESC's 2007 film *Mickey B* was shot in Northern Ireland's maximum-security prison, HMP Maghaberry and features 42 characters played by prisoners and prison staff. Roles included writers and performers, while crew work, also undertaken by the inmates, included the erection of sets, painting, editing, production assistance, sound, and make-up. ESC and Magill had an overseeing role over the production. The 39-page screenplay was written and adapted by Magill, and then rewritten into prison slang by Sam McClean and Jason Thompson (two of the prison's actors). Alongside the change to prison vernacular, 'Birnam Wood became Birnam Jail, Macbeth is Mickey B and Lady Macbeth is Ladyboy, Mickey B's bitch, the witches are bookies and Macduff is Duffer'.[18] There is the addition of a narrator in the film, the characters are reimagined, and the location of the play is shifted from a castle in Scotland to a prison in Belfast. The actor playing the role of Ladyboy/Lady Macbeth argues that it's 'appropriate to set [the film] in a jail [because] Macbeth's greatest motivating factor is his ambition ... There's plenty of boys in here that are the same'.[19] Other changes can be found in the ending of the work where there is a:

> Mutually beneficial arrangement between Malcolm and the prison authorities. Malcolm, it is suggested, has the "buckets" (staff) fighting on his side; the tyrant is ousted and, in return, the Governor regains control of the wings [...] The closing montage shows us each character now isolated, in solitary confinement and under guard (one outside each cell, heavily armed). A new coda reveals Malcolm, wearing his father's chain, playing chess with the Governor, who is back in charge'.[20]

Research suggests that companies such as ESC, by embracing a project such as *Mickey B*, raise important questions about current inequities of space and place, issues of cultural translation, notions of the Shakespearean universal, and the place of the regional in discussions of practice.[21] Projects like *Mickey B* permit a renewed attention to local-global relations and draw attention to the scope and scale of the works suggested impact. Although this provides a broad-based reaction to the impacts of the plays, it simultaneously highlights the importance of Shakespeare's work as a vehicle for cultural value and promotion of public dialogue. The work can be seen to provide impact, and ESC articulates advantage in using Shakespeare's work alongside Boalian intentions.

The work is award-wining, receiving the Roger Graff Award for Outstanding Achievement in Film, where it was acknowledged as 'an outstanding piece of work ... with mesmerising performances and [a] narrative [which] ... deserves to be seen, and on its own merits'.[22] The work has received further critical acclaim and praise from Kenneth Brannagh, Stephen Rea, Ken Loach, and Linda Smith, among others, who said *Mickey B* 'is a strong and imaginatively conceived film, the actors are remarkable and Northern Ireland's voices are very powerful'.[23] *Mickey B* also 'garnered international critical acclaim from the likes of Boal who said, "You have helped prisoners be better citizens, transforming themselves and society around them"'.[24] The work has been screened at multiple international film festivals and continues to receive praise for its ability to engage people within community-facing projects that seek to address pressing social issues and concerns. The project has also been commended for its work with socially excluded groups and at the heart of ESC is the desire to promote the marginalisation of the prisoners using applied theatre praxis to develop and transform its participants. In this regard the benefits of the work are clear: to promote the oppressed.

Although a lot of people questioned the integrity of the work and perhaps even questioned could Shakespeare's works reach even *this* audience? the feedback from the participants themselves provides an idea of the impact of the work.[25] It is documented that generally prisoners 'found in the production of *Mickey B* a way of exploring feelings around the violence that they had committed in the past'.[26] In the ESC's supporting documentary *The Making of Mickey B* (2007), the section titled *Creating Radical Transformation: Three Men Tell Their Stories* offers an even clearer interaction with the benefits of the project. Tim McCullough discusses how *Macbeth* offered a proximity to his real-life. He also documents the demands the film project placed on him in relation to process, expectations, and opportunities. He explains:

> I got involved with ESC to make a short film. I didn't think I would make a film that would be so close to who I really was. Was I committed to the film? Was I committed to the process? I struggle with that one. The process itself was a rediscovery of my creativity... it was expressing myself in a way that was directly related to my addiction. When you get in-front of the camera and then have the opportunity to look back at it, you can't deny it; you

can't say that's not me. Part of the whole process was truth and honesty. This was an opportunity for me to really sit down and look at what I was doing. I think radical is a good word to use for the transformation that has happened in my life for the change that's happened. The opportunity to look at myself and tell my story, then stand back and look at it, gave me perspective.[27]

Sam McLean, writer for *Mickey B,* acknowledges the benefits of the work for the prisoner; he explains:

My life was definitely out of control, no doubt about it. And I remember sitting in prison and that night, after I had been sentenced to 20 years in prison, and it wasn't a nice feeling. I wanted a change in my life, but I didn't know how to do it. When we set up the drama classes this was the first thing most of us have ever done, legitimate, honest thing, we achieved something and I thought hold on there's another way here, and ESC showed me that, there's no doubt. I would not steal a bar of chocolate now, and I really didn't think I could have said that, I really didn't. ESC got me a job when I came out.[28]

McClean also provides a more final and direct response to his experience, which appears appealing to all involved in the project when he states: 'I spent 26 years in prison, it cost £2.5 million pounds to keep me there, and the only time I got rehabilitated was doing *Mickey B*'.[29] McClean presents an acute awareness of the politics the work is bound to.

Tom King describes the ESC's drama as 'one of the best things' he has been involved in. He talks about the need for such projects to help prisoners transform, when stating:

Through the filmmaking aspect of it I relived my past in an upfront and honest way. In an environment with people, who I didn't realise, were experiencing very similar problems. After making the film I said to Tom, what am I to do now? I have no-one else to blame. I want to go on and achieve higher things. If ESC had got me in my early teens and helped me to see the potential that I have my life would have been radically changed.[30]

Instead of 'lock them up and throw away the key', ESC wanted to use Shakespeare's work for what they have identified as the life-changing impact it can have on its prisoners. Robin Mansfield, Director of the Northern Ireland Prison Service, states:

It is a valuable part of the resettlement process and working on this film helped those involved to gain new skills, to learn to work as a team and look at the world in an entirely new way. It is important to balance the sensitivities surrounding such a project, including potential victim's issues, with the efforts of being made to ensure that inmates leave prison as balanced individuals equipped to make a positive contribution to society.[31]

Due to the one key supporter of the project, 'a positive progressive who understood the prison culture and exactly what we were up against', the film was able to act as an education or work programme.[32]

The participants of *Mickey B* offer an insight into use of the play from the perspective of those accessing and potentially benefiting from the text. Many thought that the text was a good choice as 'you'd think [the story] was already being played out in this place'.[33] Prisoners state that 'Shakespeare writes about people. He writes about human emotion. He writes about things that really happen'.[34] Another 'translates *Macbeth*'s reality of tenth-century Scottish Thanes and clan loyalties and betrayals to existing conditions in Northern Ireland when stating "You get that [violence] on the Lower Shankill. You get that kind of problem in the New Lodge Road where I'm from … cliques and gangs"'.[35] The advantages of using the play appear bound to its ability to identify with the experiences of the prisoners that are housed there.

ESC is also commended for creating work that faced a range of challenges. Magill and Marquis-Muradaz document:

> Prison staff resistance. Maximum-security prisons are risk adverse. Fear and distrust are the dominant motivations that underlie almost every decision. Daily airtight procedures produce a monotony that numbs the senses in the name of safety […] prison staff reacted to the film and our presence with suspicion and inflexibility, appearing either blatantly apathetic or downright hostile […] we learned a great deal that scared us about the people who care for them, the people we put in charge of our most vulnerable, our most violent, our most damaged.[36]

Ultimately, some see programmes of this nature as beneficial endeavours for prisoners and prisons alike. Others see it as entertainment. What is complicated is that this type of work is heavily reliant upon 'widespread belief in fairness and effectiveness, otherwise [prisons themselves] would eventually cease to function'.[37] There is a fine line between work that is deemed transformative and work that is viewed as a prisoner 'escaping hard time'. This can be potentially damaging to the view of the penal environment itself implying that many may wish to disassociate with the field of work. This is heavily reliant upon what McAvinchey terms 'the public acceptability test', explaining how he 'tried to convince people in garage forecourts or motorway service stations why, as far as [he] was concerned, theatre and prisons did have a connection'.[38] It is difficult to fight to prove how theatre could be offered as an alternative and relevant response to crime. Public perceptions play an important role in the work and there is an increased demand for practitioners to prove the impact of their work not just to the offenders and the prisons, but to their families and the wider public. Despite wider acceptance of prison as an opportunity to promote rehabilitation, 'the tensions between the correctional and rehabilitative aspects of being in prison continue to this day' with a divide between those who are advocacies for the work and those who still need convincing that the work has value and worth.[39] From conception to fruition, ESC was fighting against some of the fundamental difficulties faced when attempting to combine theatre with a penal environment.

In considering the use of Shakespeare's work specifically alongside this project, on their website ESC states: 'We believe that we can learn from the wisdom of Shakespeare by updating and translating him for audiences today'.[40] In an interview with Werner, Magill justifies that:

> Shakespeare is too important to be used solely as a cultural sermon for the middle classes and the dwindling ancient congregations at Stratford [...] anybody can do Shakespeare given the right access and opportunity to participate with the text [...] Shakespeare's text is too important. We can learn much from these stories by engaging with them in multiple manners- and through multiple media. These stories shouldn't be sealed off, people need to see them, people need to hear them, people need to participate in them at every level of society.[41]

Complications can be found in some of the dialogue that surrounds Magill's justification for the work. At times, Magill appears to sentimentalise that Shakespeare 'is reliable and trustworthy and infinitely pliable' and is therefore a good source because it allows for adaptations to be produced.[42] By selecting the play *Macbeth*, Magill states that the play is important because 'the moral of *Macbeth* is that crime doesn't pay. The means do not justify the ends. Ill-gotten gains have only a brief period of enjoyment'.[43] Classic texts such as *Macbeth* offered Magill the ability to:

Create the necessary distance for prisoners to understand implications of their crimes safely. It can create empathy, particularly in relation to victims even fictional victims. We experienced that prisoners can come to understand the relationship between cause and effect that can, in turn, lead to transformation.[44]

Although Magill does not allude to what it is about Shakespeare's plays *specifically* that incite possibilities for transformation, he draws attention to some of the important provocations that are central to this study in promoting the importance of distancing the participant from the issues explored within Shakespeare's text.

In an accompanying educational pack, ESC states: 'we chose a play about violence and the repercussions of violence by an author we believed would excite and impress prison staff and funders'.[45] Wray states that Magill's use of Shakespeare:

It is a double-edged construction in which the Bard is regarded as a defining ingredient of the educational establishment, to the extent that any adaptation of his work carries with it acute questions not about cultural translatability but economic advantage.[46]

Wray warns that 'these gestures signal both the institutional praxes within which such organizations as ESC work (external finance and support are constant drivers) and the global marketplace in which certain appropriations of Shakespeare carry cultural capital'.[47] Wray's criticisms are important as they highlight the widest and most encompassing difficulties inherent in work that may have been influenced by readily available financial support and/or gain.

It is interesting to note that ESC has developed a series of partnerships with funders and stakeholders (LloydsTSB) to meet its mission and vision, and Magill himself reflects that 'it's useful to remember that during the making of *Mickey B*, we had disparate stakeholder groups to satisfy and a range of complex sensitivities to negotiate'.[48] ESC states that 'an independent external evaluation found that for every £1 invested in our work with prisoners and ex-prisoners, we produced a Social Return on Investment (SROI) of £10.49'.[49] This critical interpretation of using Shakespeare's work for economic advantage importantly implies that Shakespeare's work is a vital commodity to which funding may be readily given and, whilst there is no doubt that funding is important for the continuation of projects of this nature, there is criticism to be offered in the justification behind selecting Shakespeare's work due to agenda-driven incentives and his continuous links to cultural authority. This reiterates the idea that there remains a difficulty in using a source that may be firmly ingrained in a perception of financial gain, cultural heritage, and advancement.

Parts of Magill's considerations are forward-thinking and suggest the importance of using adaptation to discover differences between the past and now, translating Shakespeare's work in the areas that may not speak to an audience today. However, he is also at risk of reiterating some of the concerns raised in the earlier sections of this work which indicate that cultural values bound up with Shakespeare's work can often override the consideration of the political and cultural values embedded in Shakespeare's own theatre.

With reference to the place and space in which the work is captured, the film moves between a Shakespearean setting and a penal environment, therefore some elements of the play were removed, and some elements remained. The decisions appear to be made, not from a deep-rooted understanding of the play text, but rather from a deeper-rooted understanding of prison and the history of Northern Ireland. Cultural differences became a key context for *Mickey B*, and Shakespeare was used to cross cultural boundaries (e.g., between English and Irish, High and Low Class, straight culture and gang culture, freedom, and incarceration). Wray emphasises how:

> the project is thus a multiple form of intermediation that arises out of the differences rather than similarities which all contributes into the ways in which adaptation is intermediated into something other than the putative source text.[50]

Therefore, and although it is initially clear that the work in its application alongside prisoners has needed to consider clear, adaptive elements to be relevant and important to the prisoners, the company could also be at risk of appropriating Shakespeare to serve the purpose of fulfilling an incentive which engages with national, class and penal constructions.

The conversion of the language into prison dialect is the most significant change to the work. Interestingly not all the language was changed into Irish vernacular; some of the original language was kept at the request of the prisoners. Magill explains how converting the language of Shakespeare means it is taken from the oppressor and given to the oppressed. Prisoner William explains that 'most of us are illiterate so we've had to adapt the plot and put our own language in. The play's a bit violent and we've kept the cursing to a minimum. But, y'know, it's Shakespeare'.[51] ESC states that using prison slang instead of Shakespearean language is a purposeful choice which makes the work more accessible to a prison audience; the overarching intention being to naturalise and understand Shakespeare's language.[52]

The choice of changing the language is commendable given the target audience, and there is relevance to an argument that places the needs of the community first, in line with Boalian praxis. Changing the language into prison vernacular and relocating the place and space of the original play is also not totally illogical and the film still 'parallels many elements of plot, character and themes drawn from *Macbeth*, whilst also featuring some significant departures from or additions to Shakespeare's play'.[53] However, problems could be deduced from the implication that Shakespeare's work is 'made to fit' the intentions of ESC's work and the penal environment. Wray supports this notion when highlighting that:

> the outcome is a kind of universalizing discourse about Shakespeare that would not be acceptable in alternative critical situations [...] the work instead presents an unwillingness to challenge the precise meanings that Shakespeare has for prisoners which results in context falling out of the equation and issues of cultural specificity being overlooked.[54]

The problem is bound to the notion that Shakespeare's *name* is a cultural commodity guaranteed to achieve acceptance and afford continuation in this theatrical environment. The work becomes linked to a cultural value too important to ignore, and despite a widespread reiteration of Shakespeare's universalising force, Shakespeare's work is in danger of being seen as a source selected simply because 'the prison authorities had no objections to the text or that it was Shakespeare'.[55] The project may also not be seen as an endeavour of adaptation, but rather 'getting the prison context to fit the story of *Macbeth* in order to be true to the local prison culture'; therefore, 'Shakespeare's wisdom' could be left behind to embrace the prison context more directly in the work.[56]

The decision to include Lady Macbeth's suicide and not remove it from the adaptation offers another link to prison culture, a representation perhaps of the 29 deaths in Northern Irish prisons since 2005. The inclusion of suicide helps to remind the audience of the 'gaps in the self-harm and suicide policy' which Pauline McCabe documents in the prison ombuds-men of 2010–2011.[57] Although the inclusion of the suicide references directly and specifically the prison culture being explored, it also provides 'a chilling reminder of the power of art to replay and disrupt key tropes associated with issues of crime and punishment'.[58] It further reflects the fact that:

> Maghaberry has a notorious record in respect of suicide among the incarcer-ated. [A] damning report on deaths in gaol in 2009 noted "systemic prob-lems" in relation to the treatment of vulnerable prisoners. At this moment, *Mickey B* is insistently dialogic, working in concert with its frames of refer-ence to highlight precisely those concerns the institution has endeavoured to repress.[59]

The decision to include the suicide may be regarded as both stereotypi-cal and contradictory. Although 'the pernicious effects of colonization and violent conflict result in struggles including a desire to escape stereotypes and a promotion of reductive readings of many complex situations', here the prisoners are asked to face the issue and present the stereotype to ben-efit the project.[60] Although ESC's intentions may be to:

> mirror realities and illuminate wider instances of communities facing chal-lenges- these difficult prison realities may only be included because this helps to heighten the dialectic of the film between source and adaptation, and between text and context.[61]

ESC's decisions are presented as justified because 'of its centrality to the original—Shakespeare's revered text'; however, changes to characters' genders (Lady Macbeth to Lady Boy) or the revisionist ending to the film do not appear to be a problem for ESC, which suggests that 'Shakespeare requires updating and translating to be meaningful and relevant to an audience today'.[62] ESC uses the aspects of the work that benefit the vision of their projects but find a justification for the removal of other/similar elements. The considerations appear to be presented in line with how the changes may shape a story relevant to its prison vernacular and context and says something significantly more aligned to the incentives of the prison.

Although Magill does indicate that a safe distance from the issues of the text through its historical and fictional implications can be achieved, it remains questionable that the work is asking its participants to revisit painful memories and replay them for the purpose of an applied theatre project. By closely aligning their adaptation to Northern Irish history and prison contexts, this simultaneously means that the prisoners are required to replay and confront their past experiences, regardless of the damage this may cause. Ko states that:

> *Macbeth* has a stage history of inviting terrifying but highly sympathetic portraits of Macbeth, through studying inner psychology. The interpretive tradition has sometimes found the tension between straight moral instruction and sympathy for evil difficult to reconcile.[63]

The difficulty for any prisoner/participant, and this is by no means exclusive to the ESC, is that they are consumed in unpredictable ways by the content of the work. They are asked to build characters through the play's violent action, and in some manner re-live a similar violence that they have been incarcerated for.

It could be argued that *Mickey B* seems to set out to use the play to say something significant about prison 'particularly for those unfamiliar with the prison environment' but instead reinstates the structures of the authority that exists in the environment in which the prisoners are incarcerated.[64]

ESC's *Mickey B* faced a range of criticism. In reaction to the choice of play Magill and Marquis-Muradaz explain that:

> Some staff thought we had too many Catholics not enough Protestants. Others hated the script-citing the swearing, the drug references, and the murders. In particular, Lady Macbeth's suicide was a problem because of the recent suicides in prison. The fact that it was set in a prison at all gave rise to the fear that some people would view the film as a slice of Maghaberry prison itself. The plot, the prisoners controlling the jail was too close for comfort given the recent memory of the Maze Prison where prisoners did run their own wings.[65]

However, ESC reacted quickly to criticism and they responded to many of the concerns that surrounded the project by aiming to:

> Recruit more Protestants and set the film in a fictional private prison called Burnam. We also toned down the swearing and cut the drug referenced, and promised to emulate Hitchcock and suggest, rather than actually portray violence. The prisoners naturally, felt censored, and arguments ensued.

However, we ultimately convinced them that quitting the project would only make the naysayers happy. To their credit, they pushed forward.[66]

To their absolute credit, ESC has fought for their belief in the project, against fundamental and inherent challenges that ensue when combining applied theatre with a penal environment, for transformative purposes. Perhaps the most shocking is heard when Magill and Marquis-Muradaz explain that there were many provocations:

which included prisoner's cells being overturned staff pouring talcum powder over the prisoner's cell floors and denying the men obligatory gym visits and 'out-of-cell' time, not one of the prisoners retaliated or took the bait. In four weeks of shooting, there was not one incident with any of the prisoners on our film [...] but the security department in the prison was resistant to the idea of grouping the 'bad boys' together and rewarding them by making them into movie stars.[67]

However, ESC acknowledges that the prisoners themselves were not always easy either:

They sometimes came on set high on drugs. They didn't always know their lines. They insisted on wearing their own clothes, which presented a film continuity nightmare. They resented being quite during shooting. A few imagined we were slighting them and walked away. They complained constantly about the food and lack of pay.[68]

Taking everything into account, it is clear from the research that ESC has not been short of criticism in their creation of *Mickey B* or work with prisoners generally. They have faced much opposition in creating this work. Wray documents the project's tenuous journey when stating that:

The initial announcement that a group of serving 'lifers' had embarked upon a full-length film version of *Macbeth* also caused some controversy in the U.K. press. Reactions were hostile and pejorative, with headlines adopting a correspondingly sensationalist tone. Until recently, legal injunctions prohibited this recreation of Shakespeare from public showings and distribution.[69]

Although the work was produced in 2007, the Northern Irish office and the Northern Irish Prison Service restricted the film from being shown

96   A. HULSMEIER

or distributed in the UK or Republic of Ireland for three years after its completion. A range of events dictated the deal ESC had to strike with prison authorities in not showing the film at all in Northern Ireland. An important cast member failed to return to prison from compassionate leave. The details of his crime were broadcast all over the press, and:

> Fears that his (and others) involvement in our 'violent' film might be publicised could trigger a massive public outcry resulted in cancellation of the BBC feature about the film. The actor playing Ladyboy who had been out of jail for several months was arrested and sent back to prison. Mickey B, Duffer and others rebelled against prison authorities and were separated from other prisoners under Rule 32 which provides for good order and discipline within the prison.[70]

Unfortunately, too, ESC no longer has access to the men because the group were disbanded by prison authorities.

Mickey B is a useful and important example of 'prison Shakespeare that invites us to assess its impact on its own terms'.[71] *Mickey B* bridges the fictional with the documentary and ultimately asks, 'how can Shakespeare help?' The work demonstrates how 'Shakespeare can transcend locality of exposure via the input of the participants involved, and that institutional frameworks of dissemination are essentially interchangeable'.[72] The project helps to 'mediate local prison histories, prompt reconsideration of current political sticking-points and bring into circulation questions about guilt and memory that plague the peace process'.[73] The project as a whole:

> Has the moral that violence does not pay and the ESC's overriding intention is the idea that Shakespeare's work can provide an educative missive. *Mickey B* invites us to think anew about Shakespeare, his local utility, and the reparative cultural work his plays are still enlisted to perform Although the project can't offer guarantees that inmates will not reoffend following their release [...] the process of making *Mickey B* allowed unprecedented developmental opportunities [and] the alternative would have been to do nothing.[74]

ESC offers an important example of a prison theatre project that uses Shakespeare's work to aid transformation. There are challenges faced by ESC; however, they should be excused from reiterating some of the politics inherently tied to the work they are attempting to deliver, and instead be commended for their attempts to navigate a politically complicated terrain to benefit those involved in the work, both prisoner and prison service.

SUMMARY

Overall, the chapters on Prison Shakespeare have explored the general context of prison theatre work, its histories, origins, and influences; undertook a historic/Renaissance reading of the plays *Measure for Measure* and *Macbeth* in relation to prison and crime; and finally assessed ESC as an example of work that currently exists in combining Shakespeare's plays, prisons, and applied theatre. Ultimately the chapter, whilst not covering every single example of Shakespeare in prison, does provide an exploration of specific uses of Shakespeare in prisons, highlighting some important considerations that deserve interrogation upon the creation, production, and continuation of this type of work.

NOTES

1. Landy, R.J. & Montgomery, D.T. (2012) *Theatre for Change: Education, Social Action, and Therapy.* London: Palgrave Macmillan. p. 155.
2. ESC. *Understanding through film*: www.esc-film.com(Accessed: 30/10/16).
3. Ibid.
4. Ibid.
5. NICVA (no date) *Supporting and representing voluntary and community organisations across Northern Ireland*: www.nicva.org (Accessed: 30/10/17).
6. Since 1995 there have been three PEACE programmes, financially supported by the EU through both EU regional policy and EU contributions to the International Fund for Ireland (IFI). The programme has two main aims: (1) the cohesion between communities involved in the conflict in Northern Ireland and the border counties of Ireland and (2) economic and social stability. See Europarl. (2017) *Northern Ireland PEACE programme*: http://www.europarl.europa.eu/atyourservice/en/displayFtu.html?ftuId=FTU_3.1.9.html (Accessed: 11/04/18).
7. Magill, T. & Marquis-Muradaz, J. (2009) The making of *Mickey B*, a modern adaptation of *Macbeth* filmed in a maximum-security prison in Northern Ireland. In Jennings, S. (2009) *Dramatherapy and Social Theatre: Necessary Dialogues.* London, Routledge. Chapter 9, pp. 109–116. p. 112.

8. Ibid, p. 112.
9. Ibid, p. 113.
10. ESC. *Understanding through film:* www.esc-film.com(Accessed: 30/10/16).
11. Forum Theatre was originally created by Augusto Boal, Forum Theatre affords the audience to participate with and change the action unfolding in front of them to make a social change.
12. Landy, R.J. & Montgomery, D.T. (2012) *Theatre for Change: Education, Social Action, and Therapy.* London: Palgrave Macmillan. p. 156.
13. ESC. *Understanding through film:* www.esc-film.com (Accessed: 30/10/16).
14. NICVA (no date) *Supporting and representing voluntary and community organisations across Northern Ireland:* www.nicva.org (Accessed: 30/10/17).
15. ESC. *Understanding through film:* www.esc-film.com(Accessed: 30/10/16).
16. Ibid.
17. Ibid.
18. Landy, R.J. & Montgomery, D.T. (2012) *Theatre for Change: Education, Social Action, and Therapy.* London: Palgrave Macmillan. p. 155.
19. Wray, R. (2011) The Morals of Macbeth and Peace as Process: Adapting Shakespeare in Northern Ireland's Maximum-Security Prison' *Edinburgh Companion to Shakespeare and the Arts: Shakespeare Quarterly,* 62 (11), pp. 340–63: https://pure.qub.ac.uk/portal/en/publications/the-morals-of-macbeth-and-peace-as-process(443a3afa-a58f-435f-8fe3-d6e5bb43c949)/export.html (Accessed 26/02/19).
20. Ibid.
21. See, Burnett, M. (2012) *Shakespeare and World Cinema.* Cambridge: Cambridge University Press.
22. ESC. *Understanding through film:* www.esc-film.com(Accessed: 30/10/16).
23. Ibid.
24. Ibid.
25. See Berry, C. (2003) The uses of Shakespeare in Criminal Rehabilitation: Testing the limits of 'Universality', in Lloyd, D. (ed.) *Shakespeare Matters: History, Teaching, Performance.* Newark: University of Delaware Press, pp. 151–63.
26. ESC. *Understanding through film:* www.esc-film.com(Accessed: 30/10/16).
27. CultureNI (n.d.) Education Shakespeare Company: A Profile: https://www.youtube.com/watch?v=p9YrRVvg3-A (Accessed 19/03/19).
28. Ibid.

10 ESC: A CASE STUDY 99

29. ESC. *Understanding through film*: www.esc-film.com(Accessed: 30/10/16).
30. CultureNI (n.d.) Education Shakespeare Company: A Profile: https://www.youtube.com/watch?v=p9YrRVvg3-A (Accessed 19/03/19).
31. ESC. *Understanding through film*: www.esc-film.com(Accessed: 30/10/16).
32. Magill, T. & Marquis-Muradaz, J. (2009) The making of *Mickey B*, a modern adaptation of *Macbeth* filmed in a maximum-security prison in Northern Ireland. In Jennings, S. (2009) *Dramatherapy and Social Theatre: Necessary Dialogues*. London, Routledge. Chapter 9, pp. 109–116. p. 112. p. 109.
33. ESC. *Understanding through film*: www.esc-film.com(Accessed: 30/10/16).
34. Ibid.
35. Ibid.
36. Magill, T. & Marquis-Muradaz, J. (2009) The making of *Mickey B*, a modern adaptation of *Macbeth* filmed in a maximum-security prison in Northern Ireland. In Jennings, S. (2009) *Dramatherapy and Social Theatre: Necessary Dialogues*. London, Routledge. Chapter 9, pp. 109–116. p. 112. pp. 109–111.
37. Indemaur, D. & Hough, M. (2002) 'Strategies for Changing Public Attitudes to Punishment' in Roberts, J. & Hough, M. (ed.) *Changing Attitudes in Punishment: Public Opinion, Crime and Justice*. Cullompton: Willan Publishing, pp. 127–136. p. 198.
38. McAvinchey, C. (2011) *Theatre and Prison*. London: Palgrave Macmillan. p. xi.
39. Khutan, R. (2014) *Demonstrating Effectiveness: Competing Discourses in the use and Evaluation if Applied Theatre that contributes to Improved Health Outcomes for Prisoners*: https://www.research.manchester.ac.uk/portal/files/54564128/FULL_TEXT.PDF (Accessed: 01/02/18). p. 57.
    See, Caraher, M., Bird, L. & Hayton, P. (2000) 'Evaluation of a Campaign to Promote Mental Health in Young Offender Institutions: Problems and lessons for Future Practice'. *Health Education Journal*. 59 (2), pp. 211–227: https://journals.sagepub.com/doi/10.1177/001789690005900303 (Accessed 26/02/19).
    Caraher, M., Dixon, P., & Hayton, P. (2002) 'Are Health-Promoting Prisons an Impossibility? Lessons from England and Wales'. *Health Education Journal*, 102 (5) pp. 219–229: https://pure.york.ac.uk/portal/en/publications/are-healthpromoting-prisons-an-impossibility (2603b6f5-a962-4b63-9f43-4ef747c6eddd)/export.html (Accessed 26/02/19).
40. ESC. *Understanding through film*: www.esc-film.com(Accessed: 30/10/16).

41. Pensalfini, R. (2016) *Prison Shakespeare: For These Deep Shames and Great Indignities.* London: Palgrave Macmillan. p. 138.
42. Ibid, p. 139.
43. Magill, T. & Marquis-Muradaz, J. (2009) The making of *Mickey B,* a modern adaptation of *Macbeth* filmed in a maximum-security prison in Northern Ireland. In Jennings, S. (2009) *Dramatherapy and Social Theatre: Necessary Dialogues.* London, Routledge. Chapter 9, pp. 109–116. p. 114.
44. Ibid, p. 114.
45. ESC. *Understanding through film*: www.esc-film.com(Accessed: 30/10/16).
46. Wray, R. (2011) The Morals of Macbeth and Peace as Process: Adapting Shakespeare in Northern Ireland's Maximum-Security Prison' *Edinburgh Companion to Shakespeare and the Arts. Shakespeare Quarterly,* 62 (11), pp. 340–63: https://pure.qub.ac.uk/portal/en/publications/the-morals-of-macbeth-and-peace-as-process(443a3afa-a58f-435f-8fe3-d6e5bb43c949)/export.html (Accessed 26/02/19).
47. Ibid.
48. Pensalfini, R. (2016) *Prison Shakespeare: For These Deep Shames and Great Indignities.* London: Palgrave Macmillan. p. 177.
49. ESC Ltd. secured £135,700 during 2010/11 period from multiple funders of which £90,000 came from Trusthouse/Hollywell for a three-year period.
50. Wray, R. (2011) The Morals of Macbeth and Peace as Process: Adapting Shakespeare in Northern Ireland's Maximum-Security Prison' *Edinburgh Companion to Shakespeare and the Arts. Shakespeare Quarterly,* 62 (11), pp. 340–63: https://pure.qub.ac.uk/portal/en/publications/the-morals-of-macbeth-and-peace-as-process(443a3afa-a58f-435f-8fe3-d6e5bb43c949)/export.html (Accessed 26/02/19).
51. ESC. *Understanding through film*: www.esc-film.com(Accessed: 30/10/16).
52. Ibid.
53. Pensalfini, R. (2016) *Prison Shakespeare: For These Deep Shames and Great Indignities.* London: Palgrave Macmillan. p. 162.
54. Wray, R. (2011) The Morals of Macbeth and Peace as Process: Adapting Shakespeare in Northern Ireland's Maximum-Security Prison' *Edinburgh Companion to Shakespeare and the Arts. Shakespeare Quarterly,* 62 (11), pp. 340–63: https://pure.qub.ac.uk/portal/en/publications/the-morals-of-macbeth-and-peace-as-process(443a3afa-a58f-435f-8fe3-d6e5bb43c949)/export.html (Accessed 26/02/19).
55. Pensalfini, R. (2016) *Prison Shakespeare: For These Deep Shames and Great Indignities.* London: Palgrave Macmillan. p. 38.
56. Wray, R. (2011) The Morals of Macbeth and Peace as Process: Adapting Shakespeare in Northern Ireland's Maximum-Security Prison' *Edinburgh*

10 ESC: A CASE STUDY 101

Companion to Shakespeare and the Arts: Shakespeare Quarterly, 62 (11), pp. 340–63: https://pure.qub.ac.uk/portal/en/publications/the-morals-of-macbeth-and-peace-as-process(443a3afa-a58f-435f-8fe3-d6e5bb43c949)/export.html (Accessed 26/02/19).

57. See, McCabe, P. (2012) *Prisoner Ombudsmen for Northern Ireland:* http://www.iprt.ie/files/IPRT_Seminar_30_March_2012.pdf (Accessed: 11/04/18).
58. Wray, R. (2011) The Morals of Macbeth and Peace as Process: Adapting Shakespeare in Northern Ireland's Maximum-Security Prison' *Edinburgh Companion to Shakespeare and the Arts: Shakespeare Quarterly,* 62 (11), pp. 340–63: https://pure.qub.ac.uk/portal/en/publications/the-morals-of-macbeth-and-peace-as-process(443a3afa-a58f-435f-8fe3-d6e5bb43c949)/export.html (Accessed 26/02/19).
59. Pensalfini, R. (2016) *Prison Shakespeare: For These Deep Shames and Great Indignities.* London: Palgrave Macmillan. p. 156.
60. Wray, R. (2011) The Morals of Macbeth and Peace as Process: Adapting Shakespeare in Northern Ireland's Maximum-Security Prison' *Edinburgh Companion to Shakespeare and the Arts: Shakespeare Quarterly,* 62 (11), pp. 340–63: https://pure.qub.ac.uk/portal/en/publications/the-morals-of-macbeth-and-peace-as-process(443a3afa-a58f-435f-8fe3-d6e5bb43c949)/export.html (Accessed 26/02/19).
61. ESC. *Understanding through film:* www.esc-film.com. (Accessed: 30/10/16).
62. Ibid.
63. Ko, Y. J. (2014) *Macbeth Behind Bars* in Jensen, M. P. *What Service is here?* Borrower and Lenders article: http://www.borrowers.uga.edu/ (Accessed: 04/04/18).
64. Pensalfini, R. (2016) *Prison Shakespeare: For These Deep Shames and Great Indignities.* London: Palgrave Macmillan. p. 138.
65. Magill, T. & Marquis-Muradaz, J. (2009) The making of *Mickey B,* a modern adaptation of *Macbeth* filmed in a maximum-security prison in Northern Ireland. In Jennings, S. (2009) *Dramatherapy and Social Theatre: Necessary Dialogues.* London, Routledge. Chapter 9, pp. 109–116. p. 110.
66. Ibid, p. 110.
67. Ibid, pp. 109–111.
68. Ibid, p. 111.
69. Wray, R. (2011) The Morals of Macbeth and Peace as Process: Adapting Shakespeare in Northern Ireland's Maximum-Security Prison' *Edinburgh Companion to Shakespeare and the Arts: Shakespeare Quarterly,* 62 (11), pp. 340–63: https://pure.qub.ac.uk/portal/en/publications/the-morals-of-macbeth-and-peace-as-process(443a3afa-a58f-435f-8fe3-d6e5bb43c949)/export.html (Accessed 26/02/19).

70. Magill, T. & Marquis-Muradaz, J. (2009) The making of *Mickey B*, a modern adaptation of *Macbeth* filmed in a maximum-security prison in Northern Ireland. In Jennings, S. (2009) *Dramatherapy and Social Theatre: Necessary Dialogues*. London, Routledge. Chapter 9, pp. 109–116. p. 111.
71. Wray, R. (2011) The Morals of Macbeth and Peace as Process: Adapting Shakespeare in Northern Ireland's Maximum-Security Prison' *Edinburgh Companion to Shakespeare and the Arts*. *Shakespeare Quarterly*, 62 (11), pp. 340–63: https://pure.qub.ac.uk/portal/en/publications/the-morals-of-macbeth-and-peace-as-process(443a3afa-a58f-435f-8fe3-d6e5bb43c949)/export.html (Accessed 26/02/19).
72. Ibid.
73. Ibid.
74. Ibid.

PART III

Disabled Shakespeare

Gloucester: [Love] did corrupt frail nature with some bribe,
To shrink mine arm up like a wither'd shrub;
To make an envious mountain on my back,
Where sits deformity to mock my body;
To shape my legs of an unequal size;
To disproportion me in every part,
Like to a chaos, or an unlick'd bear-whelp
That carries no impression like the dam. [1]

Part III addresses how and where Shakespeare's work is used within Disability environments. The chapter begins with an exploration of the history of Disability theatre generally, then addresses the use of Shakespeare's work in Disability environments specifically, where it currently exists, and the articulated benefits of combining the two areas of practice. Shakespeare's *Richard III* and *Henry VI Part One* and *Two* are used as demonstrative texts to explore Shakespeare's own presentation of Disability. Finally, the chapter concludes with a case study analysis of the Blue Apple Theatre Company as an example of a community that uses Shakespeare's work for the purposes of transformation. The chapter will explore how the company articulates the benefits of using Shakespeare's work with their participants, paying particular attention to the challenges that may ensue in the application of Shakespeare alongside a Disabled community.

NOTE

1. Shakespeare, W. in Craig, W.J. (1991) (ed.) *The Complete works of Shakespeare*. Oxford: Oxford University Press. p. 580.

CHAPTER 11

The History of Disability Theatre

This chapter presents the history of Disability theatre and the progress made in reflecting upon Disability on the stage. Disabled theatre is 'a specific kind of artistic practice connected to the Disability arts and culture movement. As such, it involves artists with Disabilities who pursue an activist perspective, dismantling stereotypes, challenging stigma, and re-imagining Disability as a valued human condition'.[1] It is also a form of 'integrative theatre, for it attempts to integrate people with Disabilities into theatre and/or drama experience, either as participants or audience'.[2]

Ultimately, theatre amongst the Disabled community is:

> about ensuring that Disabled people are at the centre of the creative process, allowing Disability to influence that process. More precisely, it can be defined as theatre which involves a majority of Disabled people, explores a Disability aesthetic and mirrors in some way the lives of Disabled people.[3]

Generally, in theatre, there has been a small amount of progress in terms of reflecting Disability on stage, and in comparison to some of the other communities explored as part of this research, there is currently less written on the work and movement of theatre with Disabled people generally or cognitive Disability particularly.[4] Disability Studies has emerged only in the last twenty years or so, and Auslander and Sandahl explain that this is because:

© The Author(s), under exclusive license to Springer Nature Switzerland AG 2024
A. Hulsmeier, *Applied Shakespeare*,
https://doi.org/10.1007/978-3-031-45414-1_11

105

> Unlike race, class, and gender, [Disability] escaped recognition as an important identity rubric for performance scholars. Whereas those involved in using the arts therapeutically have formulated a concept of Disability, albeit a contested one, performance studies—out of negligence rather than overt hostility toward Disabled people or Disability studies—has had no such concept.[5]

The study of Disability in the *arts* slips between very different epistemologies: Disability studies, which explores the study of a certain group of people, and performance studies, which addresses the concepts of theatre. The two are very rarely explored together in a helpful and developed manner.[6]

Although historically it appears as though an under-interrogation of Disability's position within the realm of theatre is present, there have been more recent developments in the exploration of this field of practice. Over the past few years especially, there appears to have been a surge of interest in documenting Disability theatre, and recent publications highlight the growing interest in this area of theatre.[7] In the theatrical field, however, Disability theatre is still grappling to be recognised as having an important place within the world of theatre and the arts. Arts Consultant and Broadcaster, Andrew Miller, himself a wheelchair user, personally reflects upon the state and progress of Disability theatre. He states:

> Despite the developments by ACE in encouraging diversity, the regional support for Disabled artists and arts professionals together has yet to take full ownership of Disability. There is a lot of surface noise, but I wonder, under the radar, how much is changing? Employment of Disabled people in the arts generally remains critically low. Physical access remains a barrier, and the lack of consideration of the issues that ensure participation and equality, […] All of which could go some way to explaining just why so few of us work in this industry.[8]

Historically, there was a comparatively late establishment of theatre within this area and the inclusion of Disabled performers (in theatre predominantly) developed alongside public acceptance or integration. Companies began to form around the 1970s.

The People Players of Toronto was started in 1974, and New York City's National Theatre Workshop for the Handicapped (NTWH) was founded in 1977. Closer to home, Graeae Theatre Company was founded in 1980 by Nabil Shaban and currently still operates from Aldershot in

Hampshire. The late 1980s and early 1990s saw more of a surge in the development of Disability theatre Companies across the UK, with the formation and establishment of companies including, but not limited to: The Lawnmowers Theatre Company (Newcastle, 1986), Birds of Paradise Theatre (Glasgow, 1993), and Dark Horse Theatre (Huddersfield, 1998). The examples represent the earliest theatre companies established specifically for Disabled actors and were formed to 'combat the exclusion of Disabled people from the theatre'.[9]

Today, many of the companies who work with physically and intellectually Disabled actors all hold in common the aim to prevent isolation and often concentrate upon physical, cognitive, emotional, or sensory differences. Disability theatre companies currently operating in the USA and UK include, but are not limited to Mind the Gap, Birds of Paradise, DIY Theatre Company, The Freewheelers, Taking Flight, Twisting Ducks, About Face Theatre Company, Access Theatre, Dark Horse Theatre, Quiplash, and Ableize. Their work is successful as it involves and respects the needs, values, and cultures of people with Disabilities allowing them to shape their own artistic process. Like the prison projects, some of these companies do feature Shakespeare within their work.

NOTES

1. Johnston, K. (2012) *Stage Turns: Canadian Disability Theatre*. Quebec: McGill-Queen's University Press. p. 43.
2. Warren, B., Richard, R. J. & Brimbal, J. (2007) *Drama and the Arts for Adults with Down syndrome: Benefits, Options and Resources*. England: Down syndrome Educational Trust. p. 55.
3. Morrison, E. (1992) *Theatre and Disability Conference Report*. England: Arts Council Arts & Disability.
4. See, Hargrave, M. (2015) *Theatres of Learning Disability: Good, Bad, or Plain Ugly?* London: Palgrave Macmillan. Sealey, J. (2015) *Deaf and Disabled Artists: We will not let Government cuts make us invisible*: https://www.theguardian.com/stage/theatreblog/2015/apr/13/deaf-and-Disabled-artists-we-will-not-let-government-cuts-make-us-invisible (Accessed: 04/02/17).
5. Auslander, P. & Sandahl, C. (2009) Bodies *in Commotion: Disability and Performance*. Michigan: University Michigan Press. p. 7.
6. See Hargrave, M. (2015) *Theatres of Learning Disability: Good, Bad, or Plain Ugly?* London: Palgrave Macmillan.

7. See Johnston, K. (2016) *Disability Theatre and Modern Drama*, Kuppers, P. (2017) *Theatre & Disability*, Barton-Farcas, S. (2017) *A Practical Manual for Inclusion in the Arts*.
8. Miller, A. (2016) *My experience at Theatre*: http://www.artsprofessional. co.uk/magazine/blog/my-experience-theatre-2016 (Accessed: 04/02/17).
9. Morrison, E. (1992) *Theatre and Disability Conference Report*. England: Arts Council Arts & Disability.

CHAPTER 12

The History of Shakespeare and Disability Theatre

This chapter explores specific projects and/or performances that include the use of Shakespeare's plays alongside Disabled communities. The projects identified for the benefit of this chapter represent much more recent and sporadic work within this field, especially compared to that of Prison Shakespeare. The examples demonstrate the reach of the work, and whilst it may appear less extensive, it is work that attempts to engage a Disabled community through the purposes of applied theatre and the use of Shakespeare's plays.

Although there is evidence of development regarding work which combines Disabled theatre with Shakespeare's plays, Shakespeare's use for applied theatre purposes amongst Disabled communities appears to remain an underdeveloped area of practice. The fact that there are no individualised explorations of the use of Shakespeare's work within the Disabled community restricts the developments and recommendations for this field. Aside from theatre companies generally discussing the benefits of Shakespeare's work, academic work is also almost non-existent and therefore scholars seem slow to consider the benefits of Shakespeare's work within this area of practice and are very late in establishing Disability Shakespeare as an important field of study.

Graeae Theatre Company is a company based in the UK composed of artists and managers with physical and sensory Disabilities. It was founded in 1980 by Nabil Shaban and Richard Tomlinson and represents one of the longest running theatre companies that works with the Disabled

© The Author(s), under exclusive license to Springer Nature 109
Switzerland AG 2024
A. Hulsmeier, *Applied Shakespeare*,
https://doi.org/10.1007/978-3-031-45414-1_12

110   A. HULSMEIER

community.[1] Since 2013, the company has been working with Dhaka Theatre, Bangladesh. They offer a long-term training programme with young Disabled actors, and in 2016, they were asked to mark the 400th anniversary of Shakespeare, as part of *Shakespeare Lives*. The project was initiated by the British Council, Dhaka Theatre, and current Artistic Director of Graeae, Jenny Sealey. The project consisted of one Disabled actor who spoke and one Deaf actor who used Bengali Sign Language playing all the main characters in Shakespeare's *Romeo and Juliet*. For Sealey, the project is important because 'it challenges people's perceptions of what Deaf and Disabled people can do' and the story of *Romeo and Juliet* was regarded as an ideal source to help 'create a world where everyone has the right to love and be loved'.[2]

The company provides a well-established body of work with the Disabled community and highlights the cultural and geographical breadth to which projects of this nature can reach. They represent one of the longest serving Disabled Companies in the UK. Their interactions with Shakespeare's plays are important in highlighting where Disabled communities are interacting with Shakespeare's plays. However, it should be recognised that Graeae do not regularly produce Shakespeare's plays, and this production was aligned to a specific anniversary activity, rather than a continuous engagement with Shakespeare's plays for the purpose of transformation.

Side by Side Theatre Company, which was formed in Stourbridge in 1997, is an independent theatre company giving learning Disabled actors, many of whom have Down syndrome, the opportunity to develop skills in the performing arts.[3] In 2009, they took *Tempest in a Teacup* to the Edinburgh Fringe Festival to critical acclaim. They were then chosen to work with the RSC's Open Stages on its production Illyria-On-Sea, based on Shakespeare's *Twelfth Night* in 2014. The company describes the project as a triumph for inclusion. Their current production of *As We Like It* launched in June and August of 2018. More than 20 years of experience marks this company as well-established; their continued use of Shakespeare's work demonstrates Shakespeare's popularity amongst cast and crew.

Taking Flight Theatre Company was established in 2007 in Wales with the 'aim to work with groups of people who have traditionally been under-represented in theatre, film and television'.[4] In the summer of 2016, they performed *Romeo and Juliet* with a range of Disabled actors. Their use of Shakespeare includes the following plays: *A Winter's tale, As you Like It,*

12 THE HISTORY OF SHAKESPEARE AND DISABILITY THEATRE   111

Twelfth Night, and *A Midsummer Night's Dream.* Garside highlights the aims of the company when explaining that:

> Everyone feeling a part of the production is key to Taking Flight's ethos, inclusive theatre company- in terms of both audience and performers. This means that D/deaf actors are a part of the performance, as well as Disabled actors, and the performance is fully inclusive for the audience with both BSL interpretation and audio description. This isn't the kind of 'add on' inclusivity that audiences might expect; inclusivity is part of the performance.[5]

While being a recent addition to the collection of theatre companies that work with Disabled communities in the UK, Taking Flight is establishing opportunities to make theatre accessible. They have consistently used Shakespeare's work as a tool to aid such accessibility. Their most recent production was Shakespeare's *The Tempest* at Hijinx Theatre in the autumn of 2018.

In 2016, the BBC produced a documentary about Storme Toolis (herself a wheelchair user due to cerebral palsy) and her company of Disabled actors who attempt to redefine Juliet in their production of *Romeo and Juliet.* Toolis' *Redefining Juliet* features women in her work who would not normally be considered to play the role of Juliet. Toolis hopes to use the work to open people's minds to the abilities of all actors, to start to see Disability as a positive thing, and to embrace difference and diversity within the theatre.[6] Using a mixture of verbatim and Shakespeare's original text, six actresses explored the role of Juliet, transporting the character right into the heart of the diversity of today's twenty-first century. Toolis emphasised it was not a 'Disability-led' project but rather about difference and diversity and what that means'.[7] Toolis aims to use the project to make theatre more of a 'level playing field'. Through her work, she demonstrates how although 'there has been a small amount of progress in terms of reflecting Disability on stage, now is the time to be doing these things and having these kinds of conversations'.[8]

Toolis currently plans to tour the show and holds ambitions to audition for Juliet at the RSC. Her work represents some of the most recent explorations into the uses of Shakespeare's plays with Disabled people and demonstrates the growing fascination with the levels of inclusion Shakespeare's work is claimed to invite.

From the collection of companies presented, the range of the work is only sufficient, and currently, there appears to be only a minimal number of companies undertaking projects of this specific nature, compared to the other areas of marginalisation explored. Realistically, the field is light-years away from where it needs to be, and one of the biggest challenges of this field may in fact be the lack of interrogation and attention it has been afforded.[9] Despite this challenge, there are companies that look to Shakespeare's work as an appropriate stimulus to use amongst the Disabled community.

NOTES

1. Graeae.org. (n.d.) *Graeae Theatre Company*: http://graeae.org/ (Accessed 22/10/18).
2. British Council. (2016) *A Different Romeo and Juliet*: https://theatreand-dance.britishcouncil.org/projects/2015/a-different-romeo-and-juliet/ (Accessed: 12/04/18).
3. SBSTC (1997) *Side by Side Theatre Company*: http://www.sbstcs.org/ (Accessed: 05/06/18).
4. Garside, E. (2016) *Romeo and Juliet: Cardiff & Touring*: http://mytheatremates.com/romeo-juliet-cardiff-touring/ (Accessed: 04.02.17).
   See also Taking Flight Theatre (no date): http://www.takingflighttheatre.co.uk/blog/ (Accessed: 04/02/17).
5. Garside, E. (2016) *Taking Flight Theatre: Romeo and Juliet Theatre Review*: http://www.buzzmag.co.uk/reviews/taking-flight-theatre-romeo-juliet-stage-review/ (Accessed: 04/02/17).
6. , Toolis, S. (2016). *Drama Graduate Storme Toolis' 'Redefining Juliet' to be broadcast on BBC Four's Shakespeare Festival, School of Arts*: https://www.kent.ac.uk/arts/newsandevents/?view= 1165 (Accessed: 04/02/17).
7. Hemley, M. (2016) *BBC documentary Redefining Juliet to give Shakespeare role to Disabled actors*: https://www.thestage.co.uk/news/2016/bbc-documentary-redefining-juliet-to-give-shakespeare-role-to-Disabled-actors/ (Accessed: 04/02/17).
8. Ibid.
9. Siebers, T. (2001) 'Disability in Theory: From Social Constructionism to Realism of the Body,' *American Literary History*, 13 (4), pp. 737–754: https://www.academia.edu/2651126/Disability_in_Theory_From_Social_Constructionism_to_the_New_Realism_of_the_Body (Accessed 26/02/19).

CHAPTER 13

Shakespeare's Disabled, Disabled Shakespeare: A Renaissance Reading of Shakespeare and Disability in *Henry VI Part Two* and *Three* and *Richard III*

This chapter will explore a collection of Shakespeare's plays that feature the character of Richard/Gloucester through the lens of a modern-day interpretation of the language of Disability (as this is the only tool we have to achieve levels of understanding), but with clear and important reference to the historical implications and influences of the period in which Shakespeare was creating his work.

To be able to ascertain society's attitudes and reactions toward Disability and Disabled people would be almost impossible. Among the many suggestions that have been made is the view that Renaissance 'perceptions of impairment and Disability are coloured by a deep-rooted psychological fear of the unknown, the anomalous and the abnormal'.[1] Therefore, 'it is widely acknowledged that their perceptions of normality are partly if not wholly determined by [...] the natural transmission of ideology and culture'.[2] In developing this argument, Garland-Thomson suggests that:

> Disability is a construct which means little outside of the age which makes meaning of its metaphor. We must, then, seek to understand [Disability] within the context of its age, by looking at religion, dramatic, social, and political presumptions constructing Disability. It is only in this way that the formula which equates Disability and deviance can be understood in *its* time, rather than accepted, without question, in ours.[3]

© The Author(s), under exclusive license to Springer Nature
Switzerland AG 2024
A. Hulsmeier, *Applied Shakespeare*,
https://doi.org/10.1007/978-3-031-45414-1_13

114   A. HULSMEIER

It is therefore important to explore Renaissance ideology surrounding Disability to fully appreciate this point in history where a communally accepted set of values and beliefs influenced Shakespeare's audience and determined their reactions to the Disabled community. It is also important to acknowledge that examples of what we now call 'Disability' was not necessarily an operational identity in the Renaissance and the word itself did not circulate in England until around 1545.[4] Even then, Wilson explains:

> It most often intimated something more about an individual's general incapacity than the fact or state of having .... a physical or mental condition that prompted said incapacity [...] therefore the emergence of 'Disability' occurs later than the Renaissance and in tandem with a medical discourse that classifies, regulates, and constructs bodies as 'normal' or 'abnormal'.[5]

Disability was not a timeless universal. It was described and defined differently in the Renaissance, and therefore, it is important to look at historically specific ways in which the body was represented in the Renaissance. Whilst it should be acknowledged that individual perceptions and ideas vary slightly and there is no universal approach to Disability, historical and cultural concepts, and responses to what we now know to be Disability and/or Disabled are usually more rigid, and the chapter looks to these for an indication as to potentially significant influences upon Shakespeare's presentation of Disability.[6]

Until the seventeenth century, people with Disabilities were 'rejected by their families, along with other disadvantaged groups such as the sick, the elderly and the poor, relying upon the ineffectual tradition of Christian charity for subsistence'.[7] The seventeenth century represented vast developments in the views of people with Disabilities as, by this time, people with Disabilities were integrated into society and were allowed to marry, work, and have children. Bloy explains how Disabled people:

> were still not considered a state's responsibility and Disability was characterised as an individual's problem with the state's role to 'manage' them, however the Elizabethan Poor Law included a requirement for each parish to support Disabled people and the old – which set the tone for the next 300 years of state administration of Disabled people's lives.[8]

Discrimination however did not disappear entirely during the Elizabethan period and often continued in the form of entertainment and ridicule: 'every Disability from idiocy to insanity to diabetes and bad breath was a welcome source of amusement'.[9]

Shakespeare's first depiction of Disability may also be his funniest. It arrives in Act Two of *Henry VI* between Gloucester and Simpcox:

King Henry VI:	What, hast thou been long blind and now restored?
Simpcox:	Born blind, an't please your grace
Cardinal:	What, art thou lame?
Simpcox:	Ay, God Almighty help me!
Suffolk:	How camest thou so?
Simpcox:	A fall off of a tree.
Gloucester:	How long hast thou been blind?
Simpcox:	Born so, master.
Gloucester:	What colour is this cloak of?
Simpcox:	Red, master; red as blood.
Gloucester:	Why, that's well said. What colour is my gown of?
Simpcox:	Black, forsooth: coal-black as jet.
Gloucester:	Then, Saunder, sit there, the lyingest knave in Christendom. If thou hadst been born blind, thou mightest as well have known all our names as thus to name the several colours we do wear. Sight may distinguish of colours, but suddenly to nominate them all, it is impossible. My lords, Saint Alban here hath done a miracle; and would ye not think his cunning to be great, that could restore this cripple to his legs again?
Simpcox:	O master, that you could!
Gloucester:	Well, sir, we must have you find your legs. Sirrah beadle, whip him till he leap over that same stool. *[after the beadle hath hit him once, he leaps over the stool and runs away; and they follow and cry 'A Miracle'].*[10]

The hostility and suspicion presented throughout the scene establish an undesirable Renaissance tradition, even though Gloucester is correct in Simpcox's forgery.

116   A. HULSMEIER

Other Disabilities can be seen in the blindness of Old Gobbo in *The Merchant of Venice* and Gloucester in *King Lear*. Physical deformities can be found in Richard (*Henry VI Part Two* and *Three* and *Richard III*), Thersites (*Cymbeline*), and Caliban (*The Tempest*). Caliban in the dramatic personae for *The Tempest* is even described as "a savage and deformed slave" and is 'Shakespeare's final, and in some ways fullest, stigmatized character: he is certainly physically deformed, potentially racially different, arguably mentally challenged, and allegedly a bastard child of the devil'.[11]

Physical illness is presented in the form of epilepsy or 'the falling sickness' in *Julius Caesar, Henry IV, Othello, Macbeth,* and figuratively in *King Lear*. Although it was historically known that Caesar had epilepsy (or at least Plutarch wrote that he did), the presentation of epilepsy throughout the play *Julius Caesar* is more of a dramatization of the condition rather than the thing itself.[12] Therefore, it is not shown on stage but is presented from Cassius' interpretation of Caesar's fit:

Cassius: [...]
And when the fit was on him, I did mark
How he did shake: 'tis true, this god did shake;
His coward lips did from their colour fly,
And that same eye whose bend doth awe the world
Did lose his lustre: I did hear him groan.[13]

Of intellectual Disability, Hargrave writes that 'within the boundaries of Elizabethan drama, there was never a clear-cut distinction between what would now be called intellectual impairment and its opposite'.[14] However, the role of the fool throughout a range of Shakespeare's work points to a provisional form of this Disability, and in reaction to the historical counterpart, it was common at the time for a court jester to be a poor or Disabled boy. Minton explains that:

the Fool, in Shakespeare's time, would have been a person with developmental Disabilities, and though today we tend to see Shakespeare's fools solely as jesters and clowns, a close reading of remarks about Touchstone in *As You Like It* and Feste in *Twelfth Night* reveals the true nature of these characters.[15]

Whether or not Shakespeare presented this collection of characters as having a Disability in relation to the modern-day understanding of the word's meaning, or whether the audience is simply attaching their modern-day understanding of Disability to the character through their own interpretation of the text and traits of the role is difficult to ascertain, what is clear is that Shakespeare had an awareness of 'difference', both physical and intellectual. Through both an historical understanding of 'Disability' and through a modern lens of what Disability means today, it becomes clear that throughout the Renaissance period and as presented within Shakespeare's texts, people with Disabilities were viewed in mixed regard as humorous, as a source of entertainment and ridicule, alongside superstition, with suspicion, as a joke, or as a joker.

The character of Richard/Gloucester is often suggested to be Shakespeare's clearest interpretation of physical difference. As such, Richard is an important character to explore in relation to the content of this chapter. Gloucester and Richard are the same character. In *Henry VI Part Two and Three* he is Prince Richard, Duke of Gloucester, and Richard when he becomes King in *Richard III*. To alleviate confusion, he will be simply referenced as Richard throughout.

The presentation of Disability as a form of evil, other character's reactions to Richard, binaries presented throughout the play, Richard's own understanding of his Disability, Richard's ability to perform his Disability for purposes of manipulation, and alternative interpretations of the body within the character of Richard. The central focus of this chapter will be the character of Richard in the aforementioned plays.

Mitchell and Snyder discuss:

> The kind of early modern Disability Richard displays from contemporary discourses of Disability. Positioning the play at the "threshold" of scientific attention to Disabled bodies in the eighteenth century, *Richard III* is a Renaissance version of late medieval attitude toward deformity.[16]

However, and despite the modern implications of the term 'Disability', there is no doubt that Richard's presentation is purposefully as something 'different' and Williams' account of the play in relation to Disability theory suggests that:

> the play as a Renaissance version of late medieval attitudes toward deformity, focus attempts both to preserve Disability as an identity category that occurs later than the early modern period and to provide a trans-historical account of its emergence as identity.[17]

Throughout the plays, Richard's physical deformity is an integral focus of physical challenges and differences to the 'normative'. Metzler helps to classify Richard as one of Shakespeare's 'Disabled' characters when she explains that he falls into the category of 'extreme deformations or monstrosities; those whose physical forms did not match the most basic humans, normative standards'.[18] The inclusion of Richard's hunchback and clubfoot places the character firmly within the Renaissance classification of Disabled. Throughout the plays, Shakespeare asks the audience to pay attention to the 'deformed' body of Richard to explore the attitudes of those reacting to someone 'born into a world which placed a high premium upon physical normality'.[19] Richard's awareness of his differences is also acute when stating:

> [Love] did corrupt frail nature with some bribe,
> To shrink mine arm up like a wither'd shrub;
> To make an envious mountain on my back,
> Where sits deformity to mock my body;
> To shape my legs of an unequal size;
> To disproportion me in every part,
> Like to a chaos, or an unlick'd bear-whelp
> That carries no impression like the dam.[20]

Throughout the 'Middle-Ages people with Disabilities were the subject of superstition, persecution and rejection with Disability known to be associated with witchcraft'.[21] *Richard III* presents how ghosts, bad omens, curses, and prophetic dreams are a constant feature in his life. The supernatural is constantly present, and even Richard's downfall is the fulfilment of a prophecy of divine will. Throughout the play, there are also moments when Richard blames his Disability and physical deformity on the machinations of witches, he states:

> Then be your eyes the witness of this ill:
> See how I am bewitch'd; behold mine arm
> Is, like a blasted sapling, wither'd up:
> And this Edward's wide, that monstrous witch,
> Consorted with the harlot strumpet Shore,
> That by their witchcraft thus have marked me.[22]

However, an alternative is 'tacit and expressed emblematically throughout the plays through the choruses of women who oppose [Richard]'.[23]

The interpretation is founded in the idea that Richard's deformity is the result of the failure to grow in the woman's womb. The suggestion here is that Shakespeare had a level of medical understanding when he presents both character and narrative to diagnose Richard's difference as a matter of 'failure to form', rather than association with witchcraft. Hobgood considers this engagement (amongst many others found within the play) as an example of 'medical discourse of its own moment, pointing out that characters repeatedly read Richard's body according to emerging ideas of diagnosis and correction advanced by early modern physicians'.[24] Williams, however, emphasises that whilst the play does 'anticipate modern ideas of Disability [...] Richard III's deformity is an attempt to conceptualise the Renaissance as a time that [...] would have understood this body as evil',[25] and it is true that throughout the Middle Ages, people with a Disability were associated with evil. Barnes progresses this point of debate when explaining that:

> Those that were deformed and Disabled were seen as 'changelings' or the Devil's substitutes for humans. [...] any form of physical or mental impairment was the result of divine judgement for wrongdoing pervasive throughout this period.[26]

From the beginning of the play, the presentation of Richard as 'evil' is evident, and even Richard synonymises himself with words such as 'false', 'treacherous'; he has 'laid plots' and has 'inductions dangerous'. He successfully woos Anne after killing her husband, 'he slanders the Queen, he detains her kin and eventually, he challenges the rightful succession to the throne [...] Richard exhibits a shameless irreverence for family and for tradition and is cast immediately in opposition of good'.[27] For the Renaissance audience, Richard's Disability is the marker of evil 'because that is what lingering medieval perceptions of Disability had trained them to see'.[28] Therefore, Richard's bad actions meant that his body had to be deformed to visually reflect his moral corruption. Quayson explains that:

> 'Richard's Disability is deformity operating in a moral register, the Disabled body is one in which physical difference is overlaid with negative implications because of what it suggests about the moral character of the person who displays bodily difference'.[29]

120   A. HULSMEIER

These bodily differences are captured throughout the play via a range of important and theatrical techniques, and they go a long way in explaining medieval reactions to Disability and difference.

The insults used against Richard often reference the 'outward manifestation of the inward malignity', but they are also important as they present 'a variety of negative ways in which others view his body and attempt to employ its associations in their own struggles for political agency'.[30] The play offers viewpoints that 'anatomize and deprecate the body Richard performs'.[31] The female characters in the play often suggest that Richard displays features of monstrosity and are negative about his form. Anne and Elizabeth describe him as a 'diffused infection of a man', 'hedgehog', 'bottled spider', and 'foul bunch-backed toad', terms used to insult. Queen Margaret articulates Richard's body in bestial terms when stating:

> Thou elvish-marked, abortive, rooting hog,
> Thou that wast sealed in thy nativity
> The slave of nature and the son of hell,
> Thou slander of thy heavy mother's womb,
> Thou loathed issue of thy father's loins,
> Thou rag of honours, thou detested.[32]

Words used against Richard not only reflect the negativity towards Disabled people but connote the visual clues needed for Renaissance audiences to understand Richard's motive, desire, and evil intent.

Binaries are a further device Shakespeare utilises to highlight Richard's evil and bodily differences. Richmond is a character not only used to overthrow Richard but placed throughout the play in opposition to Richard characteristically. Richard is the evil to Richmond's pure goodness, 'when placed next to this hero, then, it is easy and exciting to see both the antagonist and protagonist on completely opposite terms; they both become binaries'.[33] Richard's body is marked as deficient, and the:

> Play ends with the figure of Richmond as the fantasy of able body: he is the warrior who is properly integrated into his family structure and will produce rightful heirs for the throne [...] his kingship will usher in a newly perfect body for the state.[34]

This is most clearly depicted in Richmond's speech in Act Five:

13 SHAKESPEARE'S DISABLED, DISABLED SHAKESPEARE: A RENAISSANCE...   121

Richmond: O, now let Richmond and Elizabeth,
The true succeeders of each royal house,
By God's fair ordinance conjoin together,
And let their heirs, God, if Thy will be so,
Enrich the time to come with smooth-faced peace,
With smiling plenty and fair prosperous days,
Abate the edge of traitors, gracious Lord,
That would reduce these bloody days again
And made poor England weep forth streams of blood.[35]

The combination of Richmond and Richard's binaries of body and state is also metaphorically important. Eyler explains that:

Historically, Richard's fictional impairment can be read as a metaphor for, not just an evil ruler, but for a corrupt state. The underlying implication is that a nation cannot function as a Disabled body-this would be understood by the Tudor dynasty, the early modern period and Shakespeare's original audience.[36]

As an historical metaphor, we accept this binary as part of the discourse of the time and the internal and external planes of Richard's operations in relation to their historical implications which are reduced to the 'demonstration of Renaissance beliefs about the continuity between inner morality and outward physical forms', power, and state. [37] However, as Williams argues:

what Shakespeare does even further is suggest that Richard is powerful in alignment with dismodern concepts of what it means to be Disabled [...] and instead Richard as a disorder subject challenges a binary of able/ Disabled bodies[...] the subject sees that the metanarratives are only socially created and accepts them as that.[38, 39]

Therefore, the binary may work in highlighting good against evil, but it doesn't necessarily mean that Disability is essential in playing the binary. Alexander explains that although:

Richard is articulate, we don't want Richmond to be bumbling [...] Richard is cunning but Richmond should not be daffy [...] equally as important, just because Richard has a Disability, should Richmond be able bodied? The answer is no.[40]

122   A. HULSMEIER

These are moral not physical binaries, and in all other manners, the characters are demonstrated to compete on the same plane.

Reading the play in its historical tradition demonstrates Shakespeare's use of the unseen being depicted in the more visual clues of Disability and therefore Shakespeare's audience are seen to need the metaphor to understand the characterisation. Williams warns that 'it should not be enough for today's audiences to accept that Richard wields evil simply because he is deformed'; therefore, other devices of character investigation are needed to understand Richard's Disability.[41]

Richard's own understanding of his Disability is important to explore regarding presentation, consideration, and understanding of the deformed body and its connections to Renaissance ideologies and concepts. It allows participants to remain at a safe distance from the issues of the play, exploring lessons that could transform experiences we currently face. At surface level, Richard may be seen to despise his body, his opening soliloquy and the way he describes that he 'has no delight to pass away the time/ unless to spy my shadow in the sun and descant on my own deformity' suggests that he hates his Disability.[42] His language also suggests that he regards himself as unable to pursue any type of norm, when stating: 'But I, that am not shaped for sportive tricks/Nor made to court an amorous looking-glass'.[43] Medieval belief too would dictate that any one of Richard's physical differences would impair him from participating in the 'normal functions of every-day society'; however, the complexities of the character suggest that this is not at all the case and that 'Richard is far more than *just* a character with physical impairment [...] and is therefore a slippery character for Disability studies to tackle'.[44] This is because Richard is successful not only in manipulating his fellow players but also in manipulating the audience as to when to see his body as associated with positive or negative rhetoric. In fact, one of the more significant aspects of Richard's interactions with his Disability is that throughout the play, he challenges the idea that people with Disabilities are lesser or more incapable beings. Furthermore, by cleverly presenting his Disabled form as an excuse for his actions, he not only presents an understanding of his form and its implications historically, but he is also able to use his deformed body as a distraction from his political manoeuvres. Williams states that Richard:

> aware of the negative associations of his body, wields his appearance as an excuse, claiming his deformity as evidence of inability [...] there is not much Richard can't do, and to do these things, he puts his body on view, using

multiple interpretations and expectations it prompts to achieve his ambition and the crown he desires.[45]

Therefore, Richard's 'misshapen' form affords him agency through manipulation, and it seems that 'Richard was more Disabled by religious, dramatic, social, and political constructs, then he was by his hunch back'.[46]

One alternative interpretation of Richard's Disability surrounds the idea that Richard's Disability works from representations of propaganda. Shakespeare's play drew from sources that make a point of Richard's appearance, for example, Thomas More's *History of King Richard III* which describes Richard as 'little of stature, ill-featured of limbs, crook-backed, his left shoulder much higher than his right, hard-favoured of visage'.[47] This text has political connotations because More needed to 'deny Richard in keeping with the Tudor monarchy in power at the time, therefore the presentation of body is also politically driven'. In modern literary studies, his body has been important in promoting a distinctive shape relative to a 'fractured and turbulent English history, a monstrous political figure who usurps the throne, and a demonstration of Renaissance beliefs about the continuity between inner morality and outward physical forms'.[48]

Buckingham's reactions to Richard in the play are of further interest. Enticed by Richard into his murderous scheming and machinations, he knows the depth of Richard's plots. By the third act, it is Buckingham who is able to plead Richard's cause without one reference to his body and instead refers to the weight of history and Richard's patriarchal lineage in shifting the focus from body to political sovereignty, particularly when Richard states: 'Withal, I did infer your lineaments/ Being the right idea of your father/Both in your form and nobleness of mind'. Williams writes that:

> most significantly, any resonance of Richard's deformed body is transferred to the nation of England as a whole, which is now situated as a precariously ailing body in need of virtuous intervention Richard himself will provide [...] Buckingham re-inscribes Richard's deformity upon the nation and casts Richard as the cure for its bodily lack.[49]

By the conclusion of the play, and through the articulation of Richard by Buckingham and Richard himself, his Disability is no longer foundational to his character. Buckingham becomes an everyman whose ultimate redemption arrives when turning his back on Richard. This is due to Buckingham realising the extent of Richard's evil, but at no stage does Buckingham infer that this is due to Richard's deformed body, suggesting that Shakespeare recognises each person's responsibility for their actions, that Richard is evil in his core, and this is not because of his physical surface. Williams progresses this argument when writing that 'the notion of deformity as physical lack is finally served from Richard's body to exist instead as a metaphysical label attached to other objects to justify political ends'.[50] Richard then can be seen to 'play' or 'perform' his Disability as a strategy for power and gain, and despite the contemporary reaction to Disability being one of pity, at no point do we have the sense that we are supposed to feel this for Richard. He frightens and intimidates and becomes the quintessential villain. The text, Richard's soliloquies, actions, interactions, and machinations allow Shakespeare to eliminate pity and move the focus from body to motive. It should be remembered that throughout the play, Richard is successful in wooing women, fulfils his duties as Duke, serves as Lord Protector, becomes King, and leads his army into battle and fights. Therefore, Shakespeare 'forces the audience to question whether or not he even has a Disability: a hunchback, the text tells us, yes; but a Disability, the text tells us, no'.[51]

Ultimately, through the character of Richard, Shakespeare uses Disability as a cultural clue to add effect to Richard's character, particularly in relation to evil. However, Richard is not limited, and Shakespeare throughout the play presents radical thinking about Disability. Jackson even goes so far as to imply that:

> in presenting Shakespeare in alignment with modern concepts of what it means to be Disabled, Shakespeare appears somewhat ahead of his time or thinking; although he does not embrace Richard's deformities, he does utilise them, and at times he appears to go so far as to understand them.[52]

Despite the limitations and liabilities of reading Richard through a Renaissance context of Disability, what this type of investigation affords is an opportunity to consider the multifarious ways in which we can speak about Disability when we encounter it in Shakespeare's texts, and therefore, as Wilson explains, Shakespeare's:

> texts can be used to generate and support theories of Disability [...] and Richard's position in the trajectory of Disabled identity offers to Shakespeare

studies a rich opportunity for new understanding about the power of the deformed body, even as careful attention to the play opens up new possibilities for thinking about Disability in the Renaissance.[53]

The differences historically in the meaning of Disability are of paramount importance throughout any investigation of this work. The play provides a depiction of the absolute adversity that Richard must endure because of the reception to his Disability. However, Richard is, in the main, able to succeed in all his endeavours. Through the character of Richard, Shakespeare can provide a dynamic consideration of the body, its challenges, limitations, and opportunities.

Richard III and *Henry VI part one* and *part two* offer opportunities to 'think about Disabled identity in the Renaissance as a complex negotiation of discourses of deformity and monstrosity as well as in relation to bodily contingency that reveals the instability of all bodies'.[54] This investigation affords an opportunity to consider the multifarious ways in which we can 'speak about Disability when we encounter it in Shakespeare's texts, and it was shown how Shakespeare's texts can be used to generate and support theories of Disability', if it is used as a tool for study and interrogation.[55]

Notes

1. Douglas, M. (1966) *Purity and Danger.* London: Routledge & Kegan Paul.
2. Barnes, C. (1991) 'A Brief History of Discrimination and Disabled People', in *Chapter 2 Disabled People in Britain and Discrimination: A case for anti-discrimination legislation:* http://Disability-studies.leeds.ac.uk/files/library/Barnes-Disabled-people-and-discrim-ch2.pdf (Accessed: 02/04/17). p. 47
3. Garland-Thomson, R. (2003) 'Making Freaks: Visual Rhetoric and the Spectacle of Julia Pastrana'. In Cohen, J.J. & Weiss, G. (eds.) *Thinking the Limits of the Body.* Albany: State University of New York Press, pp. 125–145. p. 196.
4. Barnes, C. (1991) 'A Brief History of Discrimination and Disabled People', in *Chapter 2 Disabled People in Britain and Discrimination: A case for anti-discrimination legislation:* http://Disability-studies.leeds.ac.uk/files/library/Barnes-Disabled-people-and-discrim-ch2.pdf (Accessed: 02/04/17).
5. Wilson, J, R. (2017) The Trouble with Disability in Shakespeare Studies. *Disability Studies Quarterly.* Harvard University: 2 (37): http://dsq-sds.org/article/view/5430/4644 (Accessed 21/10/18).

6. Oliver, M. (1981) 'A New Model of the Social Work Role in Relation to Disability' in Campling, J. (ed.) *The Handicapped Person: A New Perspective for Social Workers?* London: RADAR, pp. 19–36.: https://disability-studies.leeds.ac.uk/wp-content/uploads/sites/40/library/Campling-handicppaed.pdf (Accessed 26/02/19).
   Hanks, J. & Hanks, L. (1980), "The Physically Handicapped in Certain Non-Occidental Societies" in Phillips, W. & Rosenberg, J. (ed.) *Social Scientists and the Physically Handicapped*. London: Arno Press.
7. Bloy, M. (2002) *The 1601 Elizabethan Poor Law Victorian Web*: http://www.victorianweb.org/history/poorlaw/elizpl.html (Accessed: 02/02/17). p. 32.
8. Ibid, pp. 32–46.
9. Gray, P. & Cox, J.D. (ed.) (2014) *Shakespeare and Renaissance Ethics*. Cambridge: Cambridge University Print. p. 65.
10. Shakespeare, W. in Craig, W.J. (1991) (ed.) *The Complete works of Shakespeare*. Oxford: Oxford University Press. pp. 539–540.
11. Wilson, R. (1993) 'The Quality of Mercy: Discipline and Punishment in Shakespearean Comedy', in Wilson, R. (ed.) *Will Power: Essays on Shakespearean Authority*. Hemel Hempstead: Harvester Wheatsheaf, pp. 118–157.
12. It is assumed that Shakespeare referred to Plutarch's Lives to create the history plays set around this time; it is a series of biographies of famous men and an important source of information to document the times in which the Greeks and Romans lived.
13. Shakespeare, W. in Craig, W.J. (1991) (ed.) *The Complete works of Shakespeare*. Oxford: Oxford University Press. p. 822.
14. Hargrave, M. (2015) *Theatres of Learning Disability: Good, Bad, or Plain Ugly?* London: Palgrave Macmillan. p. 139.
15. Minton, E. (2011) *A Timeless Hamlet in a Dated Production*: http://www.shakespeareances.com/willpower/onscreen/Hamlet-BBCTL80.html (Accessed: 17/12/17).
16. Mitchell, D. T. & Snyder, S. L. (2002) *Narrative Prosthesis: Disability and the Dependencies of Discourse*. Ann Arbor: University of Michigan Print Press. p. 102.
17. Williams, K. S. (2009) 'Enabling Richard: The Rhetoric of Disability in *Richard III*', *Disability Studies Quarterly* 29 (4): https://www.bl.uk/shakespeare/articles/richard-iii-and-the-staging-of-Disability (Accessed: 05/01/17). p. 4.
18. Metzler, I. (2016) *Fools and Idiots? Intellectual Disability in the Middle Ages*. Manchester: Manchester University Press. p. 22.
19. Barnes, C. (1991) 'A Brief History of Discrimination and Disabled People', in *Chapter 2 Disabled People in Britain and Discrimination: A case for anti-*

13 SHAKESPEARE'S DISABLED, DISABLED SHAKESPEARE: A RENAISSANCE... 127

discrimination legislation: http://Disability-studies.leeds.ac.uk/files/library/Barnes-Disabled-people-and-discrim-ch2.pdf(Accessed: 02/04/17). p. 2.

20. Shakespeare, W. in Craig, W.J. (1991) (ed.) *The Complete works of Shakespeare*. Oxford: Oxford University Press. p.580.

21. Haffter, C. (1968) 'The Changeling: History and Psychodynamics of Attitudes to Handicapped Children in European Folklore' *Journal of the History of Behavioural Sciences*, 4 (7), pp. 55–61: https://psycnet.apa.org/record/1968-12568-001 (Accessed 26/02/19).

22. Shakespeare, W. in Craig, W.J. (1991) (ed.) *The Complete works of Shakespeare*. Oxford: Oxford University Press. p. 616.

23. West, W. N. (2009) 'What's the Matter with Shakespeare? Physics, Identity, Playin', *Northwestern University South Central Review*, 1 (232), pp. 103–126: http://www.yavanika.org/classes/reader/shakesmatter.pdf (Accessed: 18/07/18). p. 118.

24. Hobgood, A. & Houston-Wood, D. (ed.) (2009) 'Disabled Shakespeare.' *Disability Studies Quarterly*. 4 (29): http://dsq-sds.org/article/view/991/1183 (Accessed: 18/07/18).

25. Ibid.

26. Barnes, C. (1991) 'A Brief History of Discrimination and Disabled People', in *Chapter 2 Disabled People in Britain and Discrimination: A case for anti-discrimination legislation*: http://Disability-studies.leeds.ac.uk/files/library/Barnes-Disabled-people-and-discrim-ch2.pdf(Accessed: 02/04/17). p. 2.

27. Eyler, J. R. (2010) *Disability in the Middle Ages: Reconsiderations and Reverberations*. London: Routledge. p. 192.

28. Ibid, p. 192.

29. Quayson, A. (2012) *Aesthetic Nervousness*. New York: Columbia University Press. p. 97.

30. Eyler, J. R. (2010) *Disability in the Middle Ages: Reconsiderations and Reverberations*. London: Routledge. p. 194.

31. Williams, K. S. (2009) 'Enabling Richard: The Rhetoric of Disability in *Richard III*', *Disability Studies Quarterly* 29 (4): https://www.bl.uk/shakespeare/articles/richard-iii-and-the-staging-of-Disability (Accessed: 05/01/17). p. 6.

32. Shakespeare, W. in Craig, W.J. (1991) (ed.) *The Complete works of Shakespeare*. Oxford: Oxford University Press. p. 603.

33. Alexander, B. R. (2011) *Applying Disability Theory as an Actor and Director to Theatrical Texts of The Past and Present*: https://scholar.colorado.edu/honr_theses/573 (Accessed: 18/07/18). p. 15.

34. Williams, K. S. (2009) 'Enabling Richard: The Rhetoric of Disability in *Richard III*', *Disability Studies Quarterly* 29 (4): https://www.bl.uk/

shakespeare/articles/richard-iii-and-the-staging-of-Disability (Accessed: 05/01/17). p. 6.

35. Shakespeare, W. in Craig, W.J. (1991) (ed.) *The Complete works of Shakespeare*. Oxford: Oxford University Press. p. 634.

36. Eyler, J. R. (2010) *Disability in the Middle Ages: Reconsiderations and Reverberations*. London: Routledge. p. 190.

37. Williams, K. S. (2009) 'Enabling Richard: The Rhetoric of Disability in *Richard III*', *Disability Studies Quarterly* 29 (4): https://www.bl.uk/shakespeare/articles/richard-iii-and-the-staging-of-Disability (Accessed: 05/01/17). p. 2.

38. Ibid, p. 4.

39. Davis, Lennard J. *Bending over Backwards: Disability, Dismodernism, and Other Difficult Positions*. New York University Press, 2002.

40. Alexander, B. R. (2011) *Applying Disability Theory as an Actor and Director to Theatrical Texts of The Past and Present*: https://scholar.colorado.edu/honr_theses/573 (Accessed: 18/07/18). p. 120.

41. Williams, K. S. (2009) 'Enabling Richard: The Rhetoric of Disability in *Richard III*', *Disability Studies Quarterly* 29 (4): https://www.bl.uk/shakespeare/articles/richard-iii-and-the-staging-of-Disability (Accessed: 05/01/17). p. 7.

42. Shakespeare, W. in Craig, W.J. (1991) (ed.) *The Complete works of Shakespeare*. Oxford: Oxford University Press. p. 596.

43. Ibid, p. 596.

44. Eyler, J. R. (2010) *Disability in the Middle Ages: Reconsiderations and Reverberations*. London: Routledge. pp. 190–191.

45. Williams, K. S. (2009) 'Enabling Richard: The Rhetoric of Disability in *Richard III*', *Disability Studies Quarterly* 29 (4): https://www.bl.uk/shakespeare/articles/richard-iii-and-the-staging-of-Disability (Accessed: 05/01/17). p. 7.

46. Eyler, J. R. (2010) *Disability in the Middle Ages: Reconsiderations and Reverberations*. London: Routledge. p. 193.

47. More, T. (1924) *The History of King Richard the Third*. Indiana: Indianan University Press.

48. Williams, K. S. (2009) 'Enabling Richard: The Rhetoric of Disability in *Richard III*', *Disability Studies Quarterly* 29 (4): https://www.bl.uk/shakespeare/articles/richard-iii-and-the-staging-of-Disability (Accessed: 05/01/17).

49. Ibid.

50. Ibid, p. 7.

51. Eyler, J. R. (2010) *Disability in the Middle Ages: Reconsiderations and Reverberations*. London: Routledge.p.190.

52. Jackson, L. (2014) *Crouchback or Misunderstood? The Disability of Richard III*: http://www.blue-stockings.org/?p=196 (Accessed: 18/07/18). p. 4.
53. Wilson, R. (1993) 'The Quality of Mercy: Discipline and Punishment in Shakespearean Comedy', in Wilson, R. (ed.) *Will Power: Essays on Shakespearean Authority*. Hemel Hempstead: Harvester Wheatsheaf, pp. 118–157.
54. Williams, K. S. (2009) 'Enabling Richard: The Rhetoric of Disability in *Richard III*', *Disability Studies Quarterly* 29 (4): https://www.bl.uk/shakespeare/articles/richard-iii-and-the-staging-of-Disability (Accessed: 05/01/17). p. 6.
55. Wilson, R. (1993) 'The Quality of Mercy: Discipline and Punishment in Shakespearean Comedy', in Wilson, R. (ed.) *Will Power: Essays on Shakespearean Authority*. Hemel Hempstead: Harvester Wheatsheaf, pp. 118–157.

CHAPTER 14

Blue Apple Theatre Company: A Case Study

This chapter aims to look specifically at the Blue Apple Theatre Company's (Blue Apple) use of Shakespeare's work within their programme and how this programme captures some of the methodologies, impacts, and challenges tied to applied theatre's intentions for achieving transformation.

The Blue Apple Theatre Company (Blue Apple) was founded in 2005 by Jane Jessop, with support from Winchester Mencap, to 'provide opportunities for those with learning difficulties to participate in theatre and dance and to develop the social ability, behavioral and performance skills of individuals with a wide range of learning Disabilities'.[1,2] The company works with a range of participants who are aged 16 years or over and:

> while some actors do present a range of Disabilities, such as autism (including Asperger syndrome), Down's syndrome and behavioural difficulties, the company is also inclusive to people both with and without learning difficulties – what matters is a desire to take part and to make a contribution.[3]

In 2009, the company employed their first Artistic Director (Peter Clerke) and became a fully independent registered charity by 2013.[4] The company is 'based in Winchester, Hampshire but perform nationally with an established, expanding touring network. The company provides a programme of dance and drama sessions tailored to individual needs, and [they] normally work with over 70 people'.[5]

© The Author(s), under exclusive license to Springer Nature Switzerland AG 2024
A. Hulsmeier, *Applied Shakespeare*,
https://doi.org/10.1007/978-3-031-45414-1_14

131

132 A. HULSMEIER

Developments in 2008 saw the company evolve, introducing an intensive theatre training scheme for auditioned performers known as 'Apple Core'. Their website describes how 'in 2011 six Apple Core actors (four of the six had Downs syndrome) created their first major touring production *"Living without Fear"* which addressed Disability hate crime. The company is now established and produces two professional theatre shows and one touring production each year'.[6]

The overarching aims of the company can be found in their belief that the 'work enables and empowers its performers, challenging perceptions and changing expectations' and they ultimately desire to identify 'the effect its work has on the social and personal development of its members aiming to bring about widespread change in attitude towards the capabilities of learning Disabled and their ability to contribute to society'.[7] It is through the production of a range of theatre performances, dance, and film that the company aims 'to challenge prejudice and transform the lives of people with a learning Disability'.[8] They state that 'all activity is designed to build and sustain improved confidence and physical and mental wellbeing while, at the same time, producing exciting, engaging and inspiring art'.[9] In relation to its line of research, Blue Apple continues to 'influence national agendas through its live performance and films by tackling challenging issues head on [and] is leading a study to measure and demonstrate the impact of its work'.[10]

The justification for the work's existence is clear for Jane Jessop who states that the:

> lack of understanding in society about learning Disabilities can be eradicated as [...] theatre is a fantastic way in which we can show people more about the subject [...] In the end they see a real theatrical show and they forget they've been watching people with learning Disabilities. If we can go some way towards showcasing the abilities and personalities of these actors, and honestly look at them as professional actors, then we can help our audience members to do the same.[11]

Therefore, the work appears to be concerned with two overarching concerns: firstly, its desire for Disabled theatre to be an inclusive practice, and secondly, for the audience attending the performance to be afforded an opportunity to transform their understanding regarding learning Disabilities. Transformation is also mentioned in relation to the participants of the work when suggesting 'the work results in great discipline, concentration, memory, the development of language and physical skills, and the need to work collaboratively with a wide range of other people'.[12]

Although the company does not specifically reference their work as being influenced by the purposes of applied theatre, it is clear from their aims and intentions that the elements of applied theatre (relevant to social change and transformation for both participant and audience) are evident within their projects. Their overarching manifesto also supports applied theatre's intentions to promote transformation and achieve inclusion and progression. They express a desire to 'change the way people see and understand learning Disability [...] raise the ceiling of expectation for people with learning Disabilities [and] build and sustain improved confidence and physical and mental wellbeing'.[13] Such intentions can be clearly mapped onto the specific objectives, purposes, and values of applied theatre work. Blue Apple undertakes practice to touch lives, hopes the participants and audience will extend their perspectives of Disability, and imagines how it might be different, and is concerned with encouraging people to use the experience of theatre to move beyond what they already know. The company also fits the criteria for participatory work as the participants are actively involved with the projects and theatre productions. They identify the need for the work to represent Disabled people, who in turn are afforded the opportunity to engage with theatre in the role of actor. This is ultimately a company of actors with learning difficulties concerned entirely with interaction '– actor with actor, actor with text, actor with the audience. It is about trust, collaboration, and the development of bonds'.[14,15]

Of the current 24 productions created since 2005, including *The Government Inspector* (2011), *The Snow Queen* (2013), *Arabian Nights* (2014), and *The Selfish Giant* (2015), Shakespeare has provided the stimulus for some of Blue Apple's major, 'ground-breaking' productions including *A Midsummer Night's Dream* (2010), *Hamlet* (2012), and *Much Ado About Nothing* (2015).[16] Blue Apple's first performance of Shakespeare was the 2010 production of *A Midsummer Night's Dream* at the Sam Wanamaker Playhouse at the Globe Theatre, London. The company performed with a cast of over 30 actors, many of whom had Disabilities.

In 2012, the company took part in the World Shakespeare Festival and tackled their second Shakespeare performance of *Hamlet*. The production was taken on tour to twelve main-stream theatres across the South of England and was performed to over 3,500 people. Clerke explains the reasons for choosing *Hamlet*:

Shakespeare was writing a play about someone trying to find their voice, their place in this world. And, with regard directly to the character of *Hamlet*, he does finally find it. But fundamentally, it is too late. This is simply Blue Apple's attempt to identify with these themes, and to claim these words, in our own particular way, as something that can speak to all of us. Before it is, indeed, 'too late'. Too late to speak of people who are marginalised or disenfranchised because they don't 'fit in'. It is, undeniably, a cliché but, Hamlet's 'to be, or not to be' still remains the fundamental question.[17]

Although the term 'speak to all of us', appears to refer to a universalising discourse, it is in fact used by Blue Apple to achieve their inclusive intentions and allow people who are 'marginalised and disenfranchised' to have their voice.

Blue Apple's latest encounter with Shakespeare was the 2015 version of *Much Ado about Nothing*. The production included working closely with a handful of 80 Jersey Islanders with Down's syndrome and associated conditions to help them work independently and to their full potential in the community. 'To achieve this play– if we have– has been down to an enormous commitment. Many hours. Much imagination. A lot of rehearsal, discussion, and analysis. A lot of trust. And an enormous amount of belief'.[18]

The company is clear about their reasons for using Shakespeare. Jane Jessop suggests that 'this is the most famous [work] in the world. Shakespeare speaks to us all, and we should open those doors and allow everybody to taste what he has to say to us'.[19] William Jessop states Shakespeare 'is the greatest writer there's ever been. These stories are for everyone and have everything in them about humanity. Why shouldn't people with learning Disability tackle these texts?'.[20] The hope is that they 'can bring recognition from the mainstream arts world for artists with learning Disabilities, who want to take part on stage but don't usually have a chance to do so'.[21] Therefore, Blue Apple appears to be concerned with interacting with Shakespeare's work to present new visions of the plays and 'celebrate the talents of our actors through the greatest plays in the world'.[22]

Blue Apple offers a clear interrogation of the challenges a Disabled community may face when engaging with Shakespeare's plays, his vernacular and ideas about humanity. They also outline the challenges when attempting to engage people who present a range of different Disabilities with theatre generally.

14 BLUE APPLE THEATRE COMPANY: A CASE STUDY   135

Blue Apple's manner of dealing with the challenge of understanding the play *Hamlet* was to 'adapt the original script to reflect the life experiences of the learning-Disabled actors, sometimes meaning modifying the story to make it easier to understand'. It should be acknowledged that the changes to the text are made to make it more accessible and are for the participants' benefits solely. In relation to *A Midsummer Night's Dream*, William Jessop explains how the play was modernised to make it more accessible for the participants:

> One of the actors always dreamed of being a pop star, so we wrote Hermia as a pop star, and we made the whole wedding of the king and queen a celebrity VIP wedding because everyone in the group was fascinated by celebrity and gossip. We made Demetrius a footballer because the actor playing him was obsessed with football! We kept it close to the actors and their wish fulfilment.[23]

The script is also often cut in length and adapted for greater relevance to the community. Lewis describes that 'throughout the writing process the cast attended workshops led by William so that they could influence the script and greater appreciate the story'.[24] Blue Apple usually keeps the original language of Shakespeare because:

> The sound and the rhythm of the language really unlocked something within them. When you work like this with Shakespeare, you realise that it's the sounds within the language that give it such emotional depth. That is what the actors respond to when reading the lines, that is what allows them to perform without necessarily understanding the nuances of the lines' meanings.[25]

However, the inclusion of Shakespeare's original language also brings its challenges. Emma highlights difficulties when explaining that:

> Shakespeare's 16th century language was unfamiliar before the workshops started; many of the actors involved have Down's syndrome, which can make performing Shakespeare's words a bit of a challenge. The faces of people with Down's syndrome are shaped slightly differently and some have bigger tongues, so we worked with a voice coach to ensure that everyone could be heard and understood. For one of our actors, it is about learning to open her mouth wider, for another it is keeping her tongue straighter when she speaks.[26]

It is interesting to note that the challenges of the language are less to do with Shakespeare's writing and more to do with the Disability itself and its own inherent complications. Other complications tackled by Blue Apple are found when the cast faced challenges in their consideration of Hamlet and Ophelia's relationship, as 'sometimes people with Down's syndrome find it difficult to separate fiction from reality, so *Hamlet* has been blurring with their own real life, and with this comes difficulties with the emotions of the characters'.[27]

The complexities of the Disability (not necessarily the chosen text) cause a challenge, and we see again the difficulties faced when asking a member of a marginalised community to undertake character identification. The challenge here is not necessarily about what Shakespeare's work may be asking its participants to face or the issues it requires them to question or address (for the community may not be able to interact with the text at this level), but rather that the challenge is tied to the complexities of what Disabled theatre is trying to achieve when asking a community with complex Disabilities to engage with a fiction that they cannot fully separate from real life. Blue Apple's reflections surrounding the use of Shakespeare's work therefore appear to move between the physical into the intellectual considerations that need to be kept in mind when engaging with the complex profiles of Blue Apple's participants.

A further challenge in presenting this work, is held, and captured amongst members of the audience who often arrive 'not really knowing what to expect. Will they have to make any concessions? Will the show hang together?'.[28] Blue Apple aims to promote a transformation regarding the audience's views and understandings of Disability. This is not an easy feat and links to the reception of Disabled theatre generally and reiterates a similar challenge identified in the prison chapter, that of a public acceptability test and the importance of audience support for the continuation of this work (see 9). However, Blue Apple suggests that they are successful in showing an audience that, when they attend a performance by Blue Apple, 'they see a real theatrical show and they forget they've been watching people with learning Disabilities'.[29] Lewis explains that 'if we can go some way towards showcasing the abilities and personalities of these actors, and honestly look at them as professional actors, then we can help our audience members to do the same'.[30]

The challenges associated with this work can be seen as twofold. First, there are challenges presented through working with a Disabled cast (the presentation of the language and the blurred boundaries between fact and fiction that are difficult for some participants to understand). Second, there are challenges presented by the audience and their possible pre-conceived ideas about theatre and Disability and Shakespeare.

Despite the challenges identified within the work, Blue Apple has drawn a lot of critical acclaim and their work continues to be award-winning. The reception of the work appears to be continuously positive. Numerous reviews commend the work for being 'Brilliantly told and very funny,' 'Pure class and totally engaging' and 'a wonderful and joyful show'. Others state 'It always amazes me how I never see the learning Disability'.[31] The company is also commended in a reviewer's comments about *Much Ado About Nothing* when explaining that 'for the 150-strong audience who watched Blue Apple perform, it was an eye-opener to what anyone can achieve if they want to, regardless of their start in life'.[32]

Participants of the projects are also positive about the performances and their voices have a place in reflecting the overall success of the work. James Elsworth, who played Polonius and Laertes for Blue Apple offered feedback on his experience noting: 'I can be myself, people understand me'.[33] Tommy Jessop a 27-year-old actor with Down's syndrome says 'it was his dream to play Hamlet. I like the 'to be or not to be' speech because it is the most famous speech in the world and because I get to act really big to the back of the audience. The sword fighting is really fun too'.[34] Laurie Morris reflected that 'I think people out there in the world need to see that people are capable of doing Shakespeare, even with a learning Disability like we've got'.[35] Polly Troup, a performer with Blue Apple reflects more generally about the holistic experience Blue Apple affords when stating:

> Blue Apple is definitely a caring group; everyone genuinely does look out for each other. The minute something's not right, someone will say. There's a lot to cope with here: the stairs, the space, 40 plus people. This place has been the safest place for me, ever since the beginning – I know that I can come here and there are people to talk to.[36]

The work is received with positivity and enthusiasm and the impact on the participants is clear from their reactions. Their work appears successful in achieving its intentions and ambitions, and there are continuously clear links between the work of Blue Apple and the intentions of inclusive and participatory practice. They are concerned with a desire to challenge expectations, promote confidence, and develop a greater understanding of learning Disabilities. The company uses Shakespeare specifically as a tool for inclusivity, and theatre generally as a tool for transformation (not necessarily always for their participants but certainly for their audiences, although it could be argued that inclusivity for its participants is transformative). Their desire to promote inclusion within the practice of theatre generally is particularly commended, and as Lewis explains:

> taking part in theatre increases the quality of their lives outside of the company. The most rewarding element of this work is seeing the actor's blossom as people and seeing the discipline of acting giving them real confidence to take out into their lives. They realise they can learn lines and perform, and, above all, when they stand on stage in front of members of society that they don't know, they can make them laugh with them, and at the end they can be applauded and cheered for what they've done. It creates a feeling of acceptance and vindication of themselves as people.[37]

Ultimately, Blue Apple's focus is to promote inclusion, which they appear to achieve. Blue Apple presents a clear example of how a Disability Theatre Company interacts with Shakespeare's plays, and how interaction with the plays can benefit the participants by offering opportunities for increased levels of inclusion.

Summary

The chapters dedicated to Shakespeare with Disability have explored the general context of Disability theatre, its histories, origins, and influences. It has also acknowledged the importance of greater interrogation into Shakespeare's use within the Disabled community and Disability theatre's placement alongside other types of theatre. The chapter provided a Renaissance reading of Shakespeare's *Henry VI Part Two and Three,* and *Richard III* in relation to Disability, and finally assessed the Blue Apple Theatre Company as an example of work that currently exists in combining Shakespeare, Disability and applied theatre formats. The chapter overall provides an exploration of Disabled Shakespeare, and while the chapter is unable to cover every single example in this field, it does provide a comprehensive exploration of specific uses of Shakespeare's work with Disabled communities, highlighting some important findings for this practice.

NOTES

1. Blue Apple Theatre Company. (No Date) *Blue Apple Theatre*: http://blueappletheatre.com (Accessed: 01/07/16).
2. Now known as Winchester Gold, the company is a non-profit, local charity organisation that believes that people should be treated as equals and given the same respect and opportunities as everyone else. That means full choice and control in their lives, such as where to live, work, and socialise. (Winchester, n.d.) winchestergold.org.uk (Accessed: 03/11/23).
3. Blue Apple Theatre Company. (No Date) *Blue Apple Theatre*: http://blueappletheatre.com (Accessed: 01/07/16).
4. Clerke was appointed in autumn 2009 as an arts consultant and, by 2012, became the company's first Artistic Director.
5. Blue Apple Theatre Company. (No Date) *Blue Apple Theatre*: http://blueappletheatre.com (Accessed: 01/07/16).
6. Ibid.
7. Ibid.
8. Ibid.
9. Ibid.
10. Ibid.
11. Lewis, A. (2012) *A Younger Theatre: Spotlight on Blue Apple Theatre*: http://www.ayoungertheatre.com/spotlight-on-blue-apple-theatre (Accessed: 01/07/16).
12. Blue Apple Theatre Company. (No Date) *Blue Apple Theatre*: http://blueappletheatre.com (Accessed: 01/07/16).
13. Ibid.
14. Ibid.
15. **Heidi Thomas** is a UK dramatist and patron of Blue Apple Theatre Company.
16. Hamlet also featured as part of the BBC3's hour-long documentary 'Growing up Downs' which won the prestigious Creative Diversity Network Most Ground-Breaking Programme.
17. Blue Apple Theatre Company. (No Date) *Blue Apple Theatre*: http://blueappletheatre.com (Accessed: 01/07/16).
18. Ibid.
19. Lewis, A. (2012) *A Younger Theatre: Spotlight on Blue Apple Theatre*: http://www.ayoungertheatre.com/spotlight-on-blue-apple-theatre (Accessed: 01/07/16).
20. William Jessop is an award-winning, self-shooting producer and director. He was responsible for the award-winning documentary 'Growing up Downs' and has been involved with Blue Apple since his mother founded the company in 2005.

140   A. HULSMEIER

21. Lewis, A. (2012) *A Younger Theatre: Spotlight on Blue Apple Theatre*: http://www.ayoungertheatre.com/spotlight-on-blue-apple-theatre (Accessed: 01/07/16).
22. Blue Apple Theatre Company. (No Date) *Blue Apple Theatre*: http://blueappletheatre.com (Accessed: 01/07/16).
23. Lewis, A. (2012) *A Younger Theatre: Spotlight on Blue Apple Theatre:* http://www.ayoungertheatre.com/spotlight-on-blue-apple-theatre (Accessed: 01/07/16).
24. Ibid.
25. Ibid.
26. Emma. (2012) *Ouch! It's a Disability thing: Actor's with learning Disabilities perform Shakespeare's Hamlet*: http://www.bbc.co.uk/blogs/ouch/2012/05/actors_with_learning_disabilit.html (Accessed: 01/07/16).
27. Lewis, A. (2012) *A Younger Theatre: Spotlight on Blue Apple Theatre*: http://www.ayoungertheatre.com/spotlight-on-blue-apple-theatre (Accessed: 01/07/16).
28. Ibid.
29. Ibid.
30. Ibid.
31. Blue Apple Theatre Company. (No Date) *Blue Apple Theatre*: http://blueappletheatre.com (Accessed: 01/07/16).
32. Jersey Evening Post (2015): http://jerseyeveningpost.com (Accessed: 01/07/16).
33. Blue Apple Theatre Company. (No Date) *Blue Apple Theatre*: http://blueappletheatre.com (Accessed: 01/07/16).
34. Emma. (2012) *Ouch! It's a Disability thing: Actor's with learning Disabilities perform Shakespeare's Hamlet*: http://www.bbc.co.uk/blogs/ouch/2012/05/actors_with_learning_disabilit.html (Accessed: 01/07/16).
35. Payne, W. (2010) *Blue Apple Tackles the Bard*: http://www.hampshire-chronicle.co.uk/leisure/arts/8206826.Blue_Apple_tackles_the_Bard/ (Accessed: 01/07/16).
36. Blue Apple Theatre Company. (No Date) *Blue Apple Theatre*: http://blueappletheatre.com (Accessed: 01/07/16).
37. Lewis, A. (2012) *A Younger Theatre: Spotlight on Blue Apple Theatre*: http://www.ayoungertheatre.com/spotlight-on-blue-apple-theatre (Accessed: 01/07/16).

PART IV

Therapeutic Shakespeare

Hamlet: To die, to sleep-
No more- and by sleep to say we end
The heartache, and the thousand natural shocks
That flesh is heir to. T'is a consummation
Devoutly to be wish'd.[1]

Part IV addresses how and where Shakespeare's work is used within therapeutic environments. The chapter begins with an exploration of the history of theatre therapy generally, then moves into a consideration of the use of Shakespeare's work in therapeutic environments specifically, where it currently exists, and the articulated benefits and potential challenges when combining the two areas of practice. The chapter then provides a Renaissance reading of Shakespeare's *Hamlet* as a demonstrative text linked to therapeutic possibilities. Finally, the chapter concludes with a case study analysis of the Combat Veteran Plays, as an example of a therapeutic community that uses Shakespeare's work for the purposes of transformation. The work will explore how the company articulates the benefits of using Shakespeare's work to transform their participants and analyses the challenges that may ensue in the application of Shakespeare alongside combat veterans.

NOTE

1. Shakespeare, W. in Craig, W.J. (1991) (ed.) *The Complete works of Shakespeare.* Oxford: Oxford University Press. p. 886.

CHAPTER 15

The History of Theatre and Therapy

This chapter explores the history of theatre and its interactions with therapy and therapeutic outcomes for a range of different participants in a range of different contexts. Drama therapy, psychodrama, and/or theatre therapy are all forms of therapy that aim to focus on the person and/or group in reducing the symptoms of mental illness. They all follow a social model of wellness treatment.[1,2]

The chapter importantly recognises that psychodrama, dramatherapy, and theatre therapy are disparate terms. The terms are not synonymous, but 'there are obvious similarities between the disciplines as they are all based in dramatic and theatrical processes'.[3] A lot of the methods of therapy between the forms overlap, and a lot of practitioners take techniques from across the different practices.[4] Ultimately, they all aim to affect some kind of change in individuals or groups, and 'they have something in common in relation to socially and politically engaged theatre'.[5] Therefore, the terms are appropriately viewed as one and the same thing; the terms are interchangeable but their slight differences are acknowledged and retained.

Dramatic forms of therapy are 'solidly established as a viable alternative to other treatments, and it has developed into a systematic approach with established strategies and techniques'.[6] The work draws on the desire to use action techniques such as 'role play, drama games, improvisation, puppetry, masks and theatrical performance, in the service of behaviour change and personal growth'.[7] This is ultimately the use of drama as a therapeutic

© The Author(s), under exclusive license to Springer Nature
Switzerland AG 2024
A. Hulsmeier, *Applied Shakespeare*,
https://doi.org/10.1007/978-3-031-45414-1_15

143

144 A. HULSMEIER

method and the work is articulated to assist forms of mental illness, helping to work through emotional problems (Boal, 2006).[8]

At its most general, theatre therapy is often read as a form of theatre that 'can prompt us to reflect upon our own thoughts, feelings and behaviour in the presence of others, within a specific time frame'.[9] The work can be seen to 'make the hidden visible, the latent manifest, in laying bare the interior landscape of the mind and its fears and desires through a range of signifying practises'.[10] This documents the compatibility of the forms of drama and therapy in coming together to benefit and aid an individual and/or group. Chesner explains that:

> If we recognise that in each of us there are a number of sub-personalities or different facets, then our inner world can be thought of as a stage on which various conflicts, arguments and dialogues are carried out- there is interaction and there are inter-relationships. The dramatherapy process provides an opportunity for the individual to experiment with various possibilities, to re-experience and clarify perceptions of past events, aided by the drama therapist, who supplies this structure or the container for what takes place.[11]

Therefore, therapists and academics reflect that theatre therapy achieves its success 'by stepping into another person's shoes, increasing our sensitivity to others, and learning more about ourselves'.[12]

Historically, the roots of this type of theatre 'appear 45,000–35,000 years ago and tie to the beginnings of symbolic, metaphoric thought'.[13] Research indicates that 'for thousands of years drama had been used in healing rituals and the form has its roots in religion, theatre, education, social action and mental health/therapy'.[14] As a theatrical movement specifically, drama/theatre therapy emerged as a definite field of practice during the seventeenth and eighteenth centuries in some so-called 'lunatic' asylums where theatre was used as part of treatment. Naples and Palmero in Italy had theatres specially constructed in hospitals. By the 1920s, Jacob L. Moreno (psychologist, psychosociologist and educator) had started spontaneous theatre work with adult actors. By the 1930s, Peter Slade (a pioneer in the field of theatre for children and founder of dramatherapy) had begun to use dance drama with pupils who had joined the Suicide Club at boarding school.[15] Phillips documents how in 1933:

> T. D. Noble, a psychiatrist at Sheppard-Pratt Hospital in Baltimore, USA, noticed that patients who had acted in the hospital plays were able to

understand emotions better than other patients, could link their present emotional state and behaviour to their earlier trauma more easily, and were able to experiment with alternative modes of behaviour. He found drama was a vehicle for the discovery and expression of conscious and unconscious conflicts; that playing other characters helped patients release repressed emotions; that drama encouraged socialisation.[16]

From 1942 onwards, Maxwell Jones, a psychiatrist and pioneer of the therapeutic community, 'began using scripted/improvised plays and group theatrical methods for therapeutic purposes at Mill Hill Emergency Hospital, U.K'.[17] By 1955, Dr. Sue Jennings had started drama workshops with patients in a psychiatric hospital.[18] A lot of drama therapy in the UK has its roots in work developed by Jennings, who defines drama therapy as the specific application of theatre structures and drama processes with a declared intention that it is therapy. In 1964, Marian 'Billy' Lindkvist (a pioneer in the use of drama and movement therapy) founded the Sesame Institute.[19] This was 'the first training course in drama and movement therapy for occupational therapists (held at a York Clinic, Guy's Hospital, London, working with Peter Slade and Audrey Wethered and influenced by Rudolph Laban and Carl Jung)'.[20] In 1966, the Remedial Drama Group was founded by Dr. Sue Jennings and Gordon Wiseman.[21] Between 1966 and 1985, Dorothy Heathcote (influenced by Slade) 'ran drama groups in hospitals for people with mental illnesses in England, U.S.A., Australia, New Zealand and Norway, making videos of her work'.[22] By 1976, 'the British Association for Dramatherapy was founded. Queen Margaret College, Edinburgh, ran the first undergraduate course in dramatherapy, the following year saw the first dramatherapy diploma start at Hertfordshire College of Art and Design', and the USA established the National Association for Drama Therapy. The British Psychodrama Association was developed in 1984.[23]

Today, dramatherapy is recognised, through an act of Parliament, as a profession regulated through the Health Professions Council (HPC). Trained drama therapists have a code of ethics (The British Association of Dramatherapists: BADth) as well as being governed by other professional codes such as the UKCC code of conduct (United Kingdom Coaching Certificate: 1992), the UKCP (United Kingdom Council for Psychotherapy), and the British Psychodrama Association (BPA) which represents psychodrama in the HIPS Section (Humanistic and Integrative Psychotherapy: 1993). In 1997, by the act of Parliament, dramatherapy became a state-registered profession (in the Council for Professions Supplementary to Medicine (C.P.S.M) later to become the Health and Care Professionals Council (H.P.C.)) (Sesame Institute, n.d.).[24]

The history of the work, its origins, and developments are therefore vast and extremely well-documented.[25] Drama therapy represents a 'field that is now immensely flexible and used within a spectrum of mental health, forensic, education and training environments'.[26] The context of the work not only indicates its longevity but insinuates that this is a purposeful and well-supported field of study, which continues to progress, develop, and ultimately change lives.[27]

Many companies working in the area of theatre and therapy, and currently still operating in the USA and the UK include, but are not limited to Geese Theatre Company, Roundabout Dramatherapy, Encounter Theatre and Therapy, Olive Branch Arts, Odd Arts, Agape Theatre, Moving Pieces, Rowan Tree Dramatherapy, Kestrel Theatre Company, A Mind Apart Performing Arts, Rah Rah Theatre Company, Behind the Scenes, Tangled Feet, and London Playback Theatre.[28] Their work is successful as it embeds the ideals of drama therapy into its work, allowing participants to engage with theatre to heal. This work recognizes that there is a vast scope of work surrounding theatre and therapy, which is generally represented in the number of companies currently focussed upon or embedding therapy in their work. Some of these companies use Shakespeare within their projects.

NOTES

1. See, Auslander, P. & Sandahl, C. (2009) Bodies *in Commotion: Disability and Performance.* Michigan: University Michigan Press. Barnes, C. & Mercer, G. (2005) *Good Practice for Providing Reasonable Access to the Physical Built Environment for Disabled People.* Unpublished Paper. University of Leeds, Leeds: Centre for Disability Studies.

2. The social model of wellness treatment was created by Dr. Bill Hettler, Co. Founder of the National Wellness Institute. It promotes Six Dimensions of Wellness; emotional, occupational, physical, intellectual, spiritual, and social. The idea is that addressing all six dimensions of wellness in our lives builds a holistic sense of wellness and fulfilment. The model reacts against a medical model of mental health, suggesting instead that social approaches to mental health are more helpful.

    See also, Oliver, M., Baldwin, D., & Datta, S. (2018) "Health to Wellness: A Review of Wellness Models and Transitioning Back to Health."

The International Journal of Health, Wellness, and Society 9 (1): 41–56. doi:10.18848/2156-8960/CGP/v09i01/41-56.

3. Chesner, A. (1995) *Dramatherapy for People with Learning Disabilities: A World of Difference.* London: Jessica Kingsley Publishers. p. 191.

4. See, Walsh, F. (2012) *Theatre and Therapy.* London: Palgrave Macmillan. Christey-Casson, J. (2011) *seventeenth Century Theatre Therapy Shakespeare, Fletcher, Massinger, Middleton, Ford and Dekker: Six Jacobean Healing Dramas:* http://www.acacemia.edu/17783153/SIXJacobean_Plays1 (Accessed: 17/12/17).

5. Walsh, F. (2012) *Theatre and Therapy.* London: Palgrave Macmillan. p. 43.

6. Kellerman, P. F. (1992) *Focus on Psychodrama: The Therapeutic Aspects of Psychodrama.* Philadelphia: Jessica Kingsley Publishers. p. 11.

7. Ibid, p. 11.

8. See, Boal, A. (2006) *The Aesthetics of the Oppressed.* London & New York: Routledge.
Christey-Casson, J. (2011) *seventeenth Century Theatre Therapy Shakespeare, Fletcher, Massinger, Middleton, Ford and Dekker: Six Jacobean Healing Dramas:* http://www.acacemia.edu/17783153/SIXJacobean_Plays1 (Accessed: 17/12/17).
Walsh, F. (2012) *Theatre and Therapy.* London: Palgrave Macmillan.
Chesner, A. (1995) *Dramatherapy for People with Learning Disabilities: A World of Difference.* London: Jessica Kingsley Publishers.
Winn, L. C. (1994) *Post Traumatic Stress Disorder and Dramatherapy: Treatment and Risk Reduction.* London: Jessica Kingsley Publishing.
Kellerman, P. F. (1992) *Focus on Psychodrama: The Therapeutic Aspects of Psychodrama.* Philadelphia: Jessica Kingsley Publishers.

9. Walsh, F. (2012) *Theatre and Therapy.* London: Palgrave Macmillan.
Chesner, A. (1995) *Dramatherapy for People with Learning Disabilities: A World of Difference.* London: Jessica Kingsley Publishers. p. 1.

10. Campbell, P. & Kear, A. (ed.) (2001) *Psychoanalysis and Performance.* London: Routledge. p. 1.

11. Chesner, A. (1995) *Dramatherapy for People with Learning Disabilities: A World of Difference.* London: Jessica Kingsley Publishers. p. 85.

12. Walsh, F. (2012) *Theatre and Therapy.* London: Palgrave Macmillan.
Chesner, A. (1995) *Dramatherapy for People with Learning Disabilities: A World of Difference.* London: Jessica Kingsley Publishers. p. 1.

13. See, Lewis-Williams, D. (2002) *The Mind in the cave: Consciousness and the origins of art.* London: Thames & Hudson.
Mithen, S. (1996) *The Prehistory of the mind: The cognitive origins of art, religion, and science.* London: Thames & Hudson LTD.

14. Ibid.

148   A. HULSMEIER

15. Peter Slade (1947-1977) contributed to the philosophy of child drama. Slade discovered that enactments of drama prevented young men from committing suicide.

    See also, Slade, P. (2000) *Personal communication: Letter to John Casson.* 30th November 2000.

    Fleming, M., Bresler, L. & O'Toole, J. (2014) *The Routledge International Handbook of the Arts and Education (Routledge International Handbooks of Education)*. London: Routledge.

16. Phillips, M.E. (1996) 'The use of drama and puppetry in occupational therapy during the 1920s and 1930s'. *The American Journal of Occupational Therapy,* 50 (3), pp. 229-233: https://www.ncbi.nlm.nih.gov/pubmed/8822247 (Accessed 26/02/19). p. 230.

17. Ibid, p. 230.

18. Dr. Sue Jennings is a dramatherapy and playtherapy pioneer. She is a founder/full-member of the British Association of Dramatherapists; state registered with the Health Professions Council, full member of the British Association of Play Therapists and Play Therapy UK, and a member of the National Association of Drama Therapy (USA). She has written over 30 books on this area of study.

19. The Sesame Institute was based in London and focused on drama and movement therapy. The approach is still taught in a wide range of therapeutic and applied courses across the UK. It is influenced by Jung, Laban, Slade and Lindkvist, and comprises of four strands: drama, movement, myth, and movement with touch and sound. It is a non-verbal, non-direct psychotherapy.

20. Audrey Wethered puts theory and approach into practice in the field of healing and teaches students her techniques of movement and drama therapy.

    Marian 'Billy' Lindkvist (1919–2017) was the founder of the Sesame Institute, she retired in 1994.

    Rudolph Laban (1879-1958) was an Austro-Hungarian dance artist and theorist. His work laid the foundations for Laban Movement Analysis (LMA). Body, Space, Effort, and Relationships make up the four aspects of Laban's movement framework.

    Carl Jung (1875–1961) was a Swiss psychiatrist and psychoanalyst who founded analytical psychology. He influenced the Sesame Approach to Myth.

21. Gordon Wiseman (1943-2002) was a dramatherapist, political activist, and innovator in theatre arts.

22. Dorothy Heathcote (MBE) (1926–2011) was a drama teacher and academic who used the method of 'teacher in role'. She developed and defined the 'mantle of the expert' as an approach to teaching.

15 THE HISTORY OF THEATRE AND THERAPY 149

23. Phillips, M.E. (1996) 'The use of drama and puppetry in occupational therapy during the 1920s and 1930s'. *The American Journal of Occupational Therapy*, 50 (3), pp. 229–233: https://www.ncbi.nlm.nih.gov/pubmed/8822247 (Accessed 26/02/19). P. 230.
24. See, Sesame Institute. (n.d.) *Sesame Institute: Drama and Movement Therapy*: http://sesameinstitute.appspot.com/marian-lindkvist (Accessed 21/10/18).
25. Boal, A. (2006) *The Aesthetics of the Oppressed*. London & New York: Routledge.
     Christey-Casson, J. (2011) *seventeenth Century Theatre Therapy Shakespeare, Fletcher, Massinger, Middleton, Ford and Dekker: Six Jacobean Healing Dramas*: http://www.acacemia.edu/17783153/SIXJacobean_Plays1 (Accessed: 17/12/17).
     Walsh, F. (2012) *Theatre and Therapy*. London: Palgrave Macmillan.
     Chesner, A. (1995) *Dramatherapy for People with Learning Disabilities: A World of Difference*. London: Jessica Kingsley Publishers.
     Winn, L. C. (1994) *Post Traumatic Stress Disorder and Dramatherapy: Treatment and Risk Reduction*. London: Jessica Kingsley Publishing.
     Kellerman, P. F. (1992) *Focus on Psychodrama: The Therapeutic Aspects of Psychodrama*. Philadelphia: Jessica Kingsley Publishers.
26. Chesner, A. (1995) *Dramatherapy for People with Learning Disabilities: A World of Difference*. London: Jessica Kingsley Publishers. p. 5.
27. Boal, A. (2006) *The Aesthetics of the Oppressed*. London & New York: Routledge.
     Christey-Casson, J. (2011) *seventeenth Century Theatre Therapy Shakespeare, Fletcher, Massinger, Middleton, Ford and Dekker: Six Jacobean Healing Dramas*: http://www.acacemia.edu/17783153/SIXJacobean_Plays1 (Accessed: 17/12/17).
     Walsh, F. (2012) *Theatre and Therapy*. London: Palgrave Macmillan.
     Chesner, A. (1995) *Dramatherapy for People with Learning Disabilities: A World of Difference*. London: Jessica Kingsley Publishers.
     Winn, L. C. (1994) *Post Traumatic Stress Disorder and Dramatherapy: Treatment and Risk Reduction*. London: Jessica Kingsley Publishing.
     Kellerman, P. F. (1992) *Focus on Psychodrama: The Therapeutic Aspects of Psychodrama*. Philadelphia: Jessica Kingsley Publishers.
28. There are some companies here that mark a crossover between the work in therapy, Disability, and prison.

CHAPTER 16

The History of Shakespeare and Therapy

This chapter considers specific projects and/or performances that use Shakespeare's plays in therapeutic spaces. The examples demonstrate the reach of the work and the medical/therapeutic considerations that underpin Shakespeare's inclusion within theatrical programmes for therapeutic benefits. This is a collection of work that attempts to engage a community in the therapeutic space through the purposes of applied theatre supported by the plays of Shakespeare.

The idea that performing Shakespeare can help in the treatment of those suffering mental illness has been gaining popularity for several decades with actors such as Sir Mark Rylance and Sir Ian McKellen endorsing and supporting projects of this nature. Currently, there appears to be a vast amount of documentation on how Shakespeare is regarded as a prompter to therapeutic healing. There are a wide range of projects that use Shakespeare as a form of therapy and the work spans a period of approximately 30 years of activity in the field.

Cox documents that between 1989 and 1991, several of Shakespeare's tragedies were performed in the central hall of the Broadmoor Hospital's high-security Psychiatric Hospital, Crowthorne in Berkshire, England. Broadmoor Hospital is the best known of the three high-security psychiatric hospitals in England, the other two being Ashworth and Rampton. The Broadmoor Project is documented as originating as a modest enterprise developed in discussion between RSC actor, Sir Mark Rylance, and

© The Author(s), under exclusive license to Springer Nature Switzerland AG 2024
A. Hulsmeier, *Applied Shakespeare*,
https://doi.org/10.1007/978-3-031-45414-1_16

consultant psychotherapist at Broadmoor, Murray Cox. The project with the RSC added the secure psychiatric hospital, Broadmoor, to the touring schedule of its 1989 production of *Hamlet*. Prompted by this initiative, a range of other activities followed including the adaptation of three more Shakespeare plays *Romeo and Juliet* (The Royal Shakespeare Company), *King Lear* (The National Theatre), and *Measure for Measure* (the Wilde Community Theatre Company), the delivery of several after-show talks and workshops, and a book which recorded the project via the reflections of psychotherapists, actors, directors, and patients. These examples suggest the scope of Shakespeare's reach and highlight an established example of Shakespeare's use in therapy and within therapeutic settings. Their accompanying book *Shakespeare comes to Broadmoor: The performance of tragedy in a secure psychiatric hospital* provides a collection of essays by or interviews with the different departments concerned with the productions of Shakespeare at Broadmoor Hospital between 1989 and 1991.

The Madness Hotel (2012–2016) was part of a Brazilian tradition of alternative therapies based on performance, social empowerment, and interaction established by psychiatrist Vitor Pordeus to transform the suffering of his patients through creativity. Pordeus recognises that 'theatre provides stimulus for psychotic, schizophrenic and depressed patients, but questions whether it can actually improve their mental health'. [1] The Madness Hotel is based in the Nise da Silveira hospital in Rio de Janeiro:

> which has a long tradition of using art and culture to help with suffering. From 1946, the psychiatrist Nise da Silveira, a former student of Carl Jung, had patients paint and sculpt. Da Silveira was working during a brutal era of mental health treatment and fought against practices such as lobotomy and electroshock therapy in favour of more humane methods of treatment. [2]

Pordeus' performers are made up of a 20-member cast. They perform *Hamlet* at the psychiatric hospital in Rio's North Zone. Pordeus documents the benefits of the project when explaining that:

> Released from their fixed roles as catatonic, belligerent or withdrawn patients, his actors are free to don different masks as characters from Shakespeare, and to live out a different reality for a few hours. In the safe, performative setting, new things can be said or tried out. [3]

To ensure the success of the project Pordeus keeps photographs as records of the performance. He states:

> the patients review these later on [and] they can see the progress they've made, but also better understand their own behaviour and interactions with others. He claims that patients who never spoke before joining the Madness Hotel and who now smile or spontaneously interact with others are proof of the healing power of theatre. [4]

Peripheral to the application and general running of the work, McLoughlin evaluates the project as a sample of practice to academically interrogate. She states:

> at the most basic level of affect, Pordeus' performances provide a space in which patients can acknowledge each other. The Madness Hotel attempts to recover many things that are in danger of being lost, from the roots of Brazilian culture, to the idea of Shakespeare as populist street theatre instead of an art form for the elite. Most of all, it restores this idea of how vital we are to each other's recovery. [5]

Although Pordeus' work is not without contest (as other doctors believe the work agitates the patients and drugs should be used instead (alongside the project they do still receive conventional treatment and medication)), the Madness Hotel provides a long-established example of the theatre therapy's reach, taking place in a reputable and long-serving therapeutic environment. It is also theatre that attempts to subvert any level of elitism that may be attached to Shakespeare's work and the use thereof.

Jensen documents Shakespeare's *Twelfth Night* alongside Alzheimer's patients at the Stanford/VA Alzheimer's Research Centre. Throughout the project, Jensen attempts to question and raise the issue of advocacy in 'service' Shakespeare. The goal of the work 'was to find analogues between the play and life as Alzheimer's patients experience it, especially experiences that contribute to or damage self-esteem'. [6] Jensen regards Shakespeare's combination with therapy as:

> a success because the group helped patients express their concerns and frustrations and taught them coping mechanisms that would, at least for a time, make their lives better [...] these included building self-esteem, coping with

154   A. HULSMEIER

frustration, improving communication, and helping patients accept their limitations and thrive within them. [7]

He discusses his time with the patients 'why they spoke of their reading with such enthusiasm and concludes by asking whether literature might be used as a therapy to improve the lives of people with Alzheimer's disease'. [8] Not all the patients in the group had Alzheimer's, some suffered from other dementias. The group was split into two: one group for patients and one for their caregivers. The patient group had different goals in different weeks: 'this included building self-esteem, coping with frustration, improving communication, and helping patients accept their limitations and thrive within them'. [9] Jensen states that the only activity that seemed feasible was to have those who could still read and perform an abridged script of the play. He used a 90-minute annual radio version of the script and prepared topics for the group to discuss at the end of the reading. Jensen admits that Shakespeare is difficult at the best of times, but states that it:

> Shakespeare's place as a pillar of modern culture was assumed. Nobody questioned Shakespeare's status or how he came to his cultural pre-eminence. These assumptions were exactly what made a Shakespeare project desirable. [10]

Jensen offers a gentle introduction to Shakespeare's uses in therapy and Alzheimer's and again documents the reach of Shakespeare's work.

Kelly Hunter is a British actress who works with the RSC. She developed a method now known as the Hunter Heartbeat Method with special schools near London. Established over 10 years ago, the programme helped Hunter notice that students with Autism Spectrum Disorder (ASD) responded particularly well to the method, and so she began to produce one-hour therapy sessions with small groups of children with ASD. Her own company, Touchstone Shakespeare Company began in 2002 'to work with children (some autistic) who have little or no access to the arts, with the aim to release the communicative blocks within children and young people with Autism'. [11]

The work and method have also formed the basis of longitudinal research at Ohio State University from 2011 to 2015. Hunter's method is underpinned by:

two main principles: the rhythm of the iambic pentameter, which Shakespeare used and which imitates the da-dum of a human heartbeat, and an exploration of the mind's eye, allowing children to explore imaginative worlds, which may otherwise be locked away. [12]

The 'group play sensory games inspired by *The Tempest*. They act out throwing and catching a mask of "anger," for example, and make other exaggerated facial expressions'. [13] Hunter states that the reason behind her choice of *The Tempest* is 'the play's intense emotions, as personified by its characters. One of the play's main antagonists is Caliban, who personifies anger, and who must be taught how to say his name and socialize in what becomes a comic scene in the therapy sessions. The actors take the role of Caliban and the children with ASD become his teachers'. [14]

The success of the work can be found in published findings of psychologists Mehling, Tasse, and Root. [15] Their publication *Research and Practice in Intellectual and Developmental Disabilities* suggests that:

> the students showed significant improvement in standard tests conducted before and after the therapy for autism-related delays in social skills and communication, pragmatic language, and facial emotion recognition. [16]

Dr. Marc Tassé (clinical psychologist, director of the Ohio State University Wexner Medical Centre's Nisonger Centre) is leading a study to evaluate the effectiveness of Hunter's autism therapy and states that 'It's quite amazing to see how a Shakespeare play can be transformed into a therapeutic intervention that encourages students to communicate'. [17] Hunter's work demonstrates a combination of Shakespeare with therapy and highlights work which engages with both theory and practice.

The scope of the work is clear. Some of the work that falls into the category of Shakespeare and therapy may also be found under the title of Shakespeare and prison or Shakespeare and Disability, so the work is much more eclectic and all-encompassing than how it is presented here. The chapter offers isolated versions of Shakespeare in specific therapeutic environments by presenting work/projects that have not been covered in previous chapters, but readers are encouraged to revisit Part I, 7, and 12 for versions of Shakespeare that also engage with therapy.

Notes

1. Tavener, B. (2015) *From Stratford to Rio: using Shakespeare to treat mental illness*: http://www.bbc.co.uk/news/health-32241100 (Accessed: 17/12/17).
2. Ibid.
3. McLoughlin, B. (2012) *Method and madness Theatre provides stimulus for psychotic, schizophrenic and depressed patients, but can it improve their mental health?*: https://aeon.co/essays/can-performing-shakespeare-help-to-cure-mental-illness (Accessed: 21/12/17).
4. Ibid.
5. Ibid.
6. Jensen, M. P. (2014) *What Service is here?* The Borrower and Lenders article: http://www.borrowers.uga.edu/ (Accessed: 10/04/16).
7. Ibid.
8. Ibid.
9. Ibid.
10. Ibid.
11. Hunter, K. (2013) Shakespeare and autism. *Teaching Shakespeare*, 1 (3) pp. 8–10: http://www.kellyhunter.co.uk (Accessed: 17/12/17).
12. MacLellan, L. (no date) *Autistic Kids are Thriving in Shakespearean Therapy*: https://qz.com/809771/autistic-kids-are-thriving-in-shakespearean-therapy-designed-by-a-british-actress-for-the-royal-shakespeare-company/ (Accessed: 17/12/17).
13. Ibid.
14. Ibid.
15. See, Mehling, M. H., Tasse, M, J. & Root, R. (2016) 'Shakespeare and autism: an exploratory evaluation of the Hunter Heartbeat Method', *Research and Practice in Intellectual and Developmental Disabilities*, 2 (4), pp. 107–120: https://doi.org/10.1080/23297018.2016.1207202 (Accessed: 21/12/17).
16. AutismSpeaks. (2014) *Shakespeare Therapy*: https://www.autismspeaks.org/science/science-news/shakespeare-therapy-autism (Accessed: 14/04/18).
17. Hunter, K. (2013) Shakespeare and autism. *Teaching Shakespeare*, 1 (3) pp. 8–10: http://www.kellyhunter.co.uk (Accessed: 17/12/17). See also, Nisonger Centre (2014) *Shakespeare and autism*: http://nisonger.osu.edu/shakespeare-autism (Accessed: 17/12/17).

CHAPTER 17

Shakespeare's Therapy, Therapeutic Shakespeare: A Renaissance Reading of Shakespeare and Therapy in *Hamlet*

This chapter analyses *Hamlet*, a play which asks the audience to pay attention to, and question matters of the mind being considered during the Elizabethan period. Many an academic describes how Shakespeare's knowledge of 'both physical and mental illness enabled him to enlighten audiences about the soma and psyche of a character and their failure to work in harmony and there are many claims as to how Shakespeare provides important and surprising insights into medicine'. [1]

It is assumed that Shakespeare's access to medical insights derived from his relationship with his son-in-law, Doctor John Hall, although there is not a lot of evidence that suggests Hall treated the mentally ill. [2] Tosh has also suggested that Shakespeare was influenced by:

> theories of 1st century Greek physician Galen (who determined the humours) and medical writers such as Thomas Bright in his *Treatise on Melancholy* (1586), all of which helped Shakespeare to understand the causes and treatment of melancholy and madness as his contemporaries understood the conditions. [3]

Hamlet is important in providing insight into the diagnosis and treatment of the mentally ill and society's reactions to their conditions, as 'the afflictions in Shakespeare's plays help to educate modern audiences and historians about the health in Elizabethan and Jacobean England'. [4] However, it is acknowledged that there are several Shakespeare's plays that

© The Author(s), under exclusive license to Springer Nature
Switzerland AG 2024
A. Hulsmeier, *Applied Shakespeare*,
https://doi.org/10.1007/978-3-031-45414-1_17

157

158   A. HULSMEIER

consider people who suffer with mental illness. Christey-Casson states that many plays contain 'mad scenes':

> PTSD in *Titus Andronicus*, depression-induced insomnia in *Henry IV, Part Two*, anxiety in *Macbeth*, paranoia in *Coriolanus, Othello*, and *Richard III*, psychopathy in *Richard III* and dementia in *King Lear*. Some like Leontes (mad with jealousy) and Bottom (temporarily away with the fairies) recover their sanity through changes in circumstances, others tragically do not recover. [5]

It is important at this point to highlight the fact that the terms 'madness' and 'insanity' are also ascribed within Shakespeare's work. This presents vocabulary complementary to that commonly used in Renaissance England but at odds with terminology appropriate today. By providing a working definition of madness for Shakespeare's society, a better understanding of how an early modern audience would perceive and receive the theme of mental illness within the work can be ascertained, highlighting how this theme may present important insights into the notion of mental health during the Renaissance period.

Madness throughout Renaissance drama generally reflects:

> typical humoral or 'ecstatic' language, melancholic or love-sick characters. It takes place in dramatic development which passes through phases of contradiction, uncertainty and irrationality […] in tragedy, madness perpetuates the crisis to death […] in its most conventional forms, madness has always a negative potency, of signalling the failures of sovereignty and reason to guarantee meaning of the Renaissance world. [6]

All elements referenced here are represented in the play *Hamlet*. Of all the plays in which Shakespeare engages with mental health, *Hamlet* is the only text which presents issues with mental health from the beginning of the work. Characters in other work present symptoms as part of cause and effect throughout their play—a journey of dissent into madness; however, Hamlet appears in an altered mental state, perhaps that of grief and depression, from the opening act. [7]

The play asks the audience to pay attention to and question matters of the mind that were being considered during the Elizabethan period. Reimer suggests that Renaissance Madness would appear to be:

a *non-contiguous* condition characterized by *lack or loss of reasoning* capacity, *erratic behaviour*, possessing a dynamic relationship between *insanity and melancholy*, inspiring both *mirth and fear*, and falling victim to a human medical condition. [8]

His definition provides a base from which to read the character of Hamlet and his struggle with issues of mental health. It would also be appropriate to acknowledge the character of Ophelia who also offers depictions of madness and appears to possess clear characteristics of insanity. The chapter will focus on Hamlet only. This is a purposeful choice to allow the chapter to explore the differences between Hamlet's madness and Hamlet's antic-disposition. That 'there are wheels within wheels in this play, and they all spin around the blinding sun of political power' is important to acknowledge. [9] That Hamlet is an indecisive character and that the play pivots around a matter of political sovereignty, not personal animus, is also important for any reading of this play. This chapter will therefore consider Hamlet in relation to how or where he shows signs of (1) erratic behaviour, (2) lack or loss of reasoning, (3) melancholy and insanity, and/or (4) mirth and fear, as a display of Renaissance versions of madness. It will also refer to Renaissance reactions to madness and the political underlying of the play.

Hamlet is an important play to analyse in reference to mental health as it contains a developed study of mental illness. By 1601, when the play was written, a level of introspection brought a new level of respect towards those who suffered with mental health. This may be due to the developments regarding mental health which became more firmly established at the end of the sixteenth and beginning of the seventeenth century.

Hamlet is a play that unpicks a range of concepts relevant to the Renaissance audience. Madness, political sovereignty, and emotional excess are all tied up in the play, and it is important to question a period in history that questioned 'how much emotion is too much?'

Hamlet's preoccupation with a desire to murder his stepfather Claudius causes him to display a range of erratic behaviour. His actions throughout the play are what help indicate to the audience Hamlet's descent into madness. He is viewed as a mentally unstable character that, in grief, is unable to handle the overriding emotions provoked by the death of his father. In these moments, Hamlet demonstrates cruelty to Ophelia, broken sleep and bad dreams, a desire for secrecy, murder, and melancholy.

160 A. HULSMEIER

Melancholy is presented as a primary characteristic in Hamlet. Characters who interact with Hamlet ask, 'How is it that the clouds still hang on you?' and 'Good Hamlet, cast thy nighted colour off' an allusion to the grief Hamlet carries around in appearance (black attire) and characterisation. Hamlet also describes to Gertrude the manner of his mourning 'But I have that within which passeth show–/These but the trappings and the suits of woe'. [10] His grief is articulated as a deep, heavy depression. His most depressive episode appears in the 'To be or not to be' speech. Morris comments that the presentation of Hamlet's illness:

> might have been copied from the clinical notes of a student of mental disorders. We recognise all the phenomena of an attack of mental disorder consequent on a sudden and sorrowful shock; first the loss of all habitual interest in surrounding things; then, indifference to food, incapacity for customary and natural sleep. [11]

Hamlet's first soliloquy articulates this presentation of mental disorder:

> O, that this too solid flesh would melt,
> Thaw, and resolve itself into a dew,
> Or that the Everlasting had not fixed
> His canon 'gainst self-slaughter!
> Oh God, Oh God,
> How weary, stale, flat, and unprofitable
> Seem to me all the uses of this world!' [12]

Although Hamlet appears to be driven by his desire to 'avenge his father's death, he is simultaneously concerned that the ghost is a devil who will betray his soul, rather than the actual ghost of his father'. [13] Hamlet states:

> The spirit that I have seen
> May be the devil, and the devil hath power
> T' assume a pleasing shape; yea, and perhaps,
> Out of my weakness and my melancholy,
> As he is very potent with such spirits,
> Abuses me to damn me. [14]

Shakespeare appears to be referring to the pre-asylum years when madness was influenced by evil spirits, witchcraft, and the devil and when exorcism was seen as a valid treatment to madness. Frye explains that 'the popular conception of 'treatment' for mental illness drew on medieval understanding of madness as demonic possession in which the evil spirit possessing a victim had to be forced out with violence'. [15] Exorcism was seen as a valid treatment and mental illness was articulated alongside devils, fiends, witches, deception, power, and recovery through the grace, Gospel, cross, and visions of Jesus Christ. Thus, Hamlet, for a large majority of the play, remains confused as to what action he should put in place as he weighs the consequences of his actions to the reliability of their influencing source. This confusion fuels his uncontrolled behaviour throughout the remainder of the play.

Those characters who witness Hamlet's demise provide the audience with a depth of observation regarding Hamlet's mental decline. Supporting characters throughout the play (Gertrude, Claudius, Polonius, and Ophelia) all recognise and make observations or judgements about Hamlet's behaviour. Gertrude's private conversation with Claudius provides the audience with her theory of Hamlet's temperament: 'I doubt it is no other but the main/His father's death and our o'erhasty marriage'. [16] She seems to refuse to believe it is anything worse. Ophelia recalls a Hamlet speaking of 'horrors' 'as if he had been loosed out of hell'. She states:

> He took me by the wrist and held me hard.
> Then goes he to the length of all his arm,
> And, with his other hand thus o'er his brow,
> He falls to such perusal of my face
> As he would draw it. Long stayed he so.
> At last, a little shaking of mine arm,
> And thrice his head thus waving up and down,
> He raised a sigh so piteous and profound
> As it did seem to shatter all his bulk
> And end his being. That done, he lets me go,
> And, with his head over his shoulder turned,
> He seem'd to find his way without his eyes,
> For out o' doors he went without their helps
> And to the last bended their light on me. [17]

Although Hamlet is never kind to Ophelia, her death is one of the clearest moments of his undoing. At her graveside, Hamlet attacks her brother Laertes, and the pair, in the grave of Ophelia, argue over who

162   A. HULSMEIER

loved her best. Grief-stricken and outraged, Hamlet's speech becomes nonsensical and extreme. He speaks of eating crocodiles and drinking eisel (vinegar). Onlookers comment upon the madness of its content in Act Five:

King Claudius: O, he is mad, Laertes.
Queen Gertrude: For love of God, forbear him.
Hamlet: 'Swounds, show me what thou'lt do:
                     Woo't weep? woo't fight? woo't fast? woo't tear
                     thyself?
                     Woo't drink up eisel? eat a crocodile?
                     I'll do't. Dost thou come here to whine?
                     To outface me with leaping in her grave?
                     Be buried quick with her, and so will I:
                     And, if thou prate of mountains, let them throw
                     Millions of acres on us, till our ground,
                     Singeing his pate against the burning zone,
                     Make Ossa like a wart! Nay, an thou'lt mouth,
                     I'll rant as well as thou. [18]

The scene ends with Gertrude decrying her son's madness.

Queen Gertrude: This is mere madness:
                     And thus awhile the fit will work on him:
                     Anon, as patient as the female dove,
                     When that her golden couplets are disclosed,
                     His silence will sit dropping. [19]

The way Hamlet's fellow characters do not understand madness seems to provide Hamlet free reign to blame it for his wrongdoings. Hamlet's apology to Laertes is a prime example of laying the blame for his offences on 'madness':

Hamlet: 'What I have done,
                     That might your nature, honor, and exception
                     Roughly awake, I here proclaim was madness.
                     Was 't Hamlet wronged Laertes? Never Hamlet.
                     If Hamlet from himself be ta'en away,
                     And when he's not himself does wrong Laertes,

Then Hamlet does it not. Hamlet denies it.
Who does it, then? His madness.
If't be so, Hamlet is of the faction that is wronged.
His madness is poor Hamlet's enemy. [20]

Although the speech may intend to be sincere, the reasoning remains unsatisfactory. No one questions the behaviour but instead allows it to be a valid pardon.

The small role of the gravedigger goes far in suggesting a culturally predisposed attitude towards mental health when the character tells Hamlet that his madness will go unnoticed in England, because there 'the men are as mad as he'. [21] This not only says something significant about the symptoms of mental health arising in Renaissance England (which could be a reason Shakespeare wanted to reflect on this in his play) but in fact, the way Hamlet is unnoticed in the play seems to progress his dissent into madness.

For most of Shakespeare's contemporaries, madness was also a condition of darkness and fear. MacDonald writes that:

the horrors of Bedlam can easily mislead us into believing that contemporaries normally treated the insane sadistically. Chains and fetters were reserved for the most violent and menacing madmen, people who terrified their families and neighbours. The manacled lunatic was not a sign of the cruelty and stupidity of the ordinary villagers; he was an emblem of their fear. [22]

Indeed, Claudius and Gertrude depict fear in reaction to Hamlet's behaviour, they state:

Claudius: I like him not, nor stands it safe with us
To let his madness range. Therefore prepare you.
I your commission will forthwith dispatch,
And he to England shall along with you.
The terms of our estate may not endure
Hazard so dangerous as doth hourly grow
Out of his lunacies. [23]

Hamlet:	No, by the rood, not so!
	You are the Queen, your husband's brother's wife,
	And (would it were not so!) you are my mother.
Gertrude:	Nay, then I'll set those to you that can speak.
Hamlet:	Come, come, and sit you down. You shall not budge;
	You go not till I set you up a glass
	Where you may see the inmost part of you.
Gertrude:	What wilt thou do? Thou wilt not murder me?
	Help, help, ho! [24]

Despite the fears reflected in the characters of *Hamlet* being interesting depictions of our contemporaries, they are further important in drawing attention to how madness may be less about Hamlet's psychology and more about the wider political conflict which is at the heart of the play 'as *Hamlet* enacts the incoherence of the Renaissance ideology of sovereignty'. [25] Hamlet's state of indecision throughout the play is also a powerful sign of the political fears surrounding the conflicts between monochronastic powers. Hamlet projects a crisis of sovereignty: a dead father who 'warns and forebodes' and a stepfather who 'plots and schemes' but neither rule. Their indecisions are encapsulated in Hamlet's decent into madness. [26] He is unable to address the two areas of conflicting doubt and cannot commit the act of regicide.

The play also hinges around the idea of Hamlet's emotional excess. For the Renaissance audience, passions (in the modern sense) would have been described as that which 'makes one less of an individual'. Hamlet is an individual barely in control, particularly of his sovereignty. From the outset, Hamlet is in crisis between the two sovereign powers and the play depicts a political journey from order to disorder. Salkeld explains that metaphorically in the play, 'the head has been severed from the nation. And sovereignty is dead [...] a King without a body, as James well understood [...] is indeed nothing'. [27] Therefore, madness is no longer amusing or a cause to laugh at, but instead a metaphorical example of 'repressions during the 17th century for those who do not or will not conform to the power of an autocratic regime'. Madness has political significance. Hamlet's fellow character's reactions are well placed in forcing forward the fear of a populace whose sovereignty and political power suddenly fell into dispute. This culture's anxiety progresses to crisis point as bodies litter the stage at the play's conclusion. The seriousness with which these metaphors were depicted is 'indicative of the real authority which they were believed to exert'. [28] The struggle of the state and an unpopular monarchy echo throughout the play, and fears throughout *Hamlet* are palpable. The characters in presenting fear in reaction to Hamlet's behaviour also depict a deeper cultural belief about the world, its ideological struggles, and its desire for universal order.

Hamlet's behaviour is often seen to shift between melancholy and insanity, mirth and fear, normal and erratic. This links back to Reimer's initial definition of Renaissance madness and helps to highlight Hamlet's condition as non-contiguous and often contradictory. Hamlet is a complicated character which makes his diagnoses from mad, insane to merely melancholic more difficult. This is made even more complicated when questioning whether Hamlet is in in fact feigning madness or 'is he mad or mad in craft?' Madness in craft implies Hamlet can cleverly construct erratic behaviour to control and manipulate situations at his whim. Hamlet appears to put an intentional 'antic disposition' on. [29] For example, Hamlet displays pessimistic thoughts and negativity and admits to suffering from melancholy when stating:

> How strange or odd some'er I bear myself
> (As I perchance hereafter shall think meet
> To put an antic disposition on). [30]

Although given the circumstances, Hamlet's 'madness' could stem from an actual mental illness, most likely a depressive illness worsened by his father's death, Hamlet's self-awareness of his feelings is unusually acute. He recognises his strange behaviour and suggests that he can replicate the symptoms to his advantage as part of antic disposition. All of Hamlet's behaviour, then, teeters between real and fake, illusion and appearance, and it is difficult to judge whether Hamlet is erratic or considered. Through the character of Hamlet, Shakespeare plays the theme of appearance versus reality, and although Hamlet's behaviour initially appears uncontrolled, his interactions often show his ability to stay and remain focussed.

When Hamlet meets Polonius and calls him a 'fishmonger', the strangeness of his behaviour is particularly apparent. But Polonius too indicates a sense that the erratic behaviour is considered and for a cause when stating 'Though this be madness, yet there is method in't'. [31] Hamlet's actions indicate that he is more in control of his behaviour than he would have his fellow characters believe. Bynum and Neve argue that 'Shakespeare's seventeenth century audiences probably saw Hamlet as a bitter, sarcastic, cynical, and often witty malcontent, and if mad, mad rather comically, in the way that all lovers are a little mad'. [32] For example, when interacting with Polonius, Hamlet asks 'Have you a daughter?' The question leads Polonius to believe that Hamlet has a form of lovesickness. According to Polonius, after being rejected by Ophelia, Hamlet:

> Fell into a sadness, then into a fast,
> Thence to a watch, thence into a weakness,
> Thence to a lightness, and, by this declension,
> Into the madness wherein now he raves
> And all we wail for. [33]

Polonius is not being trivial in his suggestion that Hamlet was suffering from lovesickness; in the Middle-Ages, it was classed as a real disease. Williams explains that:

> the physician Gerard of Berry wrote a commentary that the lovesick sufferer becomes fixated on an object of beauty and desire because of an imbalanced constitution. This fixation causes further coldness, which perpetuates melancholia. Since the condition of melancholic lovesickness was considered to be so deeply rooted, medical treatments did exist. [34]

Wack progresses the same argument when presenting findings discovered that indicated that:

> The medical community gave serious thought to a fearsome, sometimes fatal disease then rampant among the aristocracy: love. The physicians believed that the physiological problem was an image of the loved one imprinted too deeply on the brain, which made the person obsessed. [35]

Therefore, Polonius' suggestion may be comical to a modern-day audience when he appears to misinterpret Hamlet's melancholic symptoms for a love-sick mind, however, the audience, modern or otherwise do not laugh when his daughter Ophelia descends into madness and then commits suicide due to the same malady. The difference, however, is that Polonius in this exchange is guided to the conclusion that Hamlet is love-sick by Hamlet's own endgame. Hamlet is intent on making sure Polonius and Claudius think he is mad, so they are not threatened by his behaviour. This means Hamlet will have a better advantage to exact his revenge.

Hamlet's behaviour towards his closest friends, Rosencrantz and Guildenstern, again demonstrates erratic behaviour. In his exchanges with them, he is presented in a bad mood and is often extremely critical towards his friends. He questions their presence at Elsinore and becomes preoccupied with testing their trust. When they declare they come for friendship, Hamlet asks:

> Were you not sent for?
> Is it your own inclining?
> Is it a free visitation?
> Come, come, deal justly with me.
> Come, come, nay speak
> [...]You were sent for, and there is
> a kind of confession in your looks, which your modesties have not
> craft enough to colour. [36]

It is again apparent that Hamlet's behaviour is not without aim. He discloses information about Claudius' illegally obtained position and alludes to the fact that Denmark is in hardship: 'Denmark's a prison'. [37] It is evident that Hamlet knows that anything he discloses will be relayed back to Gertrude and Claudius, he even states: 'When he [Claudius] needs what you have gleaned, it is but squeezing you and, sponge, you shall be dry again'. [38]

Hamlet's irrationality is a continuous presence around Polonius, Claudius, Gertrude, Rosencrantz, Guildenstern, and Ophelia, but around Horatio, Marcellus, and the players, he appears calm and rational. His behaviour with the players is focused; he gives clear instruction as to how he wants the play to be delivered, with precise command over the acting style and the emotions it should provoke. The scene is often viewed as a way in which Hamlet's behaviour towards the players can be viewed in contrast with other characters in the play. The scene also shows the level of Hamlet's control in plotting the unfolding of Claudius' confession to the murder of his father. *The Mousetrap* (also known as *The Murder of Gonzago*) is used by Hamlet 'to catch the conscience of the king'. [39] Hamlet's allusion to 'mad in craft' is reiterated when making arrangements with Horatio for the play. He states, 'I must be idle'. [40] He declares therefore his intent to be foolish. The ultimate explanation of behaviour is from Hamlet himself when he offers to his mother the explanation that: 'I essentially am not in madness/But mad in craft' and perhaps the true intent and nature of his behaviour are revealed. [41]

Hamlet is a tragedy and many may identify with the character's thought processes and experiences of mental illness. The play can show clear differences between then and now, as 'mental illness [in *Hamlet*] contrasts sharply with the views of the mentally ill today'. The play is therefore essential to help 'understand the social climate of the late Renaissance that allowed for these characters and their disturbed visions to flourish in popular imagination'. [42]

This reading of *Hamlet* explores the historical complexities of Renaissance interactions with madness. The reading also articulates the fine line between real madness and crafted versions of madness, and it is important to keep in mind that Shakespeare was demonstrating dramatic (rather than medical) skill, and the fact remains that 'there is no doubt that Shakespeare glorified insanity with *Hamlet*'. [43] Although there are aspects of the play that tell the audience something about a version of 'madness' or issues with mental health, the chapter warns of the danger that can arise when looking backwards 400 years to Shakespeare's texts with a modern concept of madness in the hope of learning something about modern clinical madness, 'the broad criticism to which they are open is that in the effort to get inside the character's mind and emotions, they ignore the historical conditions which enable and inform the representation of madness in the first place'. [44]

NOTES

1. Cummings, M, J. (2003) *Shakespeare and Medicine: Bard was well versed in human afflictions and their treatments*. https://www.cummingsstudyguides.net/xMedicine.html (Accessed: 17/12/17).
2. See, Morris, S. (2012) *Shakespeare's minds diseased: mental illness and its treatment*. http://theshakespeareblog.com/2012/03/shakespeares-minds-diseased-mental-illness-and-its-treatment/ (Accessed: 17/12/17).
3. Tosh, W. (2016) *Shakespeare and madness*. https://www.bl.uk/shakespeare/articles/shakespeare-and-madness# (Accessed: 17/12/17).
   See, Bright, T. (1586). *A Treatise of Melancholie* [Microfiche]. Blackfriars: London, Early English Books Online.
4. Cummings, M, J. (2003) *Shakespeare and Medicine: Bard was well versed in human afflictions and their treatments*. https://www.cummingsstudyguides.net/xMedicine.html (Accessed: 17/12/17).

5. Christey-Casson, J. (2011) *Seventeenth Century Theatre Therapy Shakespeare, Fletcher, Massinger, Middleton, Ford and Dekker: Six Jacobean Healing Dramas*: http://www.acacemia.edu/17783153/SIXJacobean_Plays1 (Accessed: 17/12/17). pp. 18–22
6. Salkeld, D. (1993) *Madness and drama in the age of Shakespeare*. Manchester: Manchester University Press. p. 284.
7. See, Minton, E. (2011) *A Timeless Hamlet in a Dated Production*: http://www.shakespeareances.com/willpower/onscreen/Hamlet-BBCTL80.html (Accessed: 17/12/17).
8. Reimer, M. (2013) *Defining Renaissance Madness*: https://english202guys.files.wordpress.com/2013/04/renaissance-madness.pdf (Accessed: 17/12/17). p. 2.
9. Critchely, S. & Webster, J. (2013) *Stay, Illusion! The Hamlet Doctrine*. New York: Pantheon Books.
10. Shakespeare, W. in Craig, W.J. (1991) (ed.) *The Complete works of Shakespeare*. Oxford: Oxford University Press. p. 873.
11. Morris, S. (2012) *Shakespeare's minds diseased: mental illness and its treatment*: http://theshakespeareblog.com/2012/03/shakespeares-minds-diseased-mental-illness-and-its-treatment/(Accessed: 17/12/17).
12. Shakespeare, W. in Craig, W.J. (1991) (ed.) *The Complete works of Shakespeare*. Oxford: Oxford University Press. p. 873.
13. Frye, R. M. (1984) *The Renaissance Hamlet: Issues and Responses In 1600*. Princeton: Princeton University Press. p. 12.
14. Shakespeare, W. in Craig, W.J. (1991) (ed.) *The Complete works of Shakespeare*. Oxford: Oxford University Press. p. 885.
15. Ibid, p. 880.
16. Ibid, p. 880.
17. Ibid, p. 879.
18. Ibid, p. 903.
19. Ibid, p. 903.
20. Ibid, p. 906.
21. Ibid, p. 902.
22. MacDonald, M. (1981) *Mystical Bedlam: Madness, Anxiety and Healing in Seventeenth Century England* Cambridge: Cambridge University Press. p. 141.
23. Shakespeare, W. in Craig, W.J. (1991) (ed.) *The Complete works of Shakespeare*. Oxford: Oxford University Press. p. 891.
24. Ibid, p. 892.
25. Salkeld, D. (1993) *Madness and drama in the age of Shakespeare*. Manchester: Manchester University Press. p. 93.
26. Ibid, p. 91.
27. Ibid, p. 123.

28. Ibid, p. 9.
29. See Cole, S, L. (2010) *The Absent One: The Mourning Ritual, Tragedy, and the Performance of Ambivalence.* USA: Penn State Press.

Cerasano, S. P., Bly, M. & Hirschfeld, H, A. (2010) *Medieval and Renaissance Drama in England- Volume 23.* New Jersey: Fairleigh Dickinson University Press.

Cowen-Orlin, L. & Johnson-Haddad, M. (ed.) (2007) *Staging Shakespeare: essays* in *honor* of *Alan C. Dessen.* Newark: University of Delaware Press.

Young, H. L. (1994) *Hamlet's Antic Disposition.* Washington: Eastern Washington University.

Rosenberg, M. (1992) *The Masks of Hamlet.* Delaware: The University of Delaware Press. Dover- Wilson, J. (1951) *What Happens in Hamlet.* Cambridge: Cambridge University Press.

Chauncy-Shackford, C. (1876) *Hamlet's Antic-Disposition.* United States: Cornell University.
30. Shakespeare, W. in Craig, W.J. (1991) (ed.) *The Complete works of Shakespeare.* Oxford: Oxford University Press. p. 78.
31. Ibid, p. 882.
32. Bynum, W. F. & Neve, M. (1986) "Hamlet on the Couch: Hamlet is a kind of touchstone by which to measure changing opinion—psychiatric and otherwise—about madness." *American Scientist.* 74 (4), pp. 390–396: https://studylib.net/doc/18744140/american-scientist%2D%2Dvol.-74%2D%2Dno.-4%2D%2Djuly (Accessed 26/02/19). p. 392.
33. Shakespeare, W. in Craig, W.J. (1991) (ed.) *The Complete works of Shakespeare.* Oxford: Oxford University Press. p. 881.
34. Williams, L. K. (2017) *Being Lovesick was a real disease in the Middle Ages:* https://theconversation.com/being-lovesick-was-a-real-disease-in-the-middle-ages-70919 (Accessed: 09/04/18).
35. Wack, M. F. (1990) *Lovesickness in the Middle Ages. The 'Viaticum' and its Commentaries.* Philadelphia. PA: University of Pennsylvania Press.
36. Shakespeare, W. in Craig, W.J. (1991) (ed.) *The Complete works of Shakespeare.* Oxford: Oxford University Press. p. 882–883.
37. Ibid, p. 882.
38. Ibid, p. 895.
39. Ibid, p. 882.
40. Ibid, p. 889.
41. Ibid, p. 894.
42. Ibid, p. 34.
43. Ibid, p. 34.
44. Salkeld, D. (1993) *Madness and drama in the age of Shakespeare.* Manchester: Manchester University Press. p. 18.

CHAPTER 18

The Combat Veteran Players: A Case Study

This chapter aims to look specifically at the Combat Veteran Players' (CVP) use of Shakespeare's work within their own theatrical programme and how this programme captures some of the methodologies, impacts, and challenges tied to applied theatre's intentions for achieving transformation.

The Combat Veteran Players is an award-winning Shakespearean theatre company of ex-Servicemen and women. Formed in 2011, the CVP is a company that has come together to overcome mental trauma, injury, and related difficulties through making professional performances of Shakespeare's work. They are predominantly concerned with individuals who have experienced or are showing symptoms of Post-Traumatic Stress Disorder (PTSD) which is defined as the 'development of certain characteristic symptoms following a psychologically distressing event which is outside the range of normal human experience'. [1]

Jaclyn McLoughlin, the founder of CVP, moved to London in 2008 to get her master's degree at the Royal Academy of Dramatic Arts (RADA). In 2009, she researched the concepts of drama therapy and applied theatre and began to explore the possibilities to combine Shakespeare's work with veterans suffering from PTSD. McLoughlin explains that:

> It was a thought I had, basically, because I was thinking breath control of delivering the verse would sort of physically manifest itself, as far as calming a heart rate. After a little bit of time working in the commercial world, I

© The Author(s), under exclusive license to Springer Nature Switzerland AG 2024
A. Hulsmeier, *Applied Shakespeare*,
https://doi.org/10.1007/978-3-031-45414-1_18

172   A. HULSMEIER

revisited the idea. That's when I approached Combat Stress and met Walter Busuttil, Combat Stress's director of medical services. [2]

Following discussions with Combat Stress (The UK's leading Veteran's mental health charity), McLoughlin created a rehabilitative, theatrical pro-gramme under the guidance of Dr. Walter Busuttil (Director of Medical Services for Combat Stress). The work was financially supported by Stoll (formerly the Sir Oswald Stoll Foundation). CVP now works in partner-ship with RSC through its Open Stages programme and Shakespeare's Globe Theatre, and the rehearsals take place at the Stoll complex in Fulham which exists to house and care for veterans of HM Armed Forces.

The aim of the company is to 'highlight the difficulties faced by veter-ans when they leave the forces and try to fit back into civilian life'. [3] Therefore, the work has a clear therapeutic and social mission. They aim to provide 'a creative and expressive outlet for active duty and former-service personnel to come together for group skill-building, training, rehearsals, & high-level performance of Shakespearean texts in industry-regarded venues'. [4] Although the company recognises that progress has been slow and sometimes painful, the results are encouraging. The com-pany understands that there is no quick fix for PTSD but develops work that helps veterans through the difficulties that PTSD presents.

The company is clear about their links to applied theatre and over time, the 'CVP has become widely recognized as a model of the practice of Applied Theatre, shown to be highly effective in mental and emotional rehabilitation and overall well-being rehabilitation for Service members'. [5] The links to social and personal change are continuously evidenced throughout their work. The company helps groups and individuals who have been isolated in the hope that drama can tackle social exclusion and change lives, while emphasizing the therapeutic and rehabilitative effects of that work. The company also fits the criteria and definition of participa-tory work as the veterans are required to be actively involved with the projects and productions, taking on all acting and performance roles within the plays explored.

The CVP has performed in several theatrical spaces to critical acclaim, ranging from Shakespeare's Globe Theatre to the RSC's Swan Theatre in Stratford-Upon-Avon. The first members of the CVP were introduced to Shakespeare in early 2011. They were initially to perform one book read-ing of *A Midsummer Night's Dream*; however, McLoughlin decided to create a full-scale production of the play. The debut was at the Old Vic

Tunnels in early 2012. The CVP followed with a tour of *Henry V* in 2013, returning to the Old Vic Tunnels, and the RSC's Dell Stage in Stratford-on-Avon, and throughout the West End. *Hamlet* was performed at Shakespeare's Globe on London's Bankside in 2014, playing to an audience of over 500 and winning the Owle Schreame award for Innovation in Classical Theatre. They have also received a nomination for an award for excellence from the Royal Society of Public Health. In 2015, the company presented their version of *Twelfth Night* at the Leicester Square Theatre. In 2016, CVP embraced the 400th anniversary commemoration of Shakespeare's death and performed an extract of *Richard III* for an audience including H.R.H. King Charles on Shakespeare's birthday on the site of Shakespeare's home.

Following the success of the CVP in the UK, McLoughlin was invited to travel to the US and expand the company there. In 2015, she visited the US for three months and opened a branch of the company in Washington, D.C. The actors in the UK at the time were into their fourth production, *Twelfth Night*. The Washington branch debuted with a performance of *The Comedy of Errors* in 2016 at the Shakespeare Theatre Company's Forum Theatre in Washington, DC. The website outlines how:

> The cast of twelve active-duty and retired servicemen and women represented branches of the U.S. Army, Navy, Marines, and Air Force. The performance was supported by the USO of Metropolitan Washington-Baltimore on the Walter Reed Military Medical Centre Campus, as well as the Fort Belvoir Army installation, Intersections International, and the National Endowment for the Arts. [6]

The success of the CVP has also resulted in an additional outreach company, *Shakespeare's Soldiers* which was launched in 2015 and led by producer Amanda Faber, working alongside director and writer Yorgo Lykouria of Soliloquy Pictures. Faber 'has since launched a series of workshop programmes where Wounded Injured and Sick Service Personnel (WIS) go into schools to inspire and teach students'. [7] The company directs the workshops under McLoughlin's instructions.

CVP explains that the combination of theatre and PTSD is important because 'military combat and acting have a number of things in common: the camaraderie, the desire to do the best possible job, and the mutual support'. [8] British Major General Richard Cripwell explains that the impact of the program has allowed:

174   A. HULSMEIER

Veterans to reconnect with family members, work through post-traumatic stress disorder and depression, gain employment and confidence. What the arts do is about life. For many of them, they didn't have another option to who they were. And what this does is give them options. [9]

Their justification for combining Shakespeare with PTSD is more complex but a common theme is that performing Shakespeare helps to break down patterns of anxiety and depression. CVP reflects that using Shakespeare within their work 'helps to navigate through the painful places they've been ... to heal the wounds most of us can't see'. [10] Ultimately, the work is about finding strategies to manage the nightmares, flashbacks, panic-attacks, and all the other many symptoms of PTSD. The participants are said to find a new purpose through Shakespeare and the way this is achieved is threefold, McLoughlin works with Shakespearean text and its calming breath patterns that are assumed to combat stress, she looks to incorporate the structure of the military regimes that the men are familiar with, and she works with identity and change from soldier to civilian.

McLoughlin discusses how Shakespeare was chosen for the calming patterns of the breath—because of its therapeutic, calming, effect. She talks about the benefit of the calming of the heart rate through Shakespeare's language. Voice Coach Victoria Williams suggests that the benefits of Shakespeare's work can be found in the fact that the participants are asked to:

> move away from flight/fight mode and they're trained into relaxing into the speech. The actual act of speaking Shakespeare can be very therapeutic it's the richness of the language and it's the fact that it's timeless as well and it's about human emotions. Often as a voice coach you strip down the words to their bare sound the sounds themselves have a cry from the soul that modern language couldn't touch. I think it's great that these guys are doing Shakespeare. [11]

The patterns of Shakespeare's speech therefore appear to offer the veterans a form of catharsis, and this method seems to reiterate some of the benefits articulated by Kelly Hunter and her Hunter Heartbeat Method (see 15), where the rhythm of the iambic pentameter imitates a calming heartbeat. McLoughlin states that:

there's a connection with stress and breathing; breathing being nature's way of mending us, which is the foundation of the CVP. Looking at breath control in Shakespearean verse and its physical effect, but there was much more to it; confidence building, bonding, discovering skills. However, I am a practitioner, not a clinician and theatre isn't a cure. [12]

Regarding the choice of plays to use amongst the veterans, in an interview, McLoughlin explains that the selection of plays chosen to explore was purposeful and progressive:

we began with *A Midsummer Night's Dream* to soften them up. It was a kind of triple whammy: Shakespeare, theatre, and fairies. The play breaks down all the walls. I thought if they could get past these three things they could do anything. [13]

Although, it appears as though the true reason for choosing and/or continuing to use Shakespeare in this setting is that:

the Veterans were the ones that didn't want to let it go. The excitement, appreciation, and pure joy of Shakespeare that they bring to the stage is unlike anything that I've ever known before in my career. They found such a love of Shakespeare; they were the ones who said, 'Well, you know, why can't we do more than an on-book reading? Why can't we do a performance? Why can't we go to a theatre?' So that was when I decided to take it up to the next level. [14]

McLoughlin attributes the military's high standards, work ethic, and team player mentality to refusing to dumb down her direction, she explains:

if anybody tells you, 'Oh, it's OK, you can hit this mark and not that one,' to me, that's patronization, and that's not doing anybody any good, but we also find that balance of, it's not life or death, and something will go wrong. I've seen this work; I know it works, that makes it less of an experiment when you're able to say, 'I've had these outcomes and this real impact. Let's just do it here. [15]

Walter Busuttil, Medical director of Combat Stress, discusses how the work ultimately allows the participants to test themselves, in terms of their emotions and how they interact with people, 'so we have the contrast of someone who is scared to go to Sainsbury's at 11am on a Saturday morning, then that individual performing in front of 200 people. It won't cure them, but it certainly will help'. [16]

Stoll showcases the advantages of the work when stating:

> the opportunity has provided them with a social reintegration into an environment with fellow Veterans; a renewed sense of achievement and accomplishment; an enhanced and re-discovered confidence; a target-driven focus for which to remain motivated and to also keep the mind occupied when it may otherwise wander (e.g. through line memorization); and a well-disguised exploration into personal identity and societal transition through projection onto characters within a canonical script. [17]

McLoughlin and CVP coherently interrogate the therapeutic processes, strategies, and techniques that are used within the project at a professional and therapeutically authenticated level and how they relate to therapeutic and psychologically approved procedures. McLoughlin interrogates aspects of the work, but her use of Shakespeare is predominantly in line with therapeutic delivery and less concerned with the analytical considerations of the plays.

It may be interesting to consider that the more robust contemplations regarding the benefits of Shakespeare's plays are in fact left to the participants to articulate. This may be a strategy of McLoughlin who affords space for the participants to provide first-hand accounts of the advantages of the work, rather than speaking on behalf of the participants. This perhaps suggests that the participants are better placed to offer connections between Shakespeare and their experiences of mental health and PTSD.

The company has worked hard to present information about the individuals participating in the programme. CVP offers a robust and comprehensive account of each individual, where they have come from and are going to, what they suffer, and why. This results in honest, first-hand reflections on the rewards of the work. The participants who discuss Shakespeare in line with PTSD provide vital reflections surrounding the work and its significance, and the veterans present interesting accounts regarding the power of the Bard. Interestingly the participants of CVP consider the significance of Shakespeare within this type of applied work and offer very clear opinions as to how Shakespeare *specifically* helps them to heal.

Androcles Scicluna, originally from Malta, was a signalman in the Royal Signals for four years. Before he joined CVP, he 'passed most days focused on survival, picking abandoned bottles and milk cartons out of trash cans and curling up in whatever public dry spot he could find to sleep at night'. [18] He has suffered from depression ('in hibernation') [19] for 20 years and left the armed forces for medical reasons. Scicluna explains that 'being used to army life, and suddenly coming to civilian life, it wasn't easy for me. It wasn't any good life, I mean, I had already experienced death ... I just stayed on my own, kind of in hibernation'. [20] This changed when 'in 2011 he was approached by a government affairs officer who pointed him towards the CVP. Four years later, Scicluna has appeared in three performances in London and holds down two part-time jobs, one as a tour guide and another as a caretaker'. [21] Of the experience of working with CVP and Shakespeare, he reflects:

> People like me sometimes are depressed over our present situation and suddenly, when we jump into a Shakespearean character, that's like leaving our own problems away and getting into another person. Once we finish the acting, being the character, and get back into our own, somehow the kind of depression has moved out. You get yourself into someone else's body and you forget yourself, and when you return you are contented and well satisfied. I can do lots of good things and I am appreciated. This is the best part of the whole thing. The subject has given us a common element to discuss between each other. [22]

He calls CVP a 'band of brothers', and thanks McLoughlin for the 'better state' he is in. Group comradeship, he concludes, is:

> the most important thing is the meeting. Getting all of us together, all ex-servicemen and women knowing each other, doing physical exercises, learning to project our voice, but also, you know, the kind of friendship we've had with one another. [23]

Scicluna's assessment of the work not only suggests a power to Shakespeare's plays and characters, but moreover he alludes to the importance of inclusion, something which is similarly suggested as powerful in the work found in Shakespeare's use amongst Disabled communities generally, and the work of Blue Apple Theatre Company specifically.

Shaun Johnson was part of the Royal Artillery until a crush injury meant he had to leave. He had wanted to do for 22 years and was

178   A. HULSMEIER

disappointed when he came out with an injury. Johnson 'saw action in Northern Ireland at the height of the troubles of the 1980s'. [24] In reaction to his declining mental health, Johnson reflects that:

> I was starting to suffer and worry and some things I saw as a young soldier were starting to bite back in my mind. I started to rapidly decline. Very, very quickly. I started to want to destroy myself. The inevitability of it is I was sitting in the car at 3am, unconscious, with a pipe in it. [25]

The Shakespeare programme is helping him with his PTSD and hyper-vigilance. Johnson generally felt that the programme was beneficial in making him feel like he was back in the armed forces, 'with the guys and the camaraderie, engaged in something that was rewarding for my condition if you will'. [26] He documents the importance of theatre when explaining that:

> when you're introduced to something like theatre and particularly with Shakespeare... you don't have time to remember or think or meditate on what's troubling you because you've got lines to learn and scenes to get on with, and all of sudden your life is filled with something which is quite exciting. [27]

He also acknowledges that people may question why Veterans? Why therapy? Why Shakespeare? To which he replies:

> Why not? It is making a difference in the lives of the people who are participating in it, and it hopes to change other's lives which will therefore have been worth it [he concludes] It helps you to under PTSD, and the stigma. You don't have to suffer in silence. It teaches you not be embarrassed. [28]

Although Johnson's reaction does not specifically confront the specific uses of Shakespeare for transformative purposes, he still voices something specific about the practice of the theatrical form and reiterates some of the considerations regarding inclusivity initially introduced in the theatre and Disability chapter.

Johnson most importantly interrogates the Shakespearean roles he is asked to perform, and it is interesting to hear the chilling comparisons between Johnson's own life and his character Hamlet. Johnson explains that:

18 THE COMBAT VETERAN PLAYERS: A CASE STUDY 179

playing Hamlet was dark and often I struggled to play him but it taught me a lot about myself and helped me to cope with my mental health condition. When I do his speech to be or not to be, when I read that through, that knocked me right back because he was talking, you know, about going through the motions of killing himself. Been there, and I immediately thought good lord – that's going to be quite a challenge. [29]

His articulation is important; it not only references a dramatic process an actor may need to undertake to understand their character more thoroughly, but it also documents a process of a person experiencing significant mental pain in their personal life being asked to explore and, in some manner, recreate some of the more torturous moments of their life for the purposes of theatre. At one point, Johnson breaks down in rehearsal, in reference to Hamlet's speech this too, too solid flesh 'I just wanted to avoid it all the time... and I dug really deep in rehearsals, to go back to what it felt like to lose myself, to become emotional. Going there is helping me face demons from the past and educating me that it's alright to let the emotions out'. [30] It remains questionable that a person with a condition of this nature is not only asked to play out his demons in the rehearsal space but also on the stage, and in the same manner that method acting has its limitations, the process of combining participants who suffer with mental health with Shakespeare's complex characters remains problematic. It is interesting to hear the brevity at which Johnson discusses a very different character Malvolio, 'a fantastic person to play. I enjoy being him although he is completely different to the real me. It's such fun exploring his mannerisms and injecting his personality into my own to create a character that is at times often hilarious'. [31] There may be something significant to say about work that allows you to escape rather than to continuously confront.

Ian Ford talks about his history as an acting sergeant in the Royal Electrical and Mechanical Engineers and discusses with *Inside Out* how he locked himself away from the 'world for a long, long time, I didn't want to see anyone and this was the first time being in a room with a bunch of squaddies again, and the joviality, believe it or not has been the most therapeutic'. [32] Ford's problems arose from his tours of duty in Bosnia in 1995; his experiences were part of the ethnic cleansing, and his group was the first to the mass grave. He states that:

eight months later when I came back, I was crying over a pint in a bar. Since leaving the army in 2006 I have found it hard to share my emotions. I have pushed everyone away. I now have no family and no friends. But put me on the stage as a frightened 12-year-old boy and I can find the emotion. It's quite liberating. Some people have noticed a big change in my anger and my attitude. I've got my self-respect back. [33]

Ford continues to reflect upon how the programme has helped with his reintegration back into civilian life and the therapeutic benefits undertaking the work has had upon his life. He states:

I was a loner and recluse. I literally would just be on my own. I was a social creature. The life and soul of the party, and I don't know how PTSD takes hold, or has hold, but it does, but this has been the biggest help since leaving the army. I should have been helped 20 years ago. I couldn't tell you what it was; I couldn't see it was a psychological problem. I don't trust people. Or myself. It's like a fight to go out there. Now because of the drama I am feeling more comfortable. [34]

Although Ford acknowledges that he is not a big reader and would not naturally know what Shakespeare was trying to say to the actors, he significantly identifies the purpose of exploring a character from a '3rd play point of view and doing things with other people's emotions without having to deal with your own is actually quite liberating and I think that in the long run I will be able to integrate them back into my own personality'; however, he does warn about the importance of the selection of the play text and states that:

Henry V is a dangerous choice, if only because Shakespeare got it so right. The early rehearsals were fraught as they dredged their memories of combat. Although sword in hand comes natural the hardest thing about the play is to confront the deep sad emotion- this has been suppressed before. [35]

Unlike Johnson, Ford is very specific about the dangers and complications inherent in the work. His reflections appear to be significantly aligned with the concerns of character identification and being positioned too closely to the issues being addressed throughout Shakespeare's plays, which have been raised previously (and continuously) throughout this research. McLoughlin also comments that 'a lot of what [she] works with is identity, and there is a lot of lost identity that happens when you're

18 THE COMBAT VETERAN PLAYERS: A CASE STUDY   181

transitioning from combat to civilian'. [36] She discusses the idea of Freud Trauma (also known as psychological trauma) and how this can break our protective shield. She states that some of these men are unable to 'cognitively absorb the traumatic experience and if we follow this approach its worth exploring being able to touch emotions of other's stories rather than our own'. [37] Therefore, promoting the importance of removing the participants from reliving their own experiences and instead exploring the experiences of others, from a safe distance.

David Wilkins 'was a Private in the Cheshire Regiment who served in Belfast during The Troubles'. [38] He states: 'I was in a local village and actually thought and believed people were spying on me, that there were men on the roof with a sniper rifle and I actually believed this. Then I realized this was just a figment of my imagination'. [39] Wilkins is the group's musician who has composed for the productions. In an interview with *The Stage*, Norman asks:

> Pouncing about as fairies in *Midsummer Night's Dream* is one thing, playing soldiers in battle in *Henry V* is quite another. Isn't that rather close to home? Wilkins responds, "there are areas we can't or don't want to go in to, but we can use some of it in the performance". [40]

Wilkins draws attention to the difficulties that character identification can present to the participants of the CVP. He offers an awareness of the limits this work can ask participants to get close to but simultaneously suggests that similarities in the text afford justification to the choice of using Shakespeare. Wilkins offers a common-sense response when he explains that:

> Soldiers are soldiers. The rank structure, the drunken soldiers, it's all the same. I'd seen it in Bosnia. The captain in tears, scared. I'm proud to be English. There is nothing different about us now to the guys in *Henry V*. Shakespeare shows that soldiers aren't just killing machines; they have emotions which is why we are all so fucked up. I want us to show the audience that soldiers aren't all bad. I hope we can give that to the audience. [41]

These are only a few of the men who reflect on the work and its benefits, many others including Cassidy Little, Andy McCabe, Julian Sayers, Alan Smith and Neil Rostron all actively promote the work on the radio, in newspapers, and in interviews on TV. [42] They clearly believe it is not

182   A. HULSMEIER

only important to experience the work but also to promote it to audiences so they too can understand the importance of understanding PTSD, and in this case, understand PTSD through Shakespeare.

What is overtly clear about the CVP's work is that there is a common interest that 'they somehow all pull through. It is quite evident that, difficult as it is for some of them, they all want to be there, to be part of the process. And many are surprisingly candid about their condition'. [43] It remains important to question whether the work has been successfully transformative to which one veteran states the project has helped 'change lives'. [44] Regardless of the therapeutic definition of transformation or change (which is not significantly explored or outlined as an intention of the work as instead development, acceptance and growth appear as the more dominant focus for the project), the work appears successful in its engagement with the veterans and it is clear from the participant's and practitioner's interrogation of the work that theatre, therapy, and Shakespeare are helpful tools in the fight against PTSD: the stigma from the outside and the suffering from the inside.

CVP appears successful in motivating and capturing the imaginations of the players in their theatrical and real lives, but there remain implicit challenges to the work in relation to the fragility of the participants and the combination of Shakespeare with therapy and a theatrical environment. Norman states that in watching the work:

> the camaraderie is there but it remains fragile. In the couple of days I spent watching rehearsals there were some difficulties with absenteeism, a tantrum or two and at least one member who admitted he had spent the previous evening self-medicating with alcohol instead of learning lines. [45]

Wilkins offers a more personal account of the challenges when he states that 'I turned into a real knob head at one time. I can get very agitated – I'm on medication for that'. [46] Therefore, the presence of the challenges presented by the varying mental health issues are continuously interlaced throughout the work, which suggests something significant about the challenges found in attempting to combine the practice of applied theatre and therapy.

CVP as a case study provides a clear example of Shakespeare's use within therapeutic environments. Their work appears successful in achieving its intentions and ambitions, and there are continuously clear links between the purposes of theatre therapy and the intentions of participatory work.

The practitioners and the participants explore some of Shakespeare's uses, intentions, impacts, and purposes and present some of the challenges faced when participants are asked to navigate the themes and issues of the texts. This is not only touched upon by observers of CVP's practice but also explored and at times questioned by the participants. The practitioners helpfully outline the rhythm and pattern of the speech as a relevant exercise for therapeutic healing, which appears to link and reiterate other examples of therapist's interactions with Shakespeare. It is evident too that the practitioners have thought significantly about what it means to combine theatre and therapy. Although, from a practitioner's perspective, more could be said about the significance of selecting the play texts, how they might align to the veteran's experiences and how the content of the work might promote opportunities for transformation, overarchingly, CVP offers a solid example, not only of Shakespeare's use alongside therapy but of therapeutic encounters through theatre.

Summary

The work across the chapters dedicated to Shakespeare with therapy has explored the general context of the work, its histories, origins, and influences, acknowledging the current level of interrogation of this field of work and its placement amongst other types of theatre. The chapter provides a Renaissance reading of Shakespeare's *Hamlet* in relation to therapy and mental health, and finally assesses The Combat Veteran Players as a successful example of work that currently exists in combining Shakespeare, therapy, and applied theatre.

The chapter overall provides an exploration of Shakespeare and therapy and whilst is unable to cover every aspect of this field, it does provide a comprehensive exploration of specific uses of Shakespeare's work within therapeutic settings and for purposes of therapeutic healing and transformation.

Notes

1. Winn, L. C. (1994) *Post Traumatic Stress Disorder and Dramatherapy: Treatment and Risk Reduction.* London: Jessica Kingsley Publishing. p. 14.
2. Donnelly, M. (2015) *Can Shakespeare Heal? One Director's Quest to Help Treat PTSD:* http://dailysignal.com/2015/09/07/can-shakespeare-heal-one-directors-quest-to-help-treat-ptsd/ (Accessed: 17/12/17).

184   A. HULSMEIER

3. CVP *The Combat Veteran Players*: https://www.britishcouncil.us/combat-veteran-players (Accessed: 12/17/12).
4. Ibid.
5. Ibid.
6. Ibid.
7. Ibid.
8. Ibid.
9. Foster, L. (2016) *Trauma to Triumph: How Shakespeare is helping veterans*: http://www.wusa9.com/news/local/dc/trauma-to-triumph-how-shakespeare-is-helping-veterans/369429671 (Accessed: 17/12/17).
10. Ibid.
11. CVP *The Combat Veteran Players*: https://www.britishcouncil.us/combat-veteran-players (Accessed: 12/17/12).
12. Ibid.
13. Norman, N. (2013) *Once More into the Breach*: https://www.thestage.co.uk/features/interviews/2013/once-more-unto-the-breech/ (Accessed: 17/12/17).
14. CVP *The Combat Veteran Players*: https://www.britishcouncil.us/combat-veteran-players (Accessed: 12/17/12).
15. Donnelly, M. (2015) *Can Shakespeare Heal? One Director's Quest to Help Treat PTSD*: http://dailysignal.com/2015/09/07/can-shakespeare-heal-one-directors-quest-to-help-treat-ptsd/ (Accessed: 17/12/17).
16. Ledgard, C. (2013) *And Calm of Mind BBC News*: http://www.bbc.co.uk/programmes/b01s09kf (Accessed: 17/12/17).
17. Stoll, (2012). *COBSEO*: https://www.cobseo.org.uk/stoll-the-combat-veteran-players-announce-date-of-first-public-performance/ (Accessed: 11/04/18).
18. Donnelly, M. (2015) *Can Shakespeare Heal? One Director's Quest to Help Treat PTSD*: http://dailysignal.com/2015/09/07/can-shakespeare-heal-one-directors-quest-to-help-treat-ptsd/ (Accessed: 17/12/17).
19. Depression in hibernation presents as melancholic features such as withdrawal from the environment, lack of energy, loss of weight from not eating, changes in sleep pattern, reduced stimulation, and emotional flatness.
20. Donnelly, M. (2015) *Can Shakespeare Heal? One Director's Quest to Help Treat PTSD*: http://dailysignal.com/2015/09/07/can-shakespeare-heal-one-directors-quest-to-help-treat-ptsd/ (Accessed: 17/12/17).
21. Ibid.
22. Ibid.
23. Ibid.
24. Dilley, S. (2015) *War Veterans Take To The Stage* Sky News: https://news.sky.com/story/war-veterans-take-to-the-stage-10348571 (Accessed: 17/12/17).

18 THE COMBAT VETERAN PLAYERS: A CASE STUDY   185

25. CVP *The Combat Veteran Players*: https://www.britishcouncil.us/combat-veteran-players (Accessed: 12/17/12).
26. Taylor, J. (2017) *Veterans with combat stress find solace in Shakespearean verse*: https://www.thetimes.co.uk/article/veterans-with-combat-stress-find-solace-in-shakespearean-verse-wq0jc5rl5jt (Accessed: 17/12/17).
27. Dilley, S. (2015) *War Veterans Take To The Stage* Sky News: https://news.sky.com/story/war-veterans-take-to-the-stage-10348571 (Accessed: 17/12/17).
28. CVP *The Combat Veteran Players*: https://www.britishcouncil.us/combat-veteran-players (Accessed: 12/17/12)
29. Ledgard, C. (2013) *And Calm of Mind BBC News*: http://www.bbc.co.uk/programmes/b01s09kf (Accessed: 17/12/17).
30. Foster, L. (2016) *Trauma to Triumph: How Shakespeare is helping veterans*: http://www.wusa9.com/news/local/dc/trauma-to-triumph-how-shakespeare-is-helping-veterans/369429671 (Accessed: 17/12/17).
31. CVP *The Combat Veteran Players*: https://www.britishcouncil.us/combat-veteran-players (Accessed: 12/17/12).
32. Inside Out. (2015) *Veterans turned into Shakespeare actors to overcome conflict stress*: https://www.youtube.com/watch?v=0605E0DwBBU (Accessed: 17/12/17).
33. Ibid.
34. Ibid.
35. Ibid.
36. Allison, E. & Hattenstone, S. (2014) *'You don't ever get over it': meet the British soldiers living with post-traumatic stress disorder*: https://www.theguardian.com/society/2014/oct/18/collateral-damage-ex-soldiers-living-with-ptsd (Accessed: 17/12/17).
37. Ibid.
38. Dilley, S. (2015) *War Veterans Take To The Stage* Sky News: https://news.sky.com/story/war-veterans-take-to-the-stage-10348571 (Accessed: 17/12/17).
39. Ledgard, C. (2013) *And Calm of Mind BBC News*: http://www.bbc.co.uk/programmes/b01s09kf (Accessed: 17/12/17).
40. Norman, N. (2013) *Once More into the Breach*: https://www.thestage.co.uk/features/interviews/2013/once-more-unto-the-breech/ (Accessed: 17/12/17).
41. Ibid.
42. Little was a serving member of 42 Commando. The former Royal Marine was severely injured by an improvised explosive device in Afghanistan. He had his right leg amputated below the knee, his left retina partially detached and various bones shattered.

43. Norman, N. (2013) *Once More into the Breach*. https://www.thestage. co.uk/features/interviews/2013/once-more-unto-the-breech/ (Accessed: 17/12/17).

44. CVP *The Combat Veteran Players*. https://www.britishcouncil.us/combat-veteran-players (Accessed: 12/17/12).

45. Norman, N. (2013) *Once More into the Breach*. https://www.thestage. co.uk/features/interviews/2013/once-more-unto-the-breech/ (Accessed: 17/12/17).

46. Ibid.

PART V

Conclusion

This chapter covers the main provocations of practice by drawing together the main findings of the book and presenting conclusive thoughts around whether Applied Shakespeare can offer transformative encounters.

This book has been positioned in relation to debates and discourses relevant to the fields of applied theatre, participatory theatre, community theatre, and Shakespearean studies.

This study aimed to provide a deeper understanding and contribute new knowledge around debate relative to combining Shakespeare's work with applied formats of theatre. Many people are articulating and engaging with the *benefits* of exploring Shakespeare's work for the purpose of transformation and documenting *where* Shakespeare's work is used as a tool for transformation in a wide range of applied theatre practices; however, more investigation is needed around the challenges this practice may face. This book centralises a range of debates regarding applied practice and its use of Shakespeare specifically. This book offered a context to the practice, introducing readers to the scope and breadth of this work, the challenges and issues of applied theatre, and the complexities bound to the bard. The book also offered the reader a selection of existing conversations regarding applied theatre's use of Shakespeare's plays that are concerned with *why* his work is regarded as an important and beneficial source to help applied practice achieve transformation.

Positively, the chapters demonstrate how Shakespeare is successfully applied alongside Disability, therapy, and prison. It is encouraging that many people support this work, and participants reflect positively on

188 CONCLUSION

projects of this nature. It is work worthy of funding and support and should continue to be developed.

I began this book by introducing the reader to Applied Shakespeare. I indicated the scope and breadth of the practice and offered the reader questions and challenges prevalent within work that aims to achieve levels of transformation, especially through engagement with Shakespeare's plays.

Chapter 3 interrogated the conversations surrounding the promotion of a universalising discourse often used in the application of Shakespeare's work, questioning the complicated political, social, and cultural implications bound up with Shakespeare's plays in the form of cultural biases. I outlined the inherent challenges of universalising discourses and complicated political, social, and cultural lessons inherent within Shakespeare's work. I also highlighted the risk of asking a (potentially vulnerable) participant to engage with compromising characters, themes, and issues found in plays that were written over 400 years ago. Chapter 3 suggested tools to help subvert the challenges of using Shakespeare's plays in applied theatre settings in the form of New Historicism, Historicization, and Verfremdungseffekt.

Using these tools to reiterate that Shakespeare's plays are examples of fiction can help participants understand the implications of their situations safely; this in turn may lead to opportunities to achieve transformation. These tools also highlight the importance of the text's historical context in suggesting ways in which Shakespeare's plays are not universal and are often a clear reflection of the time in which they were created. This demonstrates how the notion of Shakespeare's plays offering participants unparalleled insights into universal truths is questionable but provides an alternative analytical approach in which participants can engage with Shakespeare's plays and the lessons they may hold.

Shakespeare's work is challenging for any community accessing its content; hence, why a universalising discourse is ill-advised and inappropriate, particularly if transformation is to be achieved.

As there are different forms of behaviours between then and now, it remains important to question what our contemporaries did, what we do now, and the relationship between the two. By copying the surface details of the world through a universalising discourse, the world is offered as a limited vision of lived experience and makes up only one version of this experience.

The work should not be depicted as universally relevant, nor should it be used as simply a universally available resource. There must be purpose

CONCLUSION 189

and intent behind why Shakespeare's work is beneficial, and universality is unimaginative and potentially dangerous to the desires of achieving transformation, particularly when considering the complexities of the participants who may be accessing these texts and the complexities of the Shakespearean characters they may be accessing.

It is suggested that, regulated through theatrical means, Shakespeare's work can demonstrate to participants the process of historical change by illuminating the significance of differences between then and now when identifying opportunities for change and transformation. The history of Shakespeare's plays is important to acknowledge, and the overarching provocation is that by making participants aware of the history of the work, the participants are better placed to see the contents of things—its appropriateness and the success or failure of it—so that change and transformation can be considered, from a safe distance from the issue itself.

This is not a toolkit for learning or a suggestion that the findings of the chapters dealing with readings of the work are to be applied by all practitioners that use Shakespeare's work for transformative purposes, in a manner that would suggest the findings here are recommendations for practice. The findings do not suggest a creative application that has to be replicated but rather offer a range of provocations for practice in reaction to applied theatre practitioners who may want to use Shakespeare's work for transformative purposes.

Chapters 6, 7, 11, 12, 15, and 16 considered the history and context of each area of theatre (prison, Disability, and therapy) and its use of Shakespeare's plays for the purposes of transformation. It considered the different histories and epistemologies of the specific area of theatre firstly, before moving onto the consideration of how Shakespeare's work was used within these areas specifically, demonstrating the scope and breadth of this work worldwide.

Chapters 8, 9, 13, and 17 offered an historical/Renaissance reading of (a selection of) Shakespeare's plays. A logical combination between Shakespeare's work and the different marginalised communities being explored was made in the chapters concerning an historical reading of Shakespeare's plays. This did not necessarily mean that the chosen texts for chapters are used by applied theatre practitioners within that specific community or that the texts selected would always align to the related case study examples (although some examples did align such as CVP's work with *Hamlet*). However, it did mean that the researcher was able to spend

190 CONCLUSION

more time making connections between the findings, drawing upon richer research to inform the chapters.

An historical/Renaissance reading of the work was offered as a relevant tool to help understand the issues presented in the work, and through new historicism, historicization, and verfremdungseffekt, it has been suggested that a participant is offered a relevant distance from the issue, in order for their minds to remain concentrated, and for the lessons of the work to be discovered and interrogated, from a safe distance away from the issues the participants may be personally experiencing.

A critical and historical/Renaissance reading of Shakespeare's plays remains important to applied theatre practice to subvert the universalising discourse, to avoid assumptive and taken-for-granted beliefs about Shakespeare's work which may override the transformative intentions of the project, and to offer the participant's a safe distance when exploring the characters of Shakespeare's plays.

The texts explored, when undertaking critical and historical investigations into Shakespeare's works, presented a range of important considerations relevant to this area of practice, challenging the concept of universal truth and reiterating the importance of subverting a universalising discourse. By viewing Shakespeare's work as being distanced from the present, the lessons of the plays can be more effectively understood as the participant is no longer bound to make parallels to their own lives. In concentrating on a fictional past, the participants can identify opportunities for change from a safe distance, whilst still understanding the implications the opportunities for change may have today.

The readings of *Macbeth* demonstrated how the depictions of Lady Macbeth's character and behaviour are complex. One must use the lessons of this play cautiously and tread carefully when exploring her character, avoiding the suggestion that she is to be used as an example of depicting 'universal' behaviours. It would be ill-advised to suggest that she is a universal character who teaches universal truths about behaviours and attitudes. It would be dangerous even to suggest that her examples of human behaviour are 'of all time'. Taking into consideration the ideas of maternal agency, patrilineal identity and lineage, and infanticide as presented in the play Macbeth, the extent of Lady Macbeth's (sometimes imagined) crimes can be understood, and they do not appear universal. An historical reading of the work is needed when exploring this character, as the seriousness of her crimes-imaginary possibly in reference to infanticide, accurate in relation to an extinguished patrilineage can only be understood with reference

CONCLUSION 191

to the beliefs and cultural fears pervasive during the Renaissance, which are different from our own. The true extent of Lady Macbeth's evil is only comprehended when an understanding of cultural fears and traditions is explored. Although there are many relevant lessons that can be drawn from a reading of Lady Macbeth because these are predominantly historically placed, this play more than any of the others interrogated highlights the implications of historical beliefs, different to those of today. The chapter on Lady Macbeth firstly highlights the differences between then and now. The chapter secondly demonstrates the importance of undertaking an historical and critical reading of Lady Macbeth generally and her references to crime specifically. Ultimately the lessons ingrained in the work come with a warning that the practitioner of the work needs to have some level of awareness in relation to the historical references made throughout Macbeth. Distancing the participants from both character and issue would remain important; therefore, the historical implications of the work offer an appropriate distance from the play for the participants to be able to identify opportunities for change that should and potentially can take place.

The readings of *Hamlet* offer a clear presentation of how assumptions can be bound up in the readings of Shakespeare's plays and characters. Hamlet's soliloquies are often interpreted as real interactions with the complexities of the mind and are argued to provide in-depth explorations which may be helpful for anyone attempting to understand issues with mental health. There is no denying the fact that one may identify with the pain of Hamlet. There is also a relevant argument for the idea that through Hamlet one may learn more about their own state of mind. However, it is important to remember that Shakespeare is also demonstrating dramatic (rather than medical) skill, and *Hamlet* is a story of a man using a range of strategies (including madness) to exact revenge. The readings of *Hamlet*, historical or otherwise, move from real madness to crafted versions of madness, and there remain complications when participants are asked to read their own state of mental health through a theatrically constructed version of 'madness'. Although there are aspects of the play that tell the audience something about 'madness', there is a danger that from a twenty-first century perspective, we may be looking backward with a modern concept of madness with the hope to learn something about modern clinical madness. Instead, this provocation suggests using historical considerations of the work to identify the differences for change to take place. Due to mental health being a sensitive topic, one must be cautious as to how they are applying outdated views from a playwright exploring 'madness' over

192 CONCLUSION

400 years ago. They should not be promoted as universal, but rather beneficial to explore the differences that are offered between then and now.

Measure for Measure demonstrated that change is possible when exploring the differences rather than similarities between then and now. The play moves from two different penal systems of punishment: the system/age of terror (punishment of the body) and the system/age of confinement (punishment of the soul). The systems were demonstrated through the characters of Angelo and the Duke and suggested something significant about the workings of Renaissance prisons and the justice system that placed people there. The two systems of punishment were importantly only identifiable when looking back in history at the progression in prison during, and after Shakespeare was writing the play. The play offers clear considerations of the penal environment and whether its structures are beneficial for those inside the prison and/or overseeing/managing the environment. In concentrating the mind upon the historical implications of the work, it became clear that the play offers a beneficial opportunity to question the prison and justice system and the nature of crime. The play may be helpful for the prisoner and the prison service in learning more about how the different roles in a penal environment interact. Although it is important to reiterate that these plays are not saying something about these systems today, they can still be used for the purposes of change and difference. The research is not claiming that we need to learn from Renaissance law. There were many corrupt aspects to its enforcement, as demonstrated throughout *Measure for Measure*. It does suggest, however, that there are opportunities to interrogate justice, mercy, punishment, and control by participating in the work and its historical influences.

The reading of *Henry VI part Two* and *Three* and *Richard III* highlighted inherent historical implications in relation to the medical discourse and terminology that underpinned the idea of Disability in Renaissance England. Shakespeare presents a character who faces adversity, but who causes it too. In these plays, we see a mix of Renaissance values, and more modern and advanced thoughts surrounding Disability. Shakespeare's presentation appears to afford an opportunity to consider the multifarious ways in which we can speak about Disability. Through the character of Richard, Shakespeare provides a dynamic consideration of the body, its challenges, limitations, and opportunities. Richard's own experiences of Disability vastly change throughout the plays and suggest Shakespeare provides a dynamic consideration of the body, its challenges and opportunities, which would be useful to interrogate for a range of applied theatre

CONCLUSION   193

environments engaged with the considerations of Disability. The reading warns of the complexities when using modern interpretations to understand the cultural clues of Disability, which are not universal. It simultaneously highlights how the multifarious way Shakespeare's work discusses Disability is valuable to those inside and outside of this community.

Although advances have been made both medically and socially regarding Disability, the plays hold important interrogations for participants to unpick in relation to Disability and the presentation of the body (on and off stage). The plays demonstrate where changes have been made and what changes were yet to be made, in relation to its historical considerations. By combining Shakespeare's plays with a historical reading of the work, aspects of change can be identified. This should offer participants important dialogues around the historical interactions with Disability. In line with the history of Disability Theatre, it is clear there is still a long way to go in helping the Disabled become more visible in this field. The play has therefore remained important to interrogate particularly in relation to the past and to reflect upon exactly what changes have been made, and what might still need to change.

Chapters 10, 14, and 18 referenced some of the major applied theatre programmes currently in existence (predominantly in the UK and USA), which have used Shakespeare's work within applied theatre settings. It also attempted to cover a range of marginalised communities and the challenges they might face when engaging with this area of practice. The fact that new articles, projects, and investigations continue to emerge within this field demonstrates a positive surge of interest in the practice of applied theatre generally. The chapters concluded by exploring three salient case studies that took place in three specific and marginalised environments. The chapters explored companies that are currently combining Shakespeare's work with different areas of practice for purposes of healing, change, and transformation. The chapters explored Shakespeare's use with prisoners, Disabled communities, and within therapeutic settings addressing where Shakespeare's work is used as a tool in applied theatre settings, and why the work is regarded as a beneficial addition to this area of practice.

Each case study presented clear examples of the different environments and communities Shakespeare's work is 'put-to-use' in. It demonstrated success and challenges of the work and highlighted multifarious methods in which Shakespeare's work is used and *why*. These chapters explored the

194 CONCLUSION

notions, attitudes, and values about humanity that might be depicted/ promoted through Shakespeare's work.

Many reasons were offered in relation to why Shakespeare's work had been chosen as a tool for practice. ESC spoke of how 'anybody can do Shakespeare given the right access and opportunity to participate with the text […] We can learn much from these stories'. [1] Blue Apple appeared to interact with Shakespeare to 'celebrate the talents of our actors through the greatest plays in the world' because of how 'Shakespeare speaks to us all'. [2] Blue Apple used Shakespeare's plays to help aid levels of inclusion and discussed how choosing Shakespeare's plays allowed the Disabled community to join in with culture. CVP spoke of how the participants are said to find new purpose through Shakespeare and that using Shakespeare within their work 'helps to navigate through the painful places they've been … to heal the wounds most of us can't see'. [3] McLoughlin also discussed the importance of looking at breath control in Shakespearean verse and its physical effect upon the veterans. The CVP appeared to attach their thoughts regarding the value of the work more explicitly to the therapeutic environment in which they were operating. They echoed some of the sentiments regarding how Shakespeare's texts 'can be transformed into a therapeutic intervention'. [4]

The companies acknowledged that the use of Shakespeare's work could be challenging. For example, Blue Apple was aware of the challenges for their actors playing Shakespearean roles stating 'sometimes people with Down's Syndrome find it difficult to separate fiction from reality, so *Hamlet* has been blurring with their own real life, and with this comes difficulties with the emotions of the characters'. [5] CVP explained how a lot of their work was about 'identity'. Through identifying similarities with Shakespeare's characters, the men can find who they were and/or are. The participants themselves discussed the struggles in playing certain characters like *Hamlet,* and player Johnson discusses that 'When I do his speech to be or not to be […] about going through the motions of killing himself […] I immediately thought good lord- that's going to be quite a challenge'. [6] The participants themselves were offered the space to reflect upon the damaging effects of work that requires character identification, and the work acknowledges some of the limitations this may provoke. ESC documented that how, by including certain aspects of the play *Macbeth* (e.g., Lady Macbeth's suicide), the prisoners were being asked to face a particular issue despite potential vulnerabilities this may evoke.

Each case study presented complexities with the desire to combine Shakespeare's works with different and at times challenging marginalised environments. Although there were often cross-over considerations to how Shakespeare's work is 'put-to-use' it also highlighted where deviations across environments occur. This suggests that there is not one specific blueprint for applied practice and each community needs to be considered individually and independently before the work can be delivered.

Conclusively, this study has provided a deeper understanding and contributed new knowledge about debate relative to combining Shakespeare's work with applied formats of theatre. The research has highlighted how Shakespeare's work is used as a tool for transformation in a wide range of applied practices, and that many people are articulating and engaging with the *benefits* of the practice. This research centralised a range of debates regarding applied practice, and its use of Shakespeare's work specifically and drew attention to the inherent challenges that practice and practitioners may face when combining Shakespeare's plays with the purposes of Applied Theatre to achieve a transformative outcome.

Notes

1. Pensalfini, R. (2016) *Prison Shakespeare: For These Deep Shames and Great Indignities.* London: Palgrave Macmillan. p. 138.
2. Lewis, A. (2012) *A Younger Theatre: Spotlight on Blue Apple Theatre:* http://www.ayoungertheatre.com/spotlight-on-blue-apple-theatre (Accessed: 01/07/16).
3. Ibid.
4. Hunter, K. (2017) *The Hunter Heartbeat Method:* http://kellyhunter.co.uk/shakespeares-heartbeat/the-hunter-heartbeat-method/ (Accessed: 17/12/17).
5. Lewis, A. (2012) *A Younger Theatre: Spotlight on Blue Apple Theatre:* http://www.ayoungertheatre.com/spotlight-on-blue-apple-theatre (Accessed: 01/07/16).
6. Ledgard, C. (2013) *And Calm of Mind BBC News:* http://www.bbc.co.uk/programmes/b01s09kf (Accessed: 17/12/17).

CHAPTER 19

Suggestions for Further Research

This chapter suggests areas for further reading, research, and investigation relative to the practice of Applied Theatre. The suggestions are informed by the main findings of the book. Whilst this book has attempted to cover a large amount of research relative to the practice of Applied Shakespeare, it was unable to cover every topic, question, or area of query, either pre-existing or discovered as part of the book's investigations. Therefore, this section represents important (but peripheral) areas of research that could afford further research and investigation.

The hope is that, by providing additional research areas to the reader, Applied Shakespeare can continue to grow and develop, inevitably establishing more in-depth information on the topic. This chapter encourages readers to continue learning and exploring new concepts relative to Applied Shakespeare after they have finished reading this book.

More general to this research are the suggestions for further investigations more relevant to the areas of performance theory. Questions such as 'what kind of Shakespeare do we end up with when the customary purpose of playing has been altered and the play is appropriated for other uses?' would be important to explore alongside what happens to Shakespeare performed when it is subjected to other uses (e.g., morphed into some other modes of theatre). [1] Linking the explorations of Shakespeare to the fidelity debate, it would be useful to explore whether Shakespeare is still Shakespeare when the plays have been subjected to

© The Author(s), under exclusive license to Springer Nature   197
Switzerland AG 2024
A. Hulsmeier, *Applied Shakespeare*,
https://doi.org/10.1007/978-3-031-45414-1_19

other uses and forms of theatre and for different intentions (e.g., to achieve transformation, rather than to entertain).

To expand on the ideas of the importance of a historical reading in greater detail and as an entire research area of its own, it would be important to consider whether other uses of performance, more evidently so than commercial productions, help us to situate our understandings of the plays within the historical and cultural contexts that originally produced them.

Regarding the field of Applied theatre more generally, there is space to consider the inherent challenges in the practice before Shakespeare has even been considered as a tool for transformation. Although there are a vast range of benefits associated with the form of applied theatre, when exploring applied theatre projects, it is important to remain aware that aesthetic, political, and ethical discourse continually interact with the practice and may change the way the intentions and outcomes of the work are viewed/received. It would be important to interrogate applied theatre in relation to its transformative intentions, identifying the challenges inherent in this field of work. This may be relevantly considered from the perspective of transformation, the assessment of transformation, commissioning transformation, the sacrifices made to achieve transformation, and the combination of disparate forms of theatre to achieve transformation.

There also remains space to interrogate applied theatre in relation to active participation, and the challenges that arise when participants (particularly participants who are vulnerable) are expected to be actively involved in this format of theatre. This may cover the scale of participation (active = good vs passive = bad), and the perspectives that surround active and passive levels of participation. In understanding the characteristics of participation in interactive performance, communication can be employed as a medium to enable social progression and/or change. If a community is asked to participate in an issue or topic, related to their lives, then the supposition is that the work is encouraging and affords a forum for relevant discussion. Change and challenges can be addressed, and the participants are afforded a space in which to safely confront issues that they are currently facing, or resolve conflict to achieve empowerment, confidence, and transformation. However, participation can also be a limited form of performance which leaves many problems and questions open for further critical consideration, drawing attention to the challenges of applied theatre's participatory form, relevant for further investigation, consideration, and interrogation.

In breaking down each area of theatre into its subsequent part (e.g., Prison theatre, Disability theatre, Theatre Therapy), other challenges may also be interrogated, relevant to each individual area of practice. For example, Prison theatre may need to consider the challenges between freedom vs incarceration, performance vs punishment, and how theatre is used (and received) as an alternative response to crime. For Disability theatre, considerations regarding inclusion, discrimination, and exploitation would be beneficial to explore. For theatre therapy, challenges explored may include the segregated ways of knowing clients and the power dynamics between therapist and client. All will aid a deeper understanding of exactly what these forms of theatre face, and how they might be able to successfully interact with purposes of transformation before Shakespeare's plays have even been considered as a tool to aid transformation.

In relation to Shakespearean studies, and the use of Shakespeare's plays specifically with the purpose of transformation in mind, the research associated with universalising discourses, cultural values, character identification, and historical considerations, as potential challenges to the practice, could also be expanded upon further. This would help to ensure that more knowledge is offered to the practice generally and ultimately help provide practitioners with research that could potentially help to better tailor their approaches to Applied Shakespeare, maximising the effectiveness of the intentions of the work for the specific community being engaged. It could also help to address the cultural context of the work, further acknowledging that Shakespeare's plays reflect and perpetuate the social norms and prejudices of their time, which is important to acknowledge and address to create inclusive and socially responsible theatre practices complimentary to applied theatre's intentions.

NOTE

1. Herold, N. & Wallace, M. (2011) '*Time Served in Prison Shakespeare*,' Selected Papers of the Ohio Valley Shakespeare Conference, 2 (4): http://ideaexchange.uakron.edu/spovsc/vol4/iss2011/2 (Accessed: 18/07/18).

CHAPTER 20

Concluding Statement

This chapter provides the concluding thoughts for the book overall. Drawing upon existing concepts and new findings, the chapter concludes the book's overarching thoughts regarding Applied Shakespeare and its transformative possibilities.

This book has helped to acknowledge the importance of interrogating the practice of Applied Shakespeare. The original aim was to uncover Shakespeare's use within applied theatre settings (*where* and *why* Shakespeare is used for transformative purposes). The work also aimed to suggest how a historical/Renaissance reading of Shakespeare's plays could help subvert some of the inherent complications that arise when using Shakespeare's plays are used to aid transformation, allowing for important lessons within the plays to be more carefully and coherently explored.

This research has contributed to the debate surrounding Shakespeare's use in applied theatre settings, specifically for the purposes of transformation. The research demonstrates the breadth of projects that exist in using Shakespeare's plays for transformative purposes, and further highlights that much more remains to be explored in this field. The hope is that the provocations identified within this book can develop and further build on the discourses established as part of Shakespearean and applied theatre studies.

This book is a response to the need for clarity and constructive dialogue surrounding *where* and *why* Shakespeare's plays may be used as a tool to aid applied theatre practice and what challenges may also be faced in doing

© The Author(s), under exclusive license to Springer Nature Switzerland AG 2024
A. Hulsmeier, *Applied Shakespeare*,
https://doi.org/10.1007/978-3-031-45414-1_20

201

so. Throughout, the work has drawn attention to several companies, practitioners, and participants creating practice that is active, participatory, and reflective of ongoing dialogue. As the chapters identify, the field of Applied Shakespeare has broadened and is consistently changing and evolving. This means that Applied Shakespeare lands in several different locations and crosses over several different fields of praxis. Applied Shakespeare as a discourse thus finds itself in conversation with several broader critical endeavours and theories. Shakespearean studies—applied theatre studies, theatre studies, postmodernism, cultural studies, theatre in prisons, Disability theatre, and theatre therapy—all extend across the humanities and help us to think about the future of Applied Theatre praxis generally and Applied Shakespeare specifically, particularly in the context of our changing world.

The hope is that by retaining engagement and fascination with Applied Shakespeare, combined with a curiosity in the transformative, new theatre practice can continue to develop and inspire.

Bibliography

Ackroyd, J. (2001). Applied Theatre: Problems and Possibilities. *Applied Theatre Researcher*, *1*(1), 1–12. www.griffith.edu.ac/centre/cpci/atr/journal/article1_number1.htm. Accessed 5 Dec 2015.

Adams, R. (Ed.). (1985). *Teaching Shakespeare: Essays on Approaches to Shakespeare in School and College*. Robert Royce.

Adelman, J. (1987). Born of Woman': Fantasies of Maternal Power in Macbeth! In M. Garber (Ed.), *Cannibals, Witches, and Divorce: Estranging the Renaissance: Selected Papers from the English Institute* (pp. 72–91). John Hopkins University Press. https://ssologin.exeter.ac.uk/distauth/UI/Login?realm=%2Fpeople&goto=https%3A%2F%2Felibrary.exeter.ac.uk%3A443%2Fidp%2FAuthn%2FRemoteUser%3Fconversation%3De2s1. Accessed 26 Dec 2019.

Alexander, B. R. (2011). *Applying Disability Theory as an Actor and Director to Theatrical Texts of the Past and Present*. https://scholar.colorado.edu/honr_theses/573. Accessed 18 July 2018.

Allison, E., & Hattenstone, S. (2014). *'You Don't Ever Get Over It': Meet the British Soldiers Living with Post-Traumatic Stress Disorder*. https://www.theguardian.com/society/2014/oct/18/collateral-damage-ex-soldiers-living-with-ptsd. Accessed 17 Dec 2017.

Auslander, P., & Sandahl, C. (2009). *Bodies in Commotion: Disability and Performance*. University Michigan Press.

AutismSpeaks. (2014). *Shakespeare Therapy*. https://www.autismspeaks.org/science/science-news/shakespeare-therapy-autism. Accessed 14 Apr 2018.

Balfour, M. (2001). *Theatre and War, 1933-1945: Performance in Extremis*. Beghahn Books.

Balfour, M. (Ed.). (2004). *Theatre in Prison: Theory and Practice*. 4Edge.

© The Author(s), under exclusive license to Springer Nature Switzerland AG 2024
A. Hulsmeier, *Applied Shakespeare*,
https://doi.org/10.1007/978-3-031-45414-1

204 BIBLIOGRAPHY

Barnes, C. (1991). A Brief History of Discrimination and Disabled People. In *Chapter 2 Disabled People in Britain and Discrimination: A Case for Anti-discrimination Legislation*. http://Disability-studies.leeds.ac.uk/files/library/Barnes-Disabled-people-and-discrim-ch2.pdf. Accessed 2 Apr 2017.

Barnes, C., & Mercer, G. (2005). *Good Practice for Providing Reasonable Access to the Physical Built Environment for Disabled People*. Unpublished Paper, University of Leeds: Centre for Disability Studies.

Barry, P. (2017). *Beginning Theory: An Introduction to Literary and Cultural Theory*. Oxford University Press.

Barton-Farcas, S. (2017). *A Practical Manual for Inclusion in the Arts*. Taylor & Francis.

Bates, L. (2013). *Shakespeare Saved My Life: Ten Years in Solitary with the Bard*. Sourcebooks.

Bates, L. (2015). *Can Shakespeare Help Prisoners Reform?* https://www.british-council.org/voices-magazine/can-shakespeare-help-reform-prisoners. Accessed 7 Dec 2017.

Bawdy Courts. (no date). *Policing Sex*. http://hfriedberg.web.wesleyan.edu/engl205/wshakespeare/policingsex.htm. Accessed 7 Dec 2017.

Berghaus, G. (Ed.). (1996). *Fascism and Theatre*. Beghahn Books.

Berghaus, G., & Wolff, O. (Eds.). (1989). *Theatre and Film in Exile*. Berg Books.

Berry, C. (2003). The Uses of Shakespeare in Criminal Rehabilitation: Testing the Limits of 'Universality'. In D. Lloyd (Ed.), *Shakespeare Matters: History, Teaching, Performance* (pp. 151–163). University of Delaware Press.

Bloy, M. (2002). *The 1601 Elizabethan Poor Law Victorian Web*. http://www.victorianweb.org/history/poorlaw/elizpl.html. Accessed 2 Feb 2017.

Blue Apple Theatre Company. (No Date). *Blue Apple Theatre*. http://blueapple-theatre.com. Accessed 1 July 2016.

Boal, A. (2006). *The Aesthetics of the Oppressed*. Routledge.

Boal, A., & Epstein, S. (1990). The Cop in the Head: Three Hypotheses. *The Drama Review, 34*(3), 35–42. http://www.populareducation.co.za/sites/default/files/Boal%20cop%20in%20the%20head.pdf. Accessed 31 Aug 2018.

Boston, M. (2016). *Six Reasons Shakespeare Remains Relevant 400 Years After His Death*. https://news.usc.edu/91717/six-reasons-shakespeare-remains-relevant-400-years-after-his-death/. Accessed 18 July 2018.

Botelho, K. (2008). Maternal Memory and Murder in Seventeenth Century England. *Studies in English Literature 1500–1900, 48*(1), 114. https://www.academia.edu/3645009/Maternal_Memory_and_Murder_in_Early-Seventeenth-Century_England._SEL_Studies_in_English_Literature_48_1_Winter_2008_111-130. Accessed 26 Feb 2019.

Brannigan, J. (1996). *New Historicism and Cultural Materialism: A Reader*. Macmillan International.

Bratton, J. (2003). *New Readings in Theatre History*. Cambridge University Press.

BIBLIOGRAPHY 205

Brecht, B., & Willett, J. (1992). *Brecht on Theatre: The Development of an Aesthetic.* Hill and Wang.

Bright, T. (1586). *A Treatise of Melancholie* [Microfiche]. London, Early English Books Online.

Bristol, M. (1996). *Big Time Shakespeare.* Routledge.

British Council. (2016). *A Different Romeo and Juliet.* https://theatreanddance. britishcouncil.org/projects/2015/a-different-romeo-and-juliet/. Accessed 12 Apr 2018.

Burnett, M. (2012). *Shakespeare and World Cinema.* Cambridge University Press.

Bynum, W. F., & Neve, M. (1986). Hamlet on the Couch: Hamlet Is a Kind of Touchstone by Which to Measure Changing Opinion—Psychiatric and Otherwise—About Madness. *American Scientist, 74*(4), 390–396. https:// studylib.net/doc/18744140/american-scientist%2Dvol.-74%2D%2 Dno.-4%2D%2Djuly. Accessed 26 Feb 2019.

Campbell, P., & Kear, A. (Eds.). (2001). *Psychoanalysis and Performance.* Routledge.

Caraher, M., Bird, L., & Hayton, P. (2000). Evaluation of a Campaign to Promote Mental Health in Young Offender Institutions: Problems and Lessons for Future Practice. *Health Education Journal, 59*(2), 211–227. https://journals. sagepub.com/doi/10.1177/001789690005900303. Accessed 26 Feb 2019.

Caraher, M., Dixon, P., & Hayton, P. (2002). Are Health-Promoting Prisons an Impossibility? Lessons from England and Wales. *Health Education Journal, 102*(5), 219–229. https://pure.york.ac.uk/portal/en/publications/are-healthpromoting-prisons-an-impossibility(2603b6f5-a962-4b63-9f43-4ef747c6eddd)/export.html. Accessed 26 Feb 2019.

Cerasano, S. P., Bly, M., & Hirschfeld, H. A. (2010). *Medieval and Renaissance Drama in England- Volume 23.* Fairleigh Dickinson University Press.

Chamberlain, S. (2005). Fantasizing Infanticide: Lady Macbeth and the Murdering Mother in Early Modern England. *College Literature, 32*(3), 72–91. https:// www.wssd.org/cms/lib02/PA01001072/Centricity/Domain/202/ Fantacizing%20Infanticide%20Lady%20Mac%20Article.pdf. Accessed 26 Feb 2019.

Charlebois, E. (2010). Their Minds Transfigured So Together Imaginative Transformation and Transcendence in *Midsummer Night's.* In J. Shailor (Ed.), *Performing New Lives: Prison Theatre* (pp. 256–269). Jessica Kingsley Books.

Chauncy-Shackford, C. (1876). *Hamlet's Antic-Disposition.* Cornell University.

Chesner, A. (1995). *Dramatherapy for People with Learning Disabilities: A World of Difference.* Jessica Kingsley Publishers.

Christey-Casson, J. (2011). *17th Century Theatre Therapy Shakespeare, Fletcher, Massinger, Middleton, Ford and Dekker: Six Jacobean Healing Dramas.* http:// www.acacemia.edu/17783153/SIXJacobean_Plays1. Accessed 17 Dec 2017.

206   BIBLIOGRAPHY

Cochrane, C. (2015). *Theatre History and Historiography: Ethics, Evidence and Truth*. Palgrave Macmillan.

Cohen-Cruz, J., & Schultzman, M. (Eds.). (2002). *Playing Boal Theatre, Therapy, Activism*. Routledge.

Cole, S. L. (2010). *The Absent One: The Mourning Ritual, Tragedy, and the Performance of Ambivalence*. Penn State Press.

Conquergood, D. (1985). *Performing as a Moral Act: Ethical Dimensions of the Ethnography of Performance*: http://www.csun.edu/~vcspc00g/301/perfas-moralact.pdf. Accessed 5 Dec 2015.

Copeland, S. C. S. (2008). *Constructions of Infanticide in Early Modern England: Female Deviance Demographic Crisis*. https://etd.ohiolink.edu/rws_etd/document/get/osu1222046761/inlineaccessed. Accessed 4 Aug 2017.

Cowen-Orlin, L., & Johnson-Haddad, M. (Eds.). (2007). *Staging Shakespeare: Essays in Honor of Alan C. Dessen*. University of Delaware Press.

Cox, M. (Ed.). (1992). *Shakespeare Comes to Broadmoor: The Performance of Tragedy in a Secure Psychiatric Hospital*. Jessica Kingsley Publishers.

Cox, M., & Thielgaard, A. (1994). *Shakespeare as Prompter: The Amending Imagination and the Therapeutic Process*. Jessica Kingsley Publishers.

Critchely, S., & Webster, J. (2013). *Stay, Illusion! The Hamlet Doctrine*. Pantheon Books.

CultureNI. (n.d.). *Education Shakespeare Company: A Profile*. https://www.youtube.com/watch?v=p9YrRVvg3-A. Accessed 19 Mar 2019.

Cummings, M. J. (2003). *Shakespeare and Medicine: Bard Was Well Versed in Human Afflictions and Their Treatments*. https://www.cummingsstudyguides.net/xMedicine.html. Accessed 17 Dec 2017.

CVP. *The Combat Veteran Players*. https://www.britishcouncil.us/combat-veteran-players. Accessed 17 Dec 2012.

Davis, L. J. (2002). *Bending over Backwards: Disability, Dismodernism, and Other Difficult Positions*. New York University Press.

Dilley, S. (2015). *War Veterans Take to the Stage* Sky News. https://news.sky.com/story/war-veterans-take-to-the-stage-10348571. Accessed 17 Dec 2017.

Dobson, M. (2011). *Shakespeare and the Amateur Performance: A Cultural History*. Cambridge University Press.

Dolan, F. (1994). *Dangerous Familiars: Representations of Domestic Crime in England, 1550–1700*. Cornwall University Press.

Donham, M. (2016). *Theatre in Prison: How It Is Making a Difference*. http://digitalcommons.chapman.edu/cgi/viewcontent.cgi?article=1207&context=cusrd_abstracts. Accessed 7 Dec 2017.

Donnelly, M. (2015). *Can Shakespeare Heal? One Director's Quest to Help Treat PTSD*. http://dailysignal.com/2015/09/07/can-shakespeare-heal-one-directors-quest-to-help-treat-ptsd/. Accessed 17 Dec 2017.

Douglas, M. (1966). *Purity and Danger*. Routledge & Kegan Paul.

Dover-Wilson, J. (1951). *What Happens in Hamlet.* Cambridge University Press.

Dufresne, J. (2006). Crime Is Easy, Shakespeare Is Hard. *Reclaiming Children and Youth, 14*(4), 245–248.

Emma. (2012). *Ouch! It's a Disability Thing: Actor's with Learning Disabilities Perform Shakespeare's Hamlet.* http://www.bbc.co.uk/blogs/ouch/2012/05/actors_with_learning_disabilit.html. Accessed 1 July 2016.

ESC. *Understanding Through Film.* www.esc-film.com. Accessed 30 Oct 2016.

Europarl. (2017). *Northern Ireland PEACE Programme.* http://www.europarl.europa.eu/atyourservice/en/displayFtu.html?ftuId=FTU_3.1.9.html. Accessed 11 Apr 2018.

Eyler, J. R. (2010). *Disability in the Middle Ages: Reconsiderations and Reverberations.* Routledge.

Fleming, M., Bresler, L., & O'Toole, J. (2014). *The Routledge International Handbook of the Arts and Education (Routledge International Handbooks of Education).* Routledge.

Fletcher, A. (1995). *Gender, Sex, and Subordination in England? 1500–1800.* Yale University Press.

Foster, L. (2016). *Trauma to Triumph: How Shakespeare Is Helping Veterans.* http://www.wusa9.com/news/local/dc/trauma-to-triumph-how-shakespeare-is-helping-veterans/369429671. Accessed 17 Dec 2017.

Foucault, M. (1969). *The Archaeology of Knowledge.* Éditions Gallimard.

Foucault, M. (1975). *Surveiller et Punir: Naissance de la Prison.* Editions Flammarion.

Foucault, M. (1977). *Power/Knowledge: Selected Interviews and Other Writings 1972–1977.* Harvester Wheatsheaf.

Freebody, K., Balfour, M., Anderson, M., & Finnernan, M. (2018). *Applied Theatre: Understanding Change.* Springer.

Frye, R. M. (1984). *The Renaissance Hamlet: Issues and Responses in 1600.* Princeton University Press.

Funk, J. (2012). *Measuring Legal Fictions: Law and Sovereignty in Measure for Measure.* Clemson University: Tiger Prints.

Garber, M. (1997). *Coming of Age in Shakespeare.* Routledge.

Garland-Thomson, R. (2003). Making Freaks: Visual Rhetoric and the Spectacle of Julia Pastrana. In J. J. Cohen & G. Weiss (Eds.), *Thinking the Limits of the Body* (pp. 125–145). State University of New York Press.

Garside, E. (2016a). *Romeo and Juliet: Cardiff & Touring.* http://mytheatre-mates.com/romeo-juliet-cardiff-touring/. Accessed 4 Feb 2017.

Garside, E. (2016b). *Taking Flight Theatre: Romeo and Juliet Theatre Review.* http://www.buzzmag.co.uk/reviews/taking-flight-theatre-romeo-juliet-stage-review/. Accessed 4 Feb 2017.

208 BIBLIOGRAPHY

Goll, J. A. (1938). Criminal Types in Shakespeare. *Journal of Criminal Law and Justice.*, 5(29), 1–24. https://scholarlycommons.law.northwestern.edu/cgi/viewcontent.cgi?article=2829&context=jclc. Accessed 27 Sept 2018

Grady, S. (2003). Accidental Marxists? The Challenge of Critical and Feminist Pedagogies for the Practice of Applied Drama. *Youth Theatre Journal*, 17(1), 65–81. https://doi.org/10.1080/08929092.2003.10012553. http://www.tandfonline.com/doi/pdf/10.1080/08929092.2003.10012553. Accessed 7 Dec 2017. p. 75

Graeae.org. (n.d.). *Graeae Theatre Company.* http://graeae.org/. Accessed 22 Oct 2018.

Gray, P., & Cox, J. D. (Eds.). (2014). *Shakespeare and Renaissance Ethics.* Cambridge University Print.

Greenblatt, S. (2000). *Practicing New Historicism.* University of Chicago Press.

Haffter, C. (1968). The Changeling: History and Psychodynamics of Attitudes to Handicapped Children in European Folklore. *Journal of the History of Behavioural Sciences*, 4(7), 55–61. https://psycnet.apa.org/record/1968-12568-001. Accessed 26 Feb 2019.

Hanks, J., & Hanks, L. (1980). The Physically Handicapped in Certain Non-occidental Societies. In W. Phillips & J. Rosenberg (Eds.), *Social Scientists and the Physically Handicapped.* Arno Press.

Hargrave, M. (2015). *Theatres of Learning Disability: Good, Bad, or Plain Ugly?* Palgrave Macmillan.

Harpham, G. G. (1991). Foucault and the New Historicism. *American Literary History*, 3(2), 360–375. https://doi.org/10.1093/alh/3.2.360. Accessed 20 Mar 2019.

Heinemann, M. (1985). How Brecht Read Shakespeare. In J. Dollimore & A. Sinfield (Eds.), *Political Shakespeare: New Essays in Cultural Imperialism* (pp. 226–251). Manchester University Press.

Hemley, M. (2016). *BBC Documentary Redefining Juliet to Give Shakespeare Role to Disabled Actors.* https://www.thestage.co.uk/news/2016/bbc-documentary-redefining-juliet-to-give-shakespeare-role-to-Disabled-actors/. Accessed 4 Feb 2017.

Herold, N. (2014). *Prison Shakespeare and the Purpose of Performance: Repentance Rituals and the Early Modern.* Palgrave Macmillan.

Herold, N., & Wallace, M. (2011). Time Served in Prison Shakespeare. *Selected Papers of the Ohio Valley Shakespeare Conference*, 2(4) http://ideaexchange.uakron.edu/spovsc/vol4/iss2011/2. Accessed 18 July 2018.

Hobgood, A., & Houston-Wood, D. (Eds.). (2009). Disabled Shakespeare. *Disability Studies Quarterly*, 4(29). http://dsq-sds.org/article/view/991/1183. Accessed 18 July 2018.

Hunter, K. (2013). Shakespeare and Autism. *Teaching Shakespeare*, 1(3), 8–10. http://www.kellyhunter.co.uk. Accessed 17 Dec 2017.

BIBLIOGRAPHY   209

Hunter, K. (2017). *The Hunter Heartbeat Method.* http://kellyhunter.co.uk/shakespeares-heartbeat/the-hunter-heartbeat-method/. Accessed 17 Dec 2017.

Indemaur, D., & Hough, M. (2002). Strategies for Changing Public Attitudes to Punishment. In J. Roberts & M. Hough (Eds.), *Changing Attitudes in Punishment: Public Opinion, Crime and Justice* (pp. 127–136). Willan Publishing.

Ingram, M. (1987). *Church Courts, Sex and Marriage in England (1570–1640).* Cambridge University Press.

Inside Out. (2015). *Veterans Turned into Shakespeare Actors to Overcome Conflict Stress.* https://www.youtube.com/watch?v=0605E0DwBBU. Accessed 17 Dec 2017.

Irish, T. (2008). *Teaching Shakespeare: A History of the Teaching of Shakespeare in England RSC.* https://cdn2.rsc.org.uk/sitefinity/education-pdfs/articles-and-reports/rsc-education-history-of-teaching-shakespeare.pdf?sfvrsn=2. Accessed 4 Apr 2018.

Jackson, A. (2007). *Theatre, Education and the Making of Meanings.* Manchester University Press.

Jackson, L. (2014). *Crouchback or Misunderstood? The Disability of Richard III.* http://www.blue-stockings.org/?p=196. Accessed 18 July 2018.

Jelavitch, P. (1993). *Berlin Cabaret.* Harvard University Press.

Jensen, M. P. (2014) *What Service Is Here?* The Borrower and Lenders Article. http://www.borrowers.uga.edu/. Accessed 10 Apr 2016.

Jersey Evening Post. (2015). http://jerseyeveningpost.com. Accessed 1 July 2016.

Johnston, K. (2012). *Stage Turns: Canadian Disability Theatre.* McGill-Queen's University Press.

Johnston, K. (2016). *Disability Theatre and Modern Drama: Recasting Modernism.* Bloomsbury.

Kant, I. (1985). *Metaphysical Elements of Justice: Part I of the Metaphysics of Morals, Part 1.* Hackett Publishing Company Inc.

Keehan, B. (2015). Theatre, Prison & Rehabilitation: New Narratives of Purpose? *Research in Drama Education: The Journal of Applied Theatre and Performance, 3*(20), 391–394. http://www.tandfonline.com/doi/abs/10.1080/1356978 3.2015.1060118?journalCode=crde20. Accessed 7 Dec 2017.

Kellerman, P. F. (1992). *Focus on Psychodrama: The Therapeutic Aspects of Psychodrama.* Jessica Kingsley Publishers.

Kendall, G. M. (Ed.). (1998). Shakespearean Power and Punishment: A Volume of Essays. *Shakespeare Quarterly, 52*(1), 159–161. https://doi.org/10/1353/shq.2001.0012.

Kershaw, B. (1991). King Real's King Lear: Radical Shakespeare for the Nuclear Age. *Critical Survey, 3*(3), 249–259. http://www.jstor.org/stable/41556515. Accessed 14 Dec 2017.

210 BIBLIOGRAPHY

Khutan, R. (2014) *Demonstrating Effectiveness: Competing Discourses in the Use and Evaluation If Applied Theatre That Contributes to Improved Health Outcomes for Prisoners.* https://www.research.manchester.ac.uk/portal/files/54564128/FULL_TEXT.PDF. Accessed 1 Feb 2018.

Knowles, R. (2002). *Shakespeare's Argument with History.* Palgrave Macmillan.

Ko, Y. J. (2014). Macbeth Behind Bars. In M. P. Jensen (Ed.), *What Service Is Here?* Borrower and Lenders Article. http://www.borrowers.uga.edu/. Accessed 4 Apr 2018.

Kuppers, P. (2017). *Theatre and Disability.* Red Globe Press.

Landy, R. J., & Montgomery, D. T. (2012). *Theatre for Change: Education, Social Action, and Therapy.* Palgrave Macmillan.

Ledgard, C. (2013). *And Calm of Mind BBC News.* http://www.bbc.co.uk/programmes/b01s09kf. Accessed 17 Dec 2017.

Lewis, A. (2012). *A Younger Theatre: Spotlight on Blue Apple Theatre.* http://www.ayoungertheatre.com/spotlight-on-blue-apple-theatre. Accessed 1 July 2016.

Lewis-Williams, D. (2002). *The Mind in the Cave: Consciousness and the Origins of Art.* Thames & Hudson.

M, J. (2016). *Our Creative Veterans.* http://www.sandbagtimes.co.uk/creative-veterans-2/. Accessed 17 Dec 2017.

MacDonald, M. (1981). *Mystical Bedlam: Madness, Anxiety and Healing in Seventeenth Century England.* Cambridge University Press.

MacLellan, L. (no date). *Autistic Kids Are Thriving in Shakespearean Therapy.* https://qz.com/809771/autistic-kids-are-thriving-in-shakespearean-therapy-designed-by-a-british-actress-for-the-royal-shakespeare-company/. Accessed 17 Dec 2017.

Magill, T., & Marquis-Muradaz, J. (2009). The Making of *Mickey B*, a Modern Adaptation of *Macbeth* Filmed in a Maximum-Security Prison in Northern Ireland, Chapter 9. In S. Jennings (Ed.), *Dramatherapy and Social Theatre: Necessary Dialogues* (pp. 109–116). Routledge.

Martin, C., & Bial, H. (2000). *Brecht Sourcebook* (Worlds of Performance). Routledge.

Mason, M. K. (2018). *Foucault and His Panoptican.* http://www.moyak.com/papers/michel-foucault-power.html. Accessed 8 Apr 2018.

McAvinchey, C. (2011). *Theatre and Prison.* Palgrave Macmillan.

McCabe, P. (2012). *Prisoner Ombudsmen for Northern Ireland.* http://www.iprt.ie/files/IPRT_Seminar_30_March_2012.pdf. Accessed 11 Apr 2018.

McCandless, D. (no date). *"I'll Pray to Increase Your Bondage": Power and Punishment in Measure for Measure.* http://college.holycross.edu/projects/isp/measure/essays/bondage.html. Accessed 30 Oct 2016.

McLoughlin, B. (2012). *Method and Madness Theatre Provides Stimulus for Psychotic, Schizophrenic and Depressed Patients, But Can It Improve Their*

Mental Health? https://aeon.co/essays/can-performing-shakespeare-help-to-cure-mental-illness. Accessed 21 Dec 2017.

Mehling, M. H., Tasse, M. J., & Root, R. (2016). Shakespeare and Autism: An Exploratory Evaluation of the Hunter Heartbeat Method. *Research and Practice in Intellectual and Developmental Disabilities, 2*(4), 107–120. https://doi.org/10.1080/23297018.2016.1207202. Accessed 21 Dec 2017.

Metzler, I. (2016). *Fools and Idiots? Intellectual Disability in the Middle Ages.* Manchester University Press.

Miller, A. (2016). *My Experience at Theatre.* http://www.artsprofessional.co.uk/magazine/blog/my-experience-theatre-2016. Accessed 4 Feb 2017.

Minton, E. (2011). *A Timeless Hamlet in a Dated Production.* http://www.shakespeareances.com/willpower/onscreen/Hamlet-BBCTL80.html. Accessed 17 Dec 2017.

Mitchell, D. T., & Snyder, S. L. (2002). *Narrative Prosthesis: Disability and the Dependencies of Discourse.* University of Michigan Print Press.

Mithen, S. (1996). *The Prehistory of the Mind: The Cognitive Origins of Art, Religion, and Science.* Thames & Hudson LTD.

More, T. (1924). *The History of King Richard the Third.* Indianan University Press.

Morris, S. (2012). *Shakespeare's Minds Diseased: Mental Illness and Its Treatment.* http://theshakespeareblog.com/2012/03/shakespeares-minds-diseased-mental-illness-and-its-treatment/. Accessed 17 Dec 2017.

Morrison, E. (1992). *Theatre and Disability Conference Report.* Arts Council Arts & Disability.

Nicholson, H. (2005). *Applied Drama: The Gift of Theatre.* Palgrave Macmillan.

NICVA. (no date). *Supporting and Representing Voluntary and Community Organisations Across Northern Ireland.* www.nicva.org. Accessed 30 Oct 2017.

Nisonger Centre. (2014). *Shakespeare and Autism.* http://nisonger.osu.edu/shakespeare-autism. Accessed 17 Dec 2017.

Norman, N. (2013). *Once More into the Breach.* https://www.thestage.co.uk/features/interviews/2013/once-more-unto-the-breech/. Accessed 17 Dec 2017.

Oliver, M. (1981). A New Model of the Social Work Role in Relation to Disability. In J. Campling (Ed.), *The Handicapped Person: A New Perspective for Social Workers?* (pp. 19–36). RADAR. https://disability-studies.leeds.ac.uk/wp-content/uploads/sites/40/library/Campling-handicppaed.pdf. Accessed 26 Feb 2019.

Oliver, M., Baldwin, D., & Datta, S. (2018). Health to Wellness: A Review of Wellness Models and Transitioning Back to Health. *The International Journal of Health, Wellness, and Society, 9*(1), 41–56. https://doi.org/10.18848/2156-8960/CGP/v09i01/41-56

Olivier, R. (2013). *Inspirational Leadership: Timeless Lessons for Leaders from Shakespeare's Henry V.* Nicholas Brealey Publishing.

212 BIBLIOGRAPHY

Orten, J. D. (2003). 'That Perilous Stuff': Crime in Shakespeare's Tragedies. https://brage.bibsys.no/xmlui/bitstream/handle/11250/147500/Orten. pdf?sequence=1. Accessed 18 July 2018.

Payne, W. (2010). Blue Apple Tackles the Bard. http://www.hampshirechronicle. co.uk/leisure/arts/8206826.Blue_Apple_tackles_the_Bard/. Accessed 1 July 2016.

Pensalfini, R. (2016). Prison Shakespeare: For These Deep Shames and Great Indignities. Palgrave Macmillan.

Phillips, M. E. (1996). The Use of Drama and Puppetry in Occupational Therapy During the 1920s and 1930s. The American Journal of Occupational Therapy, 50(3), 229–233. https://www.ncbi.nlm.nih.gov/pubmed/8822247. Accessed 26 Feb 2019.

Popenoe, D. (1995). Sociology. Prentice Hall.

Prendergast, M., & Saxton, J. (2009). The Applied Theatre Reader. Routledge.

Prentki, T., & Preston, S. (2009). The Applied Theatre Reader. Routledge.

Quayson, A. (2012). Aesthetic Nervousness. Columbia University Press.

Reimer, M. (2013). Defining Renaissance Madness. https://english202guys.files. wordpress.com/2013/04/renaissance-madness.pdf. Accessed 17 Dec 2017.

Rosenberg, M. (1992). The Masks of Hamlet. The University of Delaware Press.

Salkeld, D. (1993). Madness and Drama in the Age of Shakespeare. Manchester University Press.

SBSTC. (1997). Side by Side Theatre Company. http://www.sbstcs.org/. Accessed 5 June 2018.

Scott-Douglass, A. (2007). Shakespeare Inside: The Bard Behind Bars. Continuum books.

Sealey, J. (2015). Deaf and Disabled Artists: We Will Not Let Government Cuts Make Us Invisible. https://www.theguardian.com/stage/theatreblog/2015/ apr/13/deaf-and-Disabled-artists-we-will-not-let-government-cuts-make-us-invisible. Accessed 4 Feb 2017.

Sesame Institute. (n.d.). Sesame Institute: Drama and Movement Therapy. http:// sesameinstitute.appspot.com/marian-lindkvist. Accessed 21 Oct 2018.

Shailor, J. (2011). Performing New Lives: Prison Theatre. Jessica Kingsley Books.

Shakespeare, W. in Craig, W. J. (1991). The Complete Works of Shakespeare. Oxford University Press.

ShakespeareMag. (2013). Crime and Punishment. http://www.shakespearemag. com/fall98/punished.asp. Accessed 7 Dec 2017.

Siebers, T. (2001). Disability in Theory: From Social Constructionism to Realism of the Body. American Literary History, 13(4), 737–754. https://www.aca-demia.edu/2651126/Disability_in_Theory_From_Social_Constructionism_ to_the_New_Realism_of_the_Body. Accessed 26 Feb 2019.

Slade, P. (2000, November 30). Personal communication: Letter to John Casson.

BIBLIOGRAPHY 213

Smith, N. (1986). Confirming Canons. *English: Journal of the English Association,* *151*(35), 57–66. https://doi.org/10.1093/english/35.151.57. Accessed 1 Aug 2018.

Sokol, B. J., & Sokol, M. (2003). *Shakespeare, Law, and Marriage.* Cambridge University Press.

Solzhenitsyn, A. (1975). *The Gulag Archipelago.* Collins & Harvill Press.

Spence, L. (2010). *Women Who Murder in Early Modern England, 1558–1700.* https://warwick.ac.uk/fac/arts/history/ecc/emforum/projects/disstheses/dissertations/spence-laura.pdf. Accessed 8 Apr 2018.

Staub, S. (2000). Early Modern Medea: Representations of Child Murder in the Street Literature of Seventeenth Century England. In N. J. Miller & N. Yavneh (Eds.), *Maternal Measures: Figuring Caregiving in the Early Modern Period* (pp. 333–347). Ashgate.

Stoll. (2012). *COBSEO.* https://www.cobseo.org.uk/stoll-the-combat-veteran-players-announce-date-of-first-public-performance/. Accessed 11 Apr 2018.

Taking Flight Theatre. (no date). http://www.takingflighttheatre.co.uk/blog/. Accessed 4 Feb 2017.

Tavener, B. (2015). *From Stratford to Rio: Using Shakespeare to Treat Mental Illness.* http://www.bbc.co.uk/news/health-32241100. Accessed 17 Dec 2017.

Taylor, J. (2017). *Veterans with Combat Stress Find Solace in Shakespearean Verse.* https://www.thetimes.co.uk/article/veterans-with-combat-stress-find-solace-in-shakespearean-verse-wq0jc5rl5jt. Accessed 17 Dec 2017.

The Newbolt Report. (1921). *The Teaching of English in England London.* HM Stationery Office. http://www.educationengland.org.uk/documents/newbolt/newbolt1921.html. Accessed 4 Apr 2018.

The Newsom Report. (1963). *Half Our Future a Report of the Central Advisory.* Council for Education (England) London: Her Majesty's Stationery Office 1963. http://www.educationengland.org.uk/documents/newsom/newsom1963.html. Accessed 4 Apr 2018.

Thompson, J. (1998). *Prison Theatre: Practices and Perspectives.* Jessica Kingsley Publishing.

Thompson, J. (2006). *Applied Theatre: Bewilderment and Beyond.* Peter Lang Publishing Incorporated.

Thompson, J. (2012). *Applied Theatre: Bewilderment and Beyond.* Peter Lang Publishing Incorporated.

Time, V. M. (1999). *Shakespeare's Criminals, Criminology, Fictions and Drama.* Greenwood Press.

Tofteland, C. (2011). The Keeper of the Keys. In J. Shailor (Ed.), *Performing New Lives: Prison Theatre* (pp. 231–246). Jessica Kingsley.

214 BIBLIOGRAPHY

Toolis, S. (2016). *Drama Graduate Storme Toolis' 'Redefining Juliet' to Be Broadcast on BBC Four's Shakespeare Festival, School of Arts.* https://www.kent. ac.uk/arts/newsandevents/?view= 1165. Accessed 4 Feb 2017.

Tosh, W. (2016). *Shakespeare and Madness.* https://www.bl.uk/shakespeare/ articles/shakespeare-and-madness#. Accessed 17 Dec 2017.

Trounstine, J. (2004). Texts as Teachers: Shakespeare Behind Bars and Changing Lives Through Literature. *Arts and Societal Learning: New Directions for Adult and Continuing Education, 116*(Winter), 65–77. https://onlinelibrary.wiley. com/doi/pdf/10.1002/ace.277. Accessed 26 Feb 2019.

Trounstine, J. (2007). *Shakespeare Behind Bars: One Teacher's Story of the Power of Drama in a Women's Prison.* The University of Michigan Press.

Wack, M. F. (1990). *Lovesickness in the Middle Ages. The 'Viaticum' and Its Commentaries.* University of Pennsylvania Press.

Walsh, F. (2012). *Theatre and Therapy.* Palgrave Macmillan.

Warren, B., Richard, R. J., & Brimbal, J. (2007). *Drama and the Arts for Adults with Down Syndrome: Benefits, Options and Resources.* Down Syndrome Educational Trust.

Weinberg, G., & Rowe, D. (1996). *Will Power! Using Shakespeare's Insights to Transform Your Life.* St Martin's Press.

Werkman, A. (2015). *Shakespeare and Prison: A Critical Reflection on Richard Wilson's Foucauldian Reading of William Shakespeare's Measure for Measure.* Utrecht University.

West, W. N. (2009). What's the Matter with Shakespeare? Physics, Identity, Playin. *Northwestern University South Central Review, 1*(232), 103–126. http://www. yavanika.org/classes/reader/shakesmatter.pdf. Accessed 18 July 2018.

White, G. (2013). *Audience Participation in Theatre: Aesthetics of the Invitation.* Palgrave Macmillan.

Williams, K. S. (2009). Enabling Richard: The Rhetoric of Disability in *Richard III. Disability Studies Quarterly, 29*(4) https://www.bl.uk/shakespeare/arti-cles/richard-iii-and-the-staging-of-Disability. Accessed 5 Jan 2017.

Williams, L. K. (2017). *Being Lovesick Was a Real Disease in the Middle Ages.* https://theconversation.com/being-lovesick-was-a-real-disease-in-the-middle-ages-70919. Accessed 9 Apr 2018.

Wilson, R. (1993). The Quality of Mercy: Discipline and Punishment in Shakespearean Comedy. In R. Wilson (Ed.), *Will Power: Essays on Shakespearean Authority* (pp. 118–157). Harvester Wheatsheaf.

Wilson, J. R. (2017). The Trouble with Disability in Shakespeare Studies. *Disability Studies Quarterly, 2*(37). Harvard University. http://dsq-sds.org/article/ view/5430/4644. Accessed 21 Oct 2018.

Winn, L. C. (1994). *Post Traumatic Stress Disorder and Dramatherapy: Treatment and Risk Reduction.* Jessica Kingsley Publishing.

Wray, R. (2011). The Morals of Macbeth and Peace as Process: Adapting Shakespeare in Northern Ireland's Maximum-Security Prison' *Edinburgh Companion to Shakespeare and the Arts. Shakespeare Quarterly, 62*(11), 340–363. https://pure.qub.ac.uk/portal/en/publications/the-morals-of-macbeth-and-peace-as-process(443a3afa-a58f-435f-8fe3-d6e5bb43c949)/export.html. Accessed 26 Feb 2019.

Young, H. L. (1994). *Hamlet's Antic Disposition*. Eastern Washington University.

INDEX

A
Ableize, 107
About Face Theatre Company, 107
Access Theatre, 107
Active Citizen Awards, 83
Agape Theatre, 146
The Age of Terror, 67–69
Alternative response to crime, 47
Alzheimer's disease, 154
Alzheimer's patients, 153
   at the Stanford/VA Alzheimer's
      Research Centre, 153
Angelo, 63–69, 192
Anne, 119
Antic disposition, 165
Antonio, 84
Apple Core, 132
Applied community, 5
Applied Shakespeare, 2, 4, 7, 9, 20
Applied Theatre, 1, 2, 4, 6, 9,
   14, 29, 30
Applied Theatre Practice, 2, 3
Applied Theatre practitioners, 2, 5
Applied Theatre settings, 1, 3, 5
Arabian Nights (2014), 133

ASD, *see* Autism Spectrum Disorder
Ashworth, 151
Askham Grange, UK, 48
Asperger syndrome, 131
As We Like It, 110
As You Like It, 110, 116
Australian convict theatres, 48
Autism, 131, 154
Autism Spectrum Disorder (ASD),
   154, 155

B
Baim, Clark, 48
Barrow, 21
Bates, Dr. Laura, 55, 56
Behind the Scenes, 146
Belfast, 181
Belfast Prison, 84
Bengali Sign Language, 110
Bergstrand, Dr. Curtis, 54
Berry, Cicely, 52
The Big Question, 84
Birds of Paradise Theatre, 107
Birnam Jail, 85

© The Author(s), under exclusive license to Springer Nature   217
Switzerland AG 2024
A. Hulsmeier, *Applied Shakespeare*,
https://doi.org/10.1007/978-3-031-45414-1

218 INDEX

Birnam Wood, 85
Blau, Herb production of *Waiting for Godot* at San Quentin Prison, California, 48
Blue Apple Theatre Company, 131–138, 177, 194
Boal, Augusto, 2, 66, 82, 83, 86
Boalian, 86, 92
Boalian praxis, 83
Bogdanov, Michael, 81
Books Behind Bars, 54
Bosnia, 179
Bottom, 158
Brannagh, Kenneth, 86
Brecht, Bertolt, 2, 38–40
  verfremdungseffekt, 3, 10
Bright, Thomas, 157
British Association for Dramatherapy, 145
The British Association of Dramatherapists: BADth, 145
British Council, 110
British Psychodrama Association (BPA), 145
Broadmoor, 13, 26
Broadmoor Hospital, 151
  high-security Psychiatric Hospital, 151
Broadmoor Project, 151
'Brothers of Hamlet', 26
Brutus, 74
Buckingham, 123, 124
Burnam, 94
Busuttil, Dr. Walter (Director of Medical Services for Combat Stress), 172, 175

C
Caesar, 52, 116
Caliban, 116, 155
Cassius, 74, 116

Claudio, 63–66
Claudius, 159, 161, 163, 166, 167
Clean Break Theatre Company, 48
Clerke, Peter (Artistic Director), 131, 133
Clinical madness, 191
Combat Stress (The UK's leading Veteran's mental health charity), 172
Combat Veteran Players (CVP), 171–177, 181–183, 189, 194
The Comedy of Errors, 173
Concentration camps, 48
Conquergood, Dwight, 30
Cops-in-the-head, 66
Coriolanus, 158
'Cornerstone of Western culture', 20
Council for Professions Supplementary to Medicine (C.P.S.M), 146
Cox, Murray, 13, 14, 152
Cripwell, British Major General Richard, 173
Crowthorne in Berkshire, England, 151
Crumlin Road Gaol, 84
Cultural biases, 3, 35, 37, 188
Cultural commodity, 92
Cultural difference, 25
Cultural distance or exclusivity, 18
Cultural Excellence, 9, 19
Cultural good, 18
Cultural heritage, 19, 20
Cultural hierarchy, 18
Cultural icon, 20
Culturally biased, 9
Cultural pretension, 17
Cultural significance, 35
Cultural success, 11
Curriculum-centred, 21
CVP, *see* Combat Veteran Players
Cymbeline, 73, 116

D

Dark Horse Theatre, 107
Demetrius, 135
Denmark, 167
Desdemona, 28
Dhaka Theatre, Bangladesh, 110
Disability, 4, 105, 106, 113–125,
131–134, 136–138, 187, 189,
192, 193
arts, 105
and Shakespeare, 4
on stage, 105
Disability Shakespeare, 109
Disability Studies, 105, 106, 122
Disability Theatre/Disability Theatre
Company, 4, 106, 138, 193,
199, 202
Disability theory, 117
Disabled, 105, 113, 114, 117–124,
132–134, 136, 193, 194
actors, 107
communities, 109–110, 112, 114,
138, 177, 193
identity, 125
theatre, 105, 109, 132, 136
Disabled Companies, 110
Disabled Shakespeare, 138
DIY Theatre Company, 107
Down's Syndrome, 110, 131, 132,
134–137, 194
Drama therapy, 143
Duffer, 85, 96
Duke, 65, 67–70, 192
Duke Vincentio, 65

E

Edinburgh Fringe Festival, 110
Educational Certificate, an Active
Citizenship Award (ASDAN), 83
Educational Shakespeare Company, 81
Educational value, 35

Eighteenth century/18th century, 62,
63, 66, 70
Elbow, 64
Elite, 17
Elitism, 3, 17, 18, 36, 37, 153
Elizabeth, 121
Elsinore, 167
Elsworth, James, 137
Encounter Theatre and
Therapy, 146
Englishness, 19, 25
English Shakespeare Company, 81
ESC, 45, 81–90, 92–97, 194
Escape Artists, 48
ESC Film, 5
ESC US, 82
Exclusion, 17
Exclusive culture, 18
Ex-Servicemen and women, 171
Extern AXIS, 84
Extern: The First Course, 84
Extern: The Second Course, 84

F

Faber, Amanda (producer), 173
Feste, 116
Financial gain, 18
Fontboone University, 54
Fool, 116
Ford, Ian, 179, 180
Forum Theatre, 83
Foucault, Michel, 62, 63, 67, 68
400th anniversary commemoration of
Shakespeare's death, 173
Framingham (MA) Women's Prison,
Massachusetts, 52
The Freewheelers, 107
Freire, Paulo, 2
Freud Trauma, 181
Friar Lodowick, 68
Funder-controlled, 21

220 INDEX

G

Galen/Galenus, Aelius/Galenus, Claudius, 157
Geese Theatre Company, 48, 146
Gertrude, 160–163, 167
Ghettos, 48
Globe Theatre, London., 133
Gloucester, 115, 116
Governmental agendas, 19
The Government Inspector (2011), 133
Graeae Theatre Company, 106, 109, 110
Greenblatt, S., 39
Guildenstern, 167
Gulags, 48
Guy's Hospital, London, 145

H

Hall, Doctor John, 157
Hamlet, 4, 5, 41, 54, 55, 133, 135–137, 152, 157–168, 173, 178, 179, 183, 189, 191, 194
Hamlet (2012), 133
Hamlet, 159, 161, 164, 166, 179, 191
Health and Care Professionals Council (H.P.C.), 146
Health Professions Council (HPC), 145
Heathcote, Dorothy, 145
Henry IV, 116
Henry IV, Part Two, 158
Henry V, 173, 180, 181
Henry VI, 115
Henry VI part one, 5, 41, 125
Henry VI Part Three, 4, 116, 117, 138, 192
Henry VI Part Two, 4, 5, 41, 116, 117, 125, 138, 192
Her Majesty's Prison Dartmoor, 52
Hermia, 135

Hertfordshire College of Art and Design, 145
Hijinx Theatre, 111
HIPS Section (Humanistic and Integrative Psychotherapy), 145
Historical reading, 37, 38, 41, 189
Historicisation, 3, 10, 35, 38, 40, 45, 188, 190
HM Armed Forces, 172
HMP Maghaberry, 84
Horatio, 167
H.R.H. King Charles, 173
Hunter Heartbeat Method, 154, 174
Hunter, Kelly, 154, 155, 174
  autism therapy, 155
Hyper-vigilance, 178

I

Iago, 74
Illyria-On-Sea, 110
Indiana Federal Prison, 55
Indiana's Correctional Facility, 56
Infanticidal, 77
Infanticide, 74, 76, 77
Infanticide Act, 76
Inside job, 84
Inside Out, 179
Internment camps, 48
Isabella, 65–67, 69, 70

J

Jennings, Dr. Sue, 145
Jensen, M. P., 153
Jersey Islanders, 134
Jessop, Jane, 131, 132, 134
Jessop, Tommy, 137
Jessop, William, 134, 135
Johnson, Shaun, 177–180, 194
Jones, Maxwell, 145
Juliet, 64, 65, 111

Julius Caesar, 52, 116
Jung, Carl, 145, 152

K
Kentucky Shakespeare Festival, 54
Kershaw, B., 21, 22
Kestrel Theatre Company, 48, 146
King Duncan, 75
King Lear, 21, 22, 116, 158
King Lear (The National
    Theatre), 152
King, Tom, 87
Ko Y. J., 27, 28

L
Laban, Rudolph, 145
Ladyboy, 85, 93, 96
Lady Macbeth, 73–78, 85, 92–94,
    190, 191, 194
Laertes, 137, 161, 162
Lawnmowers Theatre Company, 107
Learning difficulties, 133
Learning Disabilities, 132, 133, 138
Learning-Disabled, 135
Lehrstruke and Epic Theatre, 2
Leicester Square Theatre, 173
Leontes, 158
Level 4 maximum-security
    prison, 55
Lindkvist, Marian 'Billy, 145
Little, Cassidy, 181
Living without Fear, 132
Loach, Ken, 86
London Business Forum's
    Inspirational Leadership, 13
London Playback Theatre, 146
London's Bankside, 173
Luther Luckett Correctional
    Complex, 12, 54
Lykouria, Yorgo, 173

M
Macbeth, 4, 5, 41, 45, 56, 73, 74,
    76–78, 82, 84–86, 89, 92, 94,
    95, 97, 116, 158, 190, 191, 194
Macbeth, 74, 75, 85, 88
Macduff, 85
Machiavellian, 69
Madness, 158, 191
Madness Hotel, 152, 153
Maghaberry maximum-security prison,
    Ireland, Belfast, 45, 82, 93
Magill, Tom, 82–85, 88–91, 93–95
The Making of Mickey B, 86
Malcolm, 85
Malvolio, 179
Mansfield, Robin, Director of the
    Northern Ireland Prison
    Service, 87
Marcellus, 167
Marginalisation, 5, 32, 81, 112
Marginalise/marginalised, 2, 3, 30,
    32, 81, 195
  communities, 1, 5, 6, 18, 189
  environments, 3
  groups, 2
Mariana, 65
Marquis-Muradaz, Jennifer, 82,
    88, 94, 95
Maternal agency, 74, 77, 78
Matrilineal identity, 77
Maximum-security prisoners, 55
Maximum-security prisons, 88
McCabe, Andy, 181
McCabe, Pauline, 93
McClean, Sam, 85, 87
McCullough, Tim, 86
McKellen, Sir Ian, 151
McLean, Sam, 87
McLoughlin, Jaclyn, 171–177,
    180, 194
Measure for Measure, 4, 5, 41, 45, 61,
    63, 66, 69, 70, 97, 192

222 INDEX

Measure for Measure (the Wilde Community Theatre Company), 152
Mental health arts and film festival, 82
Mental illness, 151
The Merchant of Venice, 116
A Midsummer Night's Dream, 111, 133, 135, 172, 175, 181
A Midsummer Night's Dream (2010), 133
A Mind Apart Performing Arts, 146
Mickey B, 82, 84–88, 90, 91, 93–96
Mickey B, 96
Miller, Andrew (Arts Consultant and Broadcaster), 106
Mill Hill Emergency Hospital, U.K, 145
Mind the Gap, 107
Mistress Overdone, 63
Mitchell, Adrian, 21
More, Thomas, 123
    History of King Richard III, 123
Moreno, Jacob L., 2, 144
Morris, Laurie, 137
The Mousetrap, 167
Moving Pieces, 146
Much Ado About Nothing, 134, 137
Much Ado About Nothing (2015), 133
The Murder of Gonzago, 167

N
Naples, Florida, 82
National Association for Drama Therapy, 145
National heritage, 35
National identity, 19, 25
National Theatre Workshop for the Handicapped (NTWH), 106
New Historicism, 3, 10, 35, 39, 40, 45, 188, 190
New historicists, 39, 40

Newsom Report, 29
Newton, Larry, 55, 56
Nise da Silveira hospital in Rio de Janeiro, 152
Noble, T. D., 144
Norman, N., 181
Northern Ireland, 83–85, 96, 178
    maximum-security prison, HMP Maghaberry, 85
Northern Irish office, 95
Northern Irish Prison Service, 95

O
Odd Arts, 146
Ohio State University, 154
Old Gobbo, 116
Old system, 69
Old Vic Tunnels, 172–173
Olive Branch Arts, 146
Open Clasp Theatre Company, 48
Open Stages, 172
Ophelia, 136, 159, 161, 166, 167
Othello, 28, 116, 158
Outcome-driven, 21
Owle Schreame award for Innovation in Classical Theatre, 173

P
Panoptical, 67
Panopticon, 67
Parliament, dramatherapy, 145
Participatory, 22
Patrilineal castration, 74
Patrilineal identity, 74, 78
Patrilineal rights, 77
Peace II, 84
    funding, 82
Pedagogy, 2
Pedagogy of the Oppressed, 2
People Players of Toronto, 106

INDEX 223

Playing for Time, 48
Plutarch, 116
Political consciousness, 1
Polly Troup, 137
Polonius, 137, 161, 165–167
Pompey, 63, 64, 68
Pordeus, Vitor, 152, 153
Post-Traumatic Stress Disorder
    (PTSD), 171–174, 176, 178,
    180, 182
Prince Richard, Duke of
    Gloucester, 117
Prison, 4, 51, 187, 189
    and Shakespeare, 4
Prison Arts Foundation, 84
Prisoners, 57, 193
Prisoner William, 92
The Prison Service Trust, 84
Prison Shakespeare, 4
Prison Theatre, 4, 45, 47, 199
Private in the Cheshire Regiment, 181
Privilege, 17
Profitable brand, 18
Profit-making, 18
Prospero, 84
Prospero's Prison, 84, 85
Proteus in partnership with Prison Arts
    Foundation, 84
Psychodrama, 2, 143
PTSD, *see* Post-Traumatic Stress
    Disorder
The public acceptability
    test, 89

Q
Queen Margaret, 120
Queen Margaret College,
    Edinburgh, 145
Queen's University Social Work
    Department, 84
Quiplash, 107

R
Rah Rah Theatre Company, 146
Rampton, 151
Real Lear, 22
Rea, Stephen, 86
Recidivism, 47
Redefining Juliet, 111
Rehabilitation, 47, 48
Relatability, 27
Remedial Drama Group, 145
Renaissance, 113–115, 117–119,
    121, 122, 124, 125, 158,
    159, 163–165, 168,
    183, 191
    law, 192
    reading, 36, 41, 45, 189, 190, 201
Richard, 116–125, 192
Richard's Disability, 122, 123
Richard/Gloucester, 117
Richard III, 4, 5, 41, 56, 73,
    116–118, 125, 138, 158,
    173, 192
Richard III, 74, 119
Richmond, 120, 121
Rio's North Zone, 152
Roger Graff Award for
    Outstanding Achievement in
    Film, 86
Romeo and Juliet, 110, 111
Romeo and Juliet (The Royal
    Shakespeare Company), 152
Rosencrantz, 167
Rostron, Neil, 181
Roundabout Dramatherapy, 146
Rowan Tree Dramatherapy, 146
Royal Academy of Dramatic Arts
    (RADA), 171
Royal Artillery, 177
Royal Electrical and Mechanical
    Engineers, 179
Royal Society of Public
    Health., 173

224 INDEX

RSC, 52, 111, 151, 152, 172
  Dell Stage in Stratford-on-Avon, 173
  Open Stages, 110
  Swan Theatre in Stratford-Upon-Avon, 172
Rylance, Sir Mark, 26, 151

S
Sammie Bryon, 28, 29
Sam Wanamaker Playhouse, 133
Sayers, Julian, 181
SBB, *see* Shakespeare Behind Bars programme
Scicluna, Androcles, 177
Scott-Douglass, 12, 26, 54
Sealey, Jenny (Artistic Director of Graeae), 110
Secure psychiatric hospital, Broadmoor, 152
Seen but Not Heard, 84
The Selfish Giant (2015), 133
'Service' Shakespeare, 153
Sesame Institute, 145, 146
Seventeenth century, 61–63, 76
Shaban, Nabil, 106, 109
Shakespeare and Disability, 4
Shakespearean theatre company, 171
Shakespeare and Therapy, 4
Shakespeare Behind Bars programme (SBB), 54
Shakespeare in Shackles program/Shakespeare in Shackles programme, 55, 56
Shakespeare Inside: The Bard Behind Bars, 28
Shakespeare Lives, 110
Shakespeare's Globe Theatre, 172, 173
Shakespeare's Soldiers, 173
Shakespeare Theatre Company's Forum Theatre in Washington, DC, 173

Shakespeare, therapy, 183
Sheppard-Pratt Hospital in Baltimore, USA, 144
Side by Side Theatre Company, 110
Signalman in the Royal Signals, 177
Simpcox, 115
Sir Oswald Stoll Foundation, 172
Slade, Peter, 144, 145
Smith, Alan, 181
Smith, Linda, 86
The Snow Queen (2013), 133
Soliloquy Pictures, 173
Solitary Confinement in the Pendleton Correctional Facility, 55
The Stage, 181
Stakeholders, 19
Stoll, 172, 176
Stoll complex in Fulham, 172
Stourbridge, 110
String Caesar, 52
Suicide Club at boarding school, 144
Synergy Theatre Project, 48
System/age of confinement (punishment of the soul), 62, 192
System/age of terror (punishment of the body), 62, 192
System of confinement, 67

T
Taken-for-granted, 12, 38, 41, 190
  beliefs, 26, 35
Taking Flight Theatre Company, 107, 110, 111
Tangled Feet, 146
Tassé, Dr. Marc director of the Ohio State University Wexner Medical Centre's Nisonger Centre, 155
The Tempest, 84, 111, 116, 155
Tempest in a Teacup, 110
Theatre and Disability, 178

INDEX

Theatre in Prison and Probation (TIPP), 48
Theatre in prisons, 202
Theatre of the Oppressed, 2
Theatre Therapy, 4, 143, 199, 202
Theilgaard, Alice, 13, 14
Therapeutic environment, 194
Therapeutic settings, 193
Therapy, 4, 187, 189
  and Shakespeare, 4
Thersites, 116
Thompson, Jason, 85
Three high-security psychiatric hospitals in England, 151
Timeless, 1
Timelessness, 25–27
Timeless universality, 37
Timon of Athens, 73
Titus Andronicus, 158
Tofteland, Curt, 54
Tomlinson, Richard, 109
Toolis, Storme, 111
Top-down approach, 21
Touchstone, 116
Touchstone Shakespeare Company, 154
The Tragedy of King Real, 21
Transform, 21, 27
Transformation, 1, 3–6, 9, 10, 21, 23, 27, 31, 32, 35, 36, 41, 42
Transformative, 1–3, 9, 12, 17, 27, 28
  encounter, 7
  intentions, 2, 27
  outcomes, 3, 4, 9
  purposes, 6
Transforming oneself, 26
Treatise on Melancholy, 157
Trounstine, Jean, 52, 53
Twelfth Night, 110, 111, 116, 153, 173
Twisting Ducks, 107
Two Sides of the Coin, 84

U
UKCC code of conduct (United Kingdom Coaching Certificate), 145
UKCP (United Kingdom Council for Psychotherapy), 145
Ultimate form of literary achievement, 11
Universal, 5, 9, 37–39, 85, 114, 190
  discourse, 29, 37
  powers, 37
  relevance, 26
  themes, 20
  truths, 35, 190
  values, 30
Universalisation, 29, 35, 38, 41
Universalises/universalised, 27, 29–32
Universalising, 26, 27, 29, 31, 32
  discourses, 3, 25, 27, 35, 39, 40, 190, 199
  force, 9, 25
Universality, 28, 30, 35, 40, 189
Universalizing discourse, 92
Universally, 32
'Universal' themes, 1

V
Vandalia, Missouri, 54
Verbatim, 111
Verfremdungseffekt, 35, 38–40, 45, 188, 190
Veterans, 172, 175, 176, 178
Vienna, 66

W
Wabash Valley, 56
Washington, D.C., 173
Welfare State, 21, 22
Wellness treatment, 143

226 INDEX

WERDCC, *see* Women's Eastern
  Reception, Diagnostic and
  Correctional Centre
West End, 173
Wethered, Audrey, 145
Wilcox, Agnes, 54
Wilkins, David, 181
Williams, Victoria (Voice Coach), 174
*WILL POWER! Using Shakespeare's
  Insights to Transform Your Life*, 13
Winchester Mencap, 131
*The Winter's Tale/ A Winter's
  tale*, 73, 110

Wiseman, Gordon, 145
Women's Eastern Reception,
  Diagnostic and Correctional
  Centre (WERDCC), 54
Wood, Simon, 84
World Shakespeare Festival, 133
Wounded Injured and Sick
  Service Personnel
  (WIS), 173

Y
York Clinic, 145

Printed in the United States
by Baker & Taylor Publisher Services